Group Dynamics in Recreation and Leisure

Creating Conscious Groups Through an Experiential Approach

Timothy S. O'Connell, PhD

Brock University

Brent Cuthbertson, PhD

Lakehead University

Human Kinetics

Library of Congress Cataloging-in-Publication Data

O'Connell, Timothy S., 1968-
   Group dynamics in recreation and leisure : creating conscious groups through an experiential approach / Timothy S. O'Connell, Brent Cuthbertson.
      p. cm.
   Includes bibliographical references and index.
   ISBN-13: 978-0-7360-6287-9 (soft cover)
   ISBN-10: 0-7360-6287-4 (soft cover)
   1. Recreation--Sociological aspects. 2. Recreation--Psychological aspects. 3. Leisure--Sociological aspects. 4. Leisure--Psychological aspects. 5. Group relations training. 6. Social groups. 7. Experiential learning. 8. Organizational learning. I. Cuthbertson, Brent, 1961- II. Title.
   GV14.45.O36 2009
   306.4'8--dc22
                                     2008020041

ISBN-10: 0-7360-6287-4
ISBN-13: 978-0-7360-6287-9

Copyright © 2009 by Tim O'Connell and Brent Cuthbertson

The Web addresses cited in this text were current as of June 9, 2008, unless otherwise noted.

Acquisitions Editor: Gayle Kassing, PhD; **Developmental Editor:** Jacqueline Eaton Blakley; **Assistant Editors:** Lauren B. Morenz, Melissa J. Zavala, and Pamela Mazurak; **Copyeditor:** Jocelyn Engman; **Proofreader:** Anne Meyer Byler; **Indexer:** Bobbi Swanson; **Permission Manager:** Dalene Reeder; **Graphic Designer:** Joe Buck; **Graphic Artist:** Denise Lowry; **Cover Designer:** Bob Reuther; **Photographer (cover):** © Human Kinetics/Mark Anderman/The Wild Studio, © Human Kinetics/Corbis; **Photographer (interior):** © Human Kinetics, unless otherwise noted; **Photo Asset Manager:** Laura Fitch; **Visual Production Assistant:** Jason Allen; **Art Manager:** Kelly Hendren; **Associate Art Manager:** Alan L. Wilborn; **Illustrator:** Denise Lowry; **Printer:** Versa Press

Printed in the United States of America   10 9 8 7 6 5 4 3 2 1

Human Kinetics
Web site: www.HumanKinetics.com

United States: Human Kinetics, P.O. Box 5076, Champaign, IL 61825-5076
800-747-4457
e-mail: humank@hkusa.com

Canada: Human Kinetics, 475 Devonshire Road Unit 100, Windsor, ON N8Y 2L5
800-465-7301 (in Canada only)
e-mail: info@hkcanada.com

Europe: Human Kinetics, 107 Bradford Road, Stanningley, Leeds LS28 6AT, United Kingdom
+44 (0) 113 255 5665
e-mail: hk@hkeurope.com

Australia: Human Kinetics, 57A Price Avenue, Lower Mitcham, South Australia 5062
08 8372 0999
e-mail: info@hkaustralia.com

New Zealand: Human Kinetics, Division of Sports Distributors NZ Ltd., P.O. Box 300 226 Albany, North Shore City, Auckland
0064 9 448 1207
e-mail: info@humankinetics.co.nz

*This book is dedicated to the people who have
helped us understand what group dynamics is all about:
our families, students, trip groups, mentors,
colleagues, and friends.*

Contents

Preface

Can you remember a time when you were not involved with a group of some type?

On both a professional and a personal level, most of us have always belonged to a group. Our initial experience with groups started with our family. From there our experience moved to groups of friends, clubs and sports teams, work groups, professional organizations, and other collections of individuals consciously organized for some purpose. Most people choosing a career in recreation, leisure services, parks, tourism, or experiential education will spend the majority of their time working with others. Thus, understanding and applying the theory of group dynamics is of paramount importance.

Many recreation and leisure groups involve people who want to learn and grow from their experiences. They are aware that learning and growth are a primary motivation for being involved with others in recreation and leisure activities. These groups can be referred to as *conscious groups*. A conscious group recognizes that besides its other goals or productivity objectives, the personal growth of its members is a main objective. Members of a conscious group strive to better themselves and their relationships with others in the group—and probably beyond the group as well. In fact, this is why many people engage in recreation and leisure pursuits—to relax, meet others, and engage in activities they enjoy, all of which helps them become better people.

Most of the existing texts on group dynamics are not designed to meet the unique needs of recreation, leisure services, parks, tourism, and experiential education students and professionals. Framed in the context of conscious groups and experiential learning, this text integrates theory with examples, activities, and exercises designed explicitly to meet the practical needs of students and professionals in recreation, leisure services, parks, tourism, and experiential education. This combination of theory and practice provides students and professionals with the ability to recognize trends, issues, and successes in individual and group behaviors as well as provides the skills necessary to facilitate change in group interactions and celebrate group achievements.

One of our goals in writing this book was to make group dynamics meaningful and realistic for students in introductory courses. However, students, instructors, and practitioners will find that the contents of this book readily apply to other areas of study as well, including leadership, facilitation, psychology, and communication. Another of our goals was to help the reader gain a deeper understanding of what many of our students call *everyday knowledge*. In essence, we hope to challenge the reader to go beyond labeling group and individual behaviors by developing skills and knowledge to recognize implications for group development, performance, communication, and outcomes as well as to devise effective strategies to successfully work with a diverse number of groups.

Part I, Understanding the Conscious Group, introduces the reader to the theoretical foundation and contemporary research related to group dynamics. Part I focuses distinctly on knowledge related to recreation, leisure services, parks, tourism, and experiential education and working with conscious groups. Three chapters create this section:

- **Chapter 1: Introduction to Group Dynamics.** This chapter explores the history of group dynamics, the ways in which clusters of individuals come to be called *groups,* the various types of groups, and the natural benefits and barriers of groups.

- **Chapter 2: Group Formation, Development, and Function.** The second chapter examines group formation and individual motivations to join groups. Various models of group development are introduced, including sequential stage theories, cyclical models, and equilibrium theories. Additionally, chapter 2 explores the relationship between the collective and the individual. Topics include group structure, socialization, values, norms, and roles.

- **Chapter 3: The Conscious Group.** The final chapter of part I introduces the reader to conscious groups and experiential learning theory. The chapter examines the nature of conscious groups, including the definition of conscious groups, the components of a conscious group, and the application of experiential learning theory to working with conscious groups.

Part II, Developing the Conscious Group, applies the knowledge and theory discussed in part I to working with conscious groups in recreation, leisure services, parks, tourism, and experiential education settings. Part II includes the following chapters:

- **Chapter 4: Purpose, Goals, Objectives, and Expectations.** The first chapter of part II begins by clarifying the purpose of goals, objectives, and expectations. Techniques for clarifying goals and objectives are presented.

- **Chapter 5: Moral Issues in Groups.** Chapter 5 is unique in that values, ethics, and morals are rarely discussed in group dynamics textbooks. The chapter provides a rationale for including the study of these issues as well as an overview of how people develop morals and values. Several scenarios are presented to help students further understand values, ethics, and morals.

- **Chapter 6: Decision Making and Problem Solving.** Groups continuously make decisions and solve problems. Chapter 6 outlines the strengths and weaknesses of group decision making and problem solving as well as presents strategies for making decisions.

- **Chapter 7: Power and Conflict.** This chapter looks at power and how people in groups respond to it. Various sources of power are defined. Conflict is also examined, and strategies for dealing with group conflict are discussed.

- **Chapter 8: Gender in Group Dynamics.** This chapter examines how gender may influence group dynamics and individual interaction in groups. Gender is defined and an overview of how gender might affect recreation and leisure behaviors is presented.

- **Chapter 9: Group Leadership.** Leadership is a complex practice—it is as much an art as it is a science. This chapter focuses on leadership theories and their application to working with conscious groups. Style, situational, transformational, and transactional theories are discussed.

- **Chapter 10: Environmental Factors Affecting Groups.** All groups are affected by environmental factors such as weather, heat, cold, and noise. Chapter 10 examines the effects of these factors on group performance and functioning. A case study of the death of mountaineers on Mount Everest is used to highlight these effects.

Part III, Addressing Issues in the Conscious Group, examines the issues in group dynamics. Part III includes four chapters:

- **Chapter 11: Troubleshooting.** This chapter explores the signs, symptoms, and illnesses that may affect group functioning, performance, and success. Practical techniques for addressing group needs are provided, as are examples and case studies for further study.

- **Chapter 12: Crowd Dynamics.** Crowding is a common problem in recreation, leisure services, parks, tourism settings, and experiential education. Professionals in these areas are often asked to facilitate activities for large groups of people. This chapter looks at how individual and small group behaviors affect large group function and process. Case studies are used to highlight outcomes of crowd and mob behavior.

- **Chapter 13: Alternative Groups.** This chapter explores groups outside of the mainstream. Examples include cooperative living groups, consensus-based decision-making groups, and student-driven learning groups. Theory and practical strategies for working with groups of these types are provided.

- **Chapter 14: Diversity.** Diversity and difference are widely believed to enhance group dynamics. Chapter 14 covers techniques for capitalizing on the benefits as well as for avoiding the pitfalls of diversity. The chapter encourages the readers to step outside of their boundaries and consider the practical implications of interacting with diverse individuals.

Special features of this text include chapter summaries; learning activities, scenarios, and case studies appropriate to key content; examples appropriate to recreation, leisure services, parks, tourism, and experiential education practice; toolbox tips of successful strategies the reader may use in real life; and a complete reference list of sources that are cited in the text or may be interesting to the reader.

Acknowledgments

The impetus to write this book came from the various people I have worked with in a wide variety of recreation, leisure, and experiential education settings. I would like to thank those people for providing a deeper understanding of the joys and practicalities of working with groups. I am especially grateful to those participants and students from Wilderness Inquiry, Inc., Friends Seminary, SUNY Cortland, Lakehead University, and Brock University whom I have had the good fortune of traveling with in the outdoors. Thanks to Gayle Kassing for her constant support of this book in its early days and to Jackie Blakley for her editorial expertise. I would like to acknowledge Andy Young, Leo McAvoy, and Arnie Grossman for their mentorship in my journey as a student, and my parents, Tim and Sally O'Connell, for their unwavering support of my professional aspirations. Thanks to Brent Cuthbertson for agreeing to jump into this project together! Finally, I am eternally thankful to my wife, Mary Breunig, for her never-ending encouragement and love.

—Tim O'Connell

In writing on group dynamics, it is fitting to recognize that this book would not have been possible without others. Some of the contributions are overt and direct. Gayle Kassing was instrumental in getting the project off the ground, and she was patient with the bumps in my life that caused delay. Jackie Blakley has at least two talents as an editor: she has an eye for what needs yet to be explained, and she understands the motivational power of celebrating achievement. I am indebted to Tim O'Connell, my coauthor, for proposing this journey and for being so agreeable to work with. Still other contributions are less obvious. A long list of past instructors, students, and friends helped me learn the subtleties of interpersonal interaction, allowing me to refine my skills as a group member. Finally my parents, Ann and Bruce, made sure I understood and *felt* the bedrock of working and playing with others: love and respect. For the collective influence you have all had on me, I am grateful.

—Brent Cuthbertson

Part I

Understanding the Conscious Group

Because people spend so much time in groups, especially in recreation and leisure settings, they often take for granted what is required for a group to function efficiently and effectively. This is particularly true for conscious groups, or groups whose primary goal is to enhance the lived experience of its members. Understanding the historical and theoretical underpinnings of group dynamics lays the foundation for exploring contemporary concepts and research in that area. This understanding is particularly useful for recreation, leisure, and experiential education professionals who work with conscious groups on a daily basis.

We begin the exploration of group dynamics in chapter 1 by examining how the field emerged at the turn of the 20th century as a result of rapid industrialization around the world. Key concepts, terms, and figures central to the initial development of group dynamics are introduced. In chapter 2, we look at how individuals come together to form groups. In particular, the two-way interaction between the individual group members and the group as a whole is discussed in detail. In the last chapter of part I, chapter 3, we define a concept that is central to this text—the conscious group. We also examine how a common goal of recreation and leisure groups is personal growth. The chapter ends with a look at experiential education and how it relates to group dynamics.

1

Introduction to Group Dynamics

You're the head of inclusive and therapeutic recreation (ITR) at the local assisted-living facility, and in preparing your annual report, you've listed all the groups with which you've worked throughout the previous year. You realize that most of your job involves working with collections of people who are striving toward a common goal. Your list includes employees in the ITR department, executive committee members of the assisted-living facility, clients, families, and medical treatment teams. Over the course of the year, you've had to integrate new staff members into a cohesive group of employees, work to resolve conflict among executive committee members, and implement a new model of decision making involving ITR specialists, personal care attendants, and doctors. As you think about all the interactions you've had with different groups in the past year, you're thankful you took that group dynamics class when you were in school!

Working with groups is the bread and butter of most recreation and leisure professionals. They constantly interact with program participants, coworkers, community members, and committee members, among others. One of the main reasons why people participate in recreation and leisure activities is the social nature of the experience and the sense of belonging received from regular human interaction. It is through participation in these activities *with others* that people reap the most psychological, physical, emotional, intellectual, and spiritual benefits. Although some people gain these benefits from participating in solo recreation and leisure activities, taking part in group activities provides for an enriched experience.

Exploring how groups have been traditionally defined and categorized is important because it lays the foundation for how many people think about groups and group dynamics. This chapter examines how the field of group dynamics developed and how researchers became interested in studying groups. The chapter closes with a rationale that describes why a practitioner in recreation, leisure, and experiential education will find that studying group dynamics is important on both a personal and a professional level.

WHY STUDY GROUPS?

Working with groups is almost unavoidable—people move from one group context to another all the time. In a typical day, most people will spend more time with others than they will spend alone. A majority of this time with others will be with a collection of individuals that can be called a *group* for one reason or another. Although there are exceptions, most professionals spend most of their time working with groups, whether facilitating or leading programs and activities or collaborating with others to plan future events, conducting day-to-day business, or make decisions.

Understanding how and why individuals shape groups and groups shape individuals is important.

Johnson and Johnson (2003) list the following six reasons why understanding groups and group dynamics is significant:

1. Understanding group dynamics is central to maintaining a viable family.
2. Knowledge of group dynamics is central to creating effective businesses and industries.
3. Understanding group dynamics is central to education.
4. Knowledge of group dynamics is central to long-term maintenance of psychological health.
5. Knowing group dynamics theory and having small-group skills can change your life.
6. When it comes to group functioning, knowledge is power.

Groups are a basic building block in the foundation of modern society. Although countless individual transactions occur every day around the world, it is the interplay of different groups (and individuals within those groups) that makes groups incredibly influential. Groups determine how people behave and communicate and even shape people's attitudes and beliefs. Without the structure that groups provide, the world would be chaotic—everyone would be in constant conflict and it would be difficult to go about the business of daily life. Imagine if there were no groups to decide what behaviors are acceptable or unacceptable. There would be no speed limits or understanding of common social courtesies, and the world would be a much different place.

Groups provide structure for society, help people meet a variety of needs, assist the socialization process, and help people reach goals and accomplish tasks. However, groups can also be the cause of conflict, bias, and hate, and they can actually block efficient and effective productivity. Recognizing both the negative and the positive aspects of the power that groups have over shaping individuals and society is important for recreation and leisure professionals.

There are also personal benefits to studying group dynamics in the context of recreation, leisure, and experiential education. Individuals who have a firm grasp of group dynamics are able to do their jobs more effectively and efficiently. A working understanding of group dynamics may have positive financial implications, as success may be tied to a bonus, raise, or other award. Individuals who understand group dynamics are more apt to reach their own goals and objectives in a timely manner. Through this process, individuals may increase their confidence, enhance their self-concept, and feel more in control of their lives. People who understand group dynamics will also be more effective members of society. They can interject when things go astray and participate more effectively in the democratic process, thus ensuring its success.

GROUPS IN HUMAN HISTORY

From the beginning of human existence, groups have played an important role in providing basic needs such as food, shelter, clothing, protection, and company. As humans developed over time, groups changed and became more sophisticated. Hunting and gathering techniques became focused on collective endeavors instead of individual efforts, the accumulation of surplus food and materials led to trade among different small groups, and larger societies and cultures developed around shared group experiences. As groups became more refined, so did the recreation and leisure activities in which people participated. Instead of participating in activities by themselves or with immediate family, people began enjoying activities with others. Evidence of this is apparent in today's sports, travel clubs, bowling competitions, Olympic Games, and packaged group vacations.

Most people become a member of a group—their family—as soon as they enter the world. People will spend most of their lives working, playing, recreating, and living in the presence of others. The family is often the most stable group in a person's life. However, at various points in time, other groups become more important than the family. As a child grows older and progresses through school, peer groups take on value, particularly for recreation and leisure activities. This trend continues as the child reaches adulthood and moves away from the family group and is often a result of going away to college or university. As the individual continues to age, the family may again become the central group in life. However, it is usually the creation of a new family through marriage and the births of new children that reestablishes this group's central position. Human existence may be characterized by its social nature and by the fact that groups both influence and are influenced by individuals.

The family is a primary group and is often the first group to which people belong.

GROUPS DEFINED

At first glance, coming up with a definition for the term *group* doesn't appear difficult. However, when you begin to think about all the different types of groups to which people belong, it quickly becomes difficult to pinpoint a definition that captures the essence of what a group is. Understanding the key characteristics that a group exhibits will help you determine the best way to approach working with that collection of individuals. Depending on the context, the definition of the word *group* may change, especially for the individuals involved with that particular collection of people. The reason why the players on a hockey team are together is quite different from the reason why family members have gathered for camping over a summer holiday weekend. Theorists have suggested several definitions for the term *group,* but they rarely agree with one another. However, upon examining these definitions, there are seven features categorizing the nature of groups that become evident: interdependence, goals, influence, size, membership, structure, and systems.

Interdependence

Some theorists define groups as collections of individuals who are interdependent on one another (Cartwright and Zander 1968). What happens to one member affects the other members. The action or lack of action by one individual influences the experience of every other member of the group. For example, if the navigator on your canoe trip points the group in the wrong direction, everyone in the group gets lost. On the other hand, if something happens that doesn't affect each individual, then the collection of people is not a group.

Goals

Sharing a common purpose is another way in which groups have been defined (Keyton 2002). Individuals often combine their talents and resources to complete a task, reach a goal, or do something they would not be able to do on their own. In fact, all groups in some way share a common goal or purpose. The purpose depends on what the group is all about. A sports team wants to win the game, a steering committee desires to plan a special event, and a corporate group on a challenge course wishes to enhance communication skills. Each person who is a member desires the same outcome for the group and is drawn to the group because of this shared goal.

Influence

A group may be defined as people who are influenced by and influence others. Although this is similar to the definition for interdependence, it is different in that influence is bounded by the group itself. Members persuade the group, and the group persuades its members. Interdependence involves factors outside the group, while influence is an internal group process. For example, members of a softball team may choose to participate in a group cheer before the start of every game. Members are influenced by the group to participate in the cheer, while an individual member might influence what particular cheer the group does.

Size

There is some debate over the minimum number of people required to form a group. Some theorists believe two people can make up a group (referred to as a *dyad*), while others think that three people (referred to as a *triad*) is the minimum number. These theorists argue that three people are needed to create a group because in order to exert influence, two members must work with each other to pressure the third (Wilson 2002). However, two people exhibit all the components of groups listed here and thus may be considered the smallest group size.

The maximum number of people in a group is limitless. The size of a group does influence its character. Large groups may have a common purpose, and members may be interdependent, but direct links among all members are nearly impossible to establish and maintain. In small groups with only 2 to 3 members, subgroups cannot be formed, and since membership is so small, individuals cannot hide in the crowd. What these individuals say and do has a more powerful effect on the group than it would have if there were more members. On average, most groups number 2 to 7 people (Forsyth 2006).

Membership

The perception of belonging to a group has also been used to define a group (Johnson and Johnson 2003). If two or more individuals identify themselves as members of a group, then they constitute a group, particularly if others who are unaffiliated recognize them as members of that specific group. In this sense, people sharing a common social identity that is validated by nonmembers make up a group (Brown 2000). Fraternities and sororities are an excellent example of groups defined by membership. Individuals perceive their membership by going through the initiation process. Nonmembers easily identify members as those who wear clothing bearing Greek letters or who live in the fraternity or sorority house.

People may also psychologically belong to a particular group. This is especially evident in the number of Internet communities that have grown in the past number of years. Members of these groups never meet face to face and may not even know other members' real names, but they still feel as though they are members. People who share ideological viewpoints such as political or religious beliefs believe they are members of a group as well. Residents of British Columbia who consider themselves members of the Liberal Party of Canada share membership with Liberal Party members from Nova Scotia. Although they have never met one another, their shared ideological beliefs and psychological understanding of what it means to be a Liberal Party member allow them to be a group and exhibit other characteristics found in groups.

Structure

Groups have also been defined by their norms, roles, and methods of regulating or influencing members' behaviors (Sherif and Sherif 1956). These operating procedures have usually been agreed upon or accepted by group members. Those who choose to use and abide by these norms, roles, and regulatory methods are group members; those who don't are not group members. In essence, individuals buy into the structure the group has created and by doing so become group members.

Systems

Some theorists have applied systems theory to help define the term *group*. Using this framework, groups are considered to be open and complex systems (Arrow, McGrath, and Berdahl 2000). Groups are characterized not only by their inputs, processes, and outputs but also by the interactions that take place both within and outside of the group. These properties include openness to the environment, entropy, equifinality, and synergy (Beebe and Masterson 2000).

Open Systems

Systems are open when factors from the external environment can affect the interdependent relationships within the group; closed systems operate in a vacuum or some other environment in which external elements cannot affect the system in any way. Groups are open, as they are influenced continuously by the environment in which they exist. Resources such as time, money, and materials may be available or unavailable. The weather may change during the course of a backpacking trip. Members join and leave the group, bringing and taking with them their individual ideas and expertise. A book club may want to read a specific novel that happens to be out of print.

Complex Systems

Complex systems often appear disorganized and easily transformed. Small groups may be considered to be complex systems because they tend to be chaotic. Small groups also exhibit the following characteristics normally associated with complex systems: quantum change, strange attractors, phase space, bifurcation points, irreversibility of actions, double-loop learning, and sensitivity to initial conditions.

Quantum change, or second-order change, occurs when there is a fundamental shift in the way the group processes experiences or conducts itself. Quantum change should not be confused with first-order change, which is more superficial. First-order change does not require members to join or leave the group or to change the way in which they interact with one another. For example, a curling team (also called a *rink*) may change strategy during an end in order to adjust for how the other rink is playing. This is first-order change. However, if the curling team changes the order in which its players throw rocks during the game or replaces one of its players due to illness, second-order change occurs. This change reconfigures how the group goes about getting its work done.

Groups are also influenced by strange attractors. These are habits and patterns group behaviors fall into. While a habit or pattern is readily apparent, the reason why it occurs is not identifiable. However, the habits and patterns greatly influence how the group operates even though no one person can control how those habits and patterns unfold. For example, many sports teams follow certain rituals before the start of each game. The team members may wear certain T-shirts under their uniforms or eat the same food before each game. There is no clear manner in which these rituals develop, but each member of the team feels obligated to perform the ritual in the way the team has always seemed to perform it.

Phase space is the linear movement of a group through time. Chapter 2 discusses several models that try to describe the prototypical group as it moves through its life span. Phase space is affected by both strange attractors and sensitivity to initial conditions.

Groups are sensitive to their initial conditions. Any variation in group membership, resources, time frame, or decision making can produce significantly large differences in group outcomes. For example, a tournament planning committee that has the same membership as it had the previous year won't be able to produce a similar experience if its budget is cut by 50 percent.

Another way in which groups exhibit characteristics of complex systems is through double-loop learning. Groups learn from previous experiences, and when this knowledge is combined with what group members already know, new processes and procedures can be developed. Double-loop learning is the combining of different sources of knowledge and skills to create something new. For example, a football team might inadvertently come across a successful play that leads to a touchdown. The team then uses its previous knowledge of play design to refine the play and add it to the regular repertoire of plays.

The final two components of complex systems are bifurcation points and irreversibility of actions. Bifurcation points are moments in a group's existence when a certain action is taken, behavior is exhibited, or decision is made. Groups often view bifurcation points as milestones. These points often mark the choice of a specific path or course of action. Once the group embarks on that specific road, there is no turning back. This is the irreversibility of actions that

A bifurcation point.

is a characteristic of complex systems. Many groups that are planning community recreation events choose a certain theme for a festival or program. Once the theme is chosen, programs are printed, entertainment is booked, and the group is locked into that theme.

Entropy

The term *entropy* refers to the tendency for groups to become disorganized and chaotic unless there is a directed effort to maintain balance within the group. Groups that struggle to develop methods of making decisions or figure out communication networks are susceptible to entropy.

Equifinality

Equifinality suggests that groups may reach the same final goal using different means and different paths when starting from the same point and with the same resources. Conversely, groups starting at the same point with the same resources may arrive at completely different end points. For example, a goal of many outdoor adventure recreation programs is to increase the sense of community felt among the group

members. These programs send out several different groups during the course of a summer season. These groups travel different routes, follow the lead of different instructors, and involve different individuals. Yet all the groups develop an enhanced sense of community, despite the fact they use completely different means to do so. Alternatively, two teams competing in a baseball tournament have the same resources and number of people in the group: Each team has bats, gloves, and nine players on the field. However, at the end of the tournament, the outcomes of each team differ drastically. One team wins while others play only one game. Despite initial appearances of equality among teams, the events that happen to each team are quite diverse.

Synergy

The concept of synergy is best described by the phrase, "The whole is greater than the sum of its parts." Groups are more than the individual members they comprise. Synergy is the combined force of the individual members, their attitudes, and their abilities; the resources available to the group; and the ways in

Learning Activity

Box Building

Break into small groups of 5 to 6 students. Each group should receive the following materials: one standard or legal-sized file folder, five rubber bands, and one 12-inch (30-centimeter) piece of string. Additionally, each group should have access to tape, staplers, scissors, and a variety of colored markers.

All groups should design a gift box from the materials provided. They may decorate the gift box as they see fit. They do not have to use all the materials, but they are not allowed to use any materials other than those provided and a pen or pencil. Each group must take at least three minutes to formulate a plan before cutting, marking, or manipulating any of the materials.

When all the groups are finished creating their gift box, one representative from each group should present the group's creation to the larger class and note any special features the gift box may have. Once all the groups have presented their boxes, discuss the following questions as a class:

1. What were the initial conditions for all the groups?
2. Was there a bifurcation point for your group? Was the action irreversible?
3. How does this activity exhibit the characteristics of an open and a complex system?
4. How is the concept of equifinality displayed through this activity?

which these relate to the purpose of the group (Barker, Wahlers, and Watson 2001). Synergy may affect groups both positively and negatively. When groups work well together, the outcomes are far superior to those that individuals are capable of producing. However, synergy may also allow groups to fail miserably. This may be evident in poor decision making and problem solving and may result in outcomes that are dramatically worse than those an individual working alone might achieve in the same situation.

All groups have two types of synergy: maintenance synergy and effective synergy (Barker, Wahlers, and Watson 2001). Maintenance synergy is the energy a group uses to sustain relationships, maintain communication networks, determine roles and norms, and resolve conflicts. Effective synergy, sometimes called *action synergy,* is the energy a group uses to reach goals and objectives, to complete the task at hand, and to otherwise be productive. Although capitalizing on the positive effects of synergy to address maintenance issues is crucial to a group's success, using effective synergy is preferable, as groups use this energy to be industrious and reach their goals.

Historically, there have been many ideas of what constitutes a group, many of which overlap. Although each conceptualization has merit in its own right, combining the features of these definitions allows for a more inclusive understanding of the term. Thus, a group may be considered to be two or more individuals who exhibit one or more of the following characteristics: social connections, interdependence, shared or common goals, mutual influence, perceived membership, structure, and components of complex systems. Many groups will exhibit all of these characteristics, while others may exhibit only one or two. Regardless, recreation and leisure professionals should understand the variety of ways in which a collection of individuals may be considered a group. What creates a group in one setting may not create a group in another.

CLASSIFICATIONS OF GROUPS

Once it is determined that the collection of individuals you are working with is actually a group, it is helpful to figure out what type of group it is. Doing so will help you make decisions, choose a leadership style, and design programs, among other things. Classifying groups also gives you clues as to why people are members and helps you meet both individual and group needs.

Primary and Secondary Groups

The first group most people become a member of is their family. The family is called a *primary group,* and it meets different needs than those met by other groups to which people belong. Primary groups provide affection and inclusion and often provide basic physiological needs such as food, shelter, and clothing. This type of group is characterized by high levels of interdependence and influence as well as by clear perceptions of membership. Primary groups are long-term groups, and face-to-face interaction is common. Often primary groups are responsible for the socialization process, or the means by which people learn how to interact with others and within society. The socialization process also shapes an individual's attitudes, beliefs, and values. Other groups, such as those people have long-term exposure to, are defined as primary groups. For example, collections of friends or housemates may be considered primary groups.

Most of the other groups that people belong to are secondary groups. The purpose of these groups is to accomplish a goal or solve problems. Secondary groups usually don't last as long as primary groups do, and secondary groups are more formally organized. A good example of a secondary group is a youth soccer league committee in the local recreation department. Secondary groups are more often focused on the task at hand than on the social relationships among members. This arrangement requires less emotional energy. Secondary groups influence members' socialization, but they do not affect it to the extent that primary groups do. Often, secondary groups are used to characterize an individual's place in society. For example, Patrick is a member of the Clark family. However, if you asked his friends to describe Patrick, they would most likely describe him as being a member of the local climbing club, as working at a civil engineering firm, and as belonging to a certain group of friends from college.

There are many types of secondary groups, all of which exist for different functions. The purposes of many of these secondary groups are familiar to most people. Secondary groups include work groups, study groups, therapy groups, committees, focus groups, clubs, and groups of friends (Beebe and Masterson 2000). Most professionals work with both primary groups and secondary groups. Some primary groups may look more like secondary groups, and some secondary groups may closely resemble primary groups. Figuring out why a group exists will help determine whether a group is a primary group or a secondary group.

Emergent and Planned Groups

Another way to describe groups is by how they came to exist in the first place. Emergent groups form by chance. A group of this type develops suddenly because people happen to be in the same spot for something. For example, a scheduled flight between Minneapolis, Minnesota, and Thunder Bay, Ontario, is canceled. A group of passengers decides to rent a car to drive the seven hours in order to get home that evening rather than wait until the next afternoon for another flight. This group emerges out of the situation. The individuals in this group develop a loose-knit understanding of the group's goal (to get home) as well as a few basic structures to help members deal with the situation, such as deciding who will drive and who will rent the car.

Emergent groups may also form slowly over time as individuals consistently find themselves in the same place with others. In recreation and leisure settings, individuals who work out at the same time every week or play pickup basketball during the lunch hour may develop an identity as a group and figure out structures that define their group. During the pickup basketball games that occur daily over the lunch hour at the local gym, there are clear ways of doing things that the emergent group members have come to agree on. Some of the structures that might exist include the following: the winning team stays on the floor until it loses a game; in order to challenge the winners, a team must have five players; if there are more than five people waiting to play on the team, they must shoot free throws to decide who makes up the five-person team; and one team is shirts and the other is skins. Emergent groups are fluid—members may come and go, structures may change, and the group may suddenly cease to exist without causing any adverse effects on people who were associated with it.

Planned groups are those that are formed on purpose, usually to complete a specific task or serve a particular function. Planned groups usually have well-defined structures that are formalized through bylaws or spelled out in publications such as a staff

Learning Activity

Group Categorization

List the groups you have belonged to in the last five years. Then complete the following:

1. Describe to what extent each group on your list displayed the characteristics of groups (interdependence, goals, influence, size, membership, structure, and systems).
2. Categorize each group as the following:
   a. Primary or secondary
   b. Emergent or planned
3. Explain why you think each group is primary or secondary and emergent or planned. Discuss your answers with someone else.

manual or a book of operating procedures. Planned groups also have clear roles and norms for members, and leadership positions are assigned to specific individuals. Usually, a planned group has clearly defined intended outcomes, such as making a decision, planning an event, or finishing an experiential education activity.

Membership in planned groups may be exclusive, as people are invited to join because of the specific expertise they bring with them. For example, as a recreation professional, you might create a planned group for the purpose of designing a new skateboard park. You specifically include a local contractor who specializes in cement structures, a youth worker, the organizer of the school's skateboard club, a parent, and the owner of the skateboard shop. Your recreation department has developed operating guidelines for committees like this, which require the group to keep minutes, elect a chairperson, and complete its plan in four months. Recognizing whether a group is emergent or planned has implications for approaches to working with that particular group. One of the best ways to understand the various facets of how groups work is to study group dynamics.

GROUP DYNAMICS

Group dynamics is the scientific study of human behavior in groups. It involves studying the formation and development of groups, the group processes, the individual and collective behaviors, and the interaction of groups with others, including individuals, other groups, and society at large.

Groups, and the individuals who are members of groups, have interested researchers and theorists from a wide array of academic disciplines. The interdisciplinary nature of group dynamics has allowed for a rich description of what happens when individuals come together to form a group. Some of the fields that have contributed to the study of groups are education, recreation and sport management, psychology, sociology, communications, business, and social work. Although group dynamics was studied first by sociologists and psychologists, almost all social science fields have added, in some way, to the current understanding of groups.

History of Group Dynamics

Although the study of groups was of interest to some theorists in the late 1700s and early 1800s, it wasn't until the late 19th century and the early 20th century that theorists began to examine seriously how people worked in the presence of others. One of the first studies looked at how race times decreased for cyclists biking against another racer instead of racing alone against the clock. This study was extended to a different context when it was determined that a child winds a fishing reel faster when in the presence of another child (Triplett 1898). Eventually it was discovered that most people perform better when others are around. During the formative years of group dynamics, most of the research that was done described practical situations in which individuals and groups interact daily. This focus soon grew, and the interaction of groups and society became the center of attention of the studies that were being conducted. Theorists attempted to explain how groups affect common social phenomena such as politics, religion, education, and business.

After the turn of the 20th century, people began to notice that groups were having a greater influence on society. Groups began to be studied through a number of lenses. One of the first ways in which group dynamics was examined was from the perspective of business management. More and more people recognized that groups are more effective than individuals are in a number of ways. Researchers focused on decision making and problem solving and refined their focus on how people perform in front of others. They discovered that the nature of the task influences how well individuals can perform in front of others. When completing simple tasks, individuals perform better in a group; when executing complex tasks, individuals work better when alone (Allport 1924).

Perhaps one of the most famous demonstrations of the effects of performing in front of others was the study conducted by Elton Mayo and his colleagues at the Hawthorne Works of the Western Electric Company. In this study, factory workers were subjected to a number of changes in their working conditions. Regardless of how their working conditions were manipulated, the workers always increased their productivity when they were being observed by others. Today this observation is referred to as the *Hawthorne effect,* which is defined as the changes in behavior that result when people are being watched or studied by others (Mayo 1945).

This scientific study of groups led others to examine communication and discussion patterns and leadership within groups as well as the effects of groups on attitudes. As a result of this deeper understanding of groups and group processes, the research findings began to be implemented in the daily practice of working with groups. Much like the group dynamics classes of today, the results of these early studies were used to train people to make group processes more efficient and effective. This was of particular importance, as during this time World War I, the

Great Depression, World War II, and resultant focus on industrial efficiency weighed heavily on the minds of most people.

Kurt Lewin and Field Theory of Group Dynamics

The field of group dynamics grew most rapidly in the 1930s and 1940s, during which a few prominent social scientists centered their attention on understanding group processes and interactions. Led by sociologist Kurt Lewin, group dynamics became a popular topic. Lewin's approach, which contrasted with that of earlier theorists such as Allport (1924), asserted that individuals are best understood in a group context. Lewin believed that groups have the power to influence individuals and society and to cause action and that they are dynamic and potent entities (Lewin 1943, 1944, 1948). In fact, Lewin is credited with coining the term *group dynamics* and is considered by many as the founder of the field (Forsyth 2006).

Kurt Lewin was born in the late 1800s in what is now part of Poland. After graduating from the University of Berlin with a doctorate degree in philosophy and psychology, Lewin fought in World War I as an infantryman. He immigrated to the United States in the 1930s and worked at several prestigious institutions, including the University of Iowa, Cornell University, and the Massachusetts Institute of Technology (MIT). It was at MIT that he created the Research Center for Group Dynamics, from which numerous studies were conducted.

Lewin was a firm believer in the connections among research, theory, and the practical application of both. Building on this belief, Lewin studied social situations involving individuals and groups in a laboratory setting and then generalized his observations to everyday life. In essence, he thought that solutions to social problems could be uncovered through research and the resulting development of theories to explain human behavior in those settings. As such, Lewin is credited with the creation of action research, which encourages people studying group dynamics to think about how they can best address societal problems through the practical application of their findings. As a proponent of the idea that there is a relationship between the practical needs of practitioners and the ability of theorists to

Toolbox Tips

As a recreation and leisure professional, you can gain a better understanding of an individual group member's lifespace through a number of ways:

- Review each registration form to get an idea of each person's past experiences.
- Before starting an activity, check with group members to determine if they are prepared to commence the activity. A couple of minutes spent centering people's attention to the task at hand leads to success.
- During the initial stages of a group's existence, encourage individuals to share their experiences so that the others are aware of their group members' lifespaces.

assist in addressing those needs, Lewin permanently influenced social science research.

Perhaps one of Lewin's greatest contributions to the study of groups is his field theory of group dynamics (1948). This theory assumes that groups are open and complex systems (as introduced earlier in this chapter) and that both internal and external forces affect the group's behavior (Barker, Wahlers, and Watson 2001). Lewin also introduced the concept of *lifespace,* or the physical space in which a person currently exists. A person's perception of this lifespace is influenced by his interpretation of the situation, by the others involved, and by his personal history. For example, Mary's interaction with the rest of the Clark family at the annual picnic depends on her previous experiences with her cousins, her familiarity with the setting, and the feelings she is facing that day. Mary's experience may vary dramatically by how she interprets her lifespace from situation to situation. This is called *interactionism.*

A second component of Lewin's field theory is the idea that groups are a dynamic whole. Change to one part of a group changes other parts of the group. An individual group member's choice to abide by agreed-upon rules or to break these rules directly affects others in the group. For example, Kristen chooses to have people on her canoe trip participate in a tip test to practice what to do when a boat rolls over. However, Diego decides not to participate in this exercise. Later on, while the group is paddling on a windy day, the canoe tips and Diego doesn't know what to do. Diego's behavior has affected the rest of the group. Hopefully, his lifespace changes after this event and he changes

his behavior and participates in the tip test the next time he goes canoeing with his group. His perceptions of paddling on a windy day and his understanding of what could happen change his future behaviors.

Lewin's field theory asserts that an individual's behavior is a function of personality and personal qualities, group context or social environment, and lifespace (how the person interacts with this context). In order to fully understand a group and its processes, the interaction of individual behaviors as well as group behaviors must be examined as a single phenomenon. Lewin believed that it is impossible to truly understand a group unless you look at it from a global perspective (Forsyth 2006). While change in one part of the group affects other parts of the group, the group as a whole is greater than the sum of its parts. Groups are capable of doing more than individuals can do alone.

SUMMARY

People around the world spend a majority of their time living and working in groups. For recreation and leisure professionals, understanding how interdependence, goals, influence, size, membership, and structure affect how a group functions is important for success. It is also necessary to be aware of how a group operates as a system, is open to the environment, and is subject to entropy, equifinality, and synergy. Classifying a group as primary or secondary and as emergent or planned can give a leader or facilitator a head start on developing strategies for working effectively with that group. Primary and planned groups differ greatly from groups that are secondary or emergent.

Kurt Lewin, a pioneer in group dynamics, contributed the idea of field theory to our understanding of how people work and interact as a collection of individuals. He believed that personality and personal qualities, group context or social environment, and lifespace affect a group and that groups must be examined from a holistic, all-encompassing perspective.

Studying group dynamics will be valuable to students not only in their future profession but also in all aspects of their lives. Learning about group functioning and group dynamics is a lifelong process. A strong foundation, such as the one provided by this text, will enable students to work successfully with all types of groups in a variety of settings.

RESOURCES

Allport, F. 1924. *Social psychology.* Boston: Houghton Mifflin.

Arrow, H., J.E. McGrath, and J.L. Berdahl. 2000. *Small groups as complex systems: Formation, coordination, development and adaptation.* Thousand Oaks, CA: Sage.

Barker, L.L., K.J. Wahlers, and K.W. Watson. 2001. *Groups in process: An introduction to small group communication.* 6th ed. Boston: Allyn & Bacon.

Beebe, S.A., and J.T. Masterson. 2000. *Communicating in small groups: Principles and practices.* 6th ed. New York: Longman.

Brown, R. 2000. *Group processes.* 2nd ed. Malden, MA: Blackwell.

Cartwright, D., and A. Zander, eds. 1968. *Group dynamics: Research and theory.* 3rd ed. New York: Harper & Row.

Forsyth, D. 2006. *Group dynamics.* 4th ed. Belmont, CA: Thompson-Wadsworth.

Johnson, D.W., and F.P. Johnson. 2003. *Joining together: Group theory and group skills.* 8th ed. Boston: Pearson Education.

Keyton, J. 2002. *Communicating in groups: Building relationships for effective decision making.* New York: McGraw-Hill.

Lewin, K. 1943. Forces behind food habits and methods of change. *Bulletin of the National Research Council* 108:35-36.

Lewin, K. 1944. Dynamics of group action. *Educational Leadership* 1:195-200.

Lewin, K. 1948. *Resolving social conflicts: Selected papers on group dynamics.* New York: Harper.

Mayo, E. 1945. *The social problems of an industrial civilization.* Cambridge, MA: Harvard University Press.

Sherif, M., and C.W. Sherif. 1956. *An outline of social psychology.* New York: Harper & Row.

Triplett, N. 1898. The dynamogenic factors in pacemaking and competition. *American Journal of Psychology* 9:507-33.

Wilson, G. 2002. *Groups in context: Leadership and participation in small groups.* 6th ed. Boston: McGraw-Hill.

2

Group Formation, Development, and Function

You've just walked into the room for the first meeting of the Waterfront Extravaganza steering committee. Sitting around the table are several members of your staff from the parks and recreation department, as well as community members, business people, and local politicians.

As the Director of Special Events, you are responsible for planning, running, and evaluating the Waterfront Extravaganza that is six months away. You know that each individual present has different reasons for attending the planning committee meeting. One person is an advocate for increased public use of the waterfront, while another person owns property bordering the event site. A businesswoman is interested in profiting from increased sales during the event. A senior citizen who regularly volunteers for park events and whose wife recently passed away is there, and one of the politicians attending is running for reelection in the fall. The group has several decisions to make—for example, they must choose a theme and entertainment. Most of the people attending the meeting don't know each other, and the businesswoman and politicians haven't been involved with the parks and recreation department before. You know that six months isn't a lot of time to plan such a large event, especially when working with a group like this!

Although each member has an interest in a group's success, there are many different reasons why people join groups. Some join for friendship and affiliation or because they like other members of the group. The group might meet at a convenient place or time. The activities in which the group engages might be of value to a person. The group could provide a means of increasing a member's public exposure. Whatever the reason, people join groups for both personal and situational motivations. How will you work with your particular collection of individuals? What will you do if there is conflict within the group? How will you lead this group? The answers to these questions are rooted in a basic understanding of why and how groups form and develop.

WHY PEOPLE JOIN GROUPS

People join groups for a number of reasons. Usually these reasons are based on a need. Knowing the needs that people fulfill by joining a group will help you as the group leader; you will be able to recognize and adapt to unique circumstances and to help people maximize their group experience. Both William Schutz and Abraham Maslow developed theories that describe the needs people have and the ways in which people go about fulfilling these needs.

Fundamental Interpersonal Relationship Orientation (FIRO) Theory

In 1958, William Schutz wrote the book *FIRO: A Three Dimensional Theory of Interpersonal Behavior.* Schutz thought that people want social interaction and relationships with other people and that through these associations people meet their needs for inclusion, control, and affection. He called this concept the *fundamental interpersonal relationship orientation (FIRO) theory,* which is based on four ideas:

1. As a group develops, it goes through distinct phases of inclusion, control, and affection. When a group begins to disband, it reverses this order and goes from affection to control and ends with inclusion.

2. Each individual has the need for inclusion, control, and affection.

3. Individuals bring with them behaviors they have learned from previous group experiences. Behaviors people experience in their relationship with their parents at an early age are especially important.

4. A group's compatibility in terms of inclusion, control, and affection affects the group's cohesiveness, effectiveness, and operating efficiency.

Figure 2.1 shows how these four ideas interact to form the FIRO theory. Each row represents one of the three needs Schutz identified as part of his theory (i.e., inclusion, control, and affection). Each row also

represents a continuum related to each of these needs, as well as behaviors a person might exhibit depending on his or her level of need. For example, a person who needs to have a greater effect on the group and more power over others (or a strong need for control) would exhibit autocratic (or directive) behaviors.

Inclusion

In general, people are social creatures. We like to be with others, share experiences with others, and feel accepted by others. Our need to belong and to be recognized as an individual causes us to join groups. The need for inclusion may also be viewed as the need for affiliation, as shown in the third row in figure 2.1. Schutz argued that people may be categorized as oversocial, social, or undersocial when it comes to their need for inclusion. This categorization ranges from having a need for high levels of interaction to a need for no interaction.

People who need affiliation might be involved with several groups at one time, are more engaged with group processes, and spend more time with others

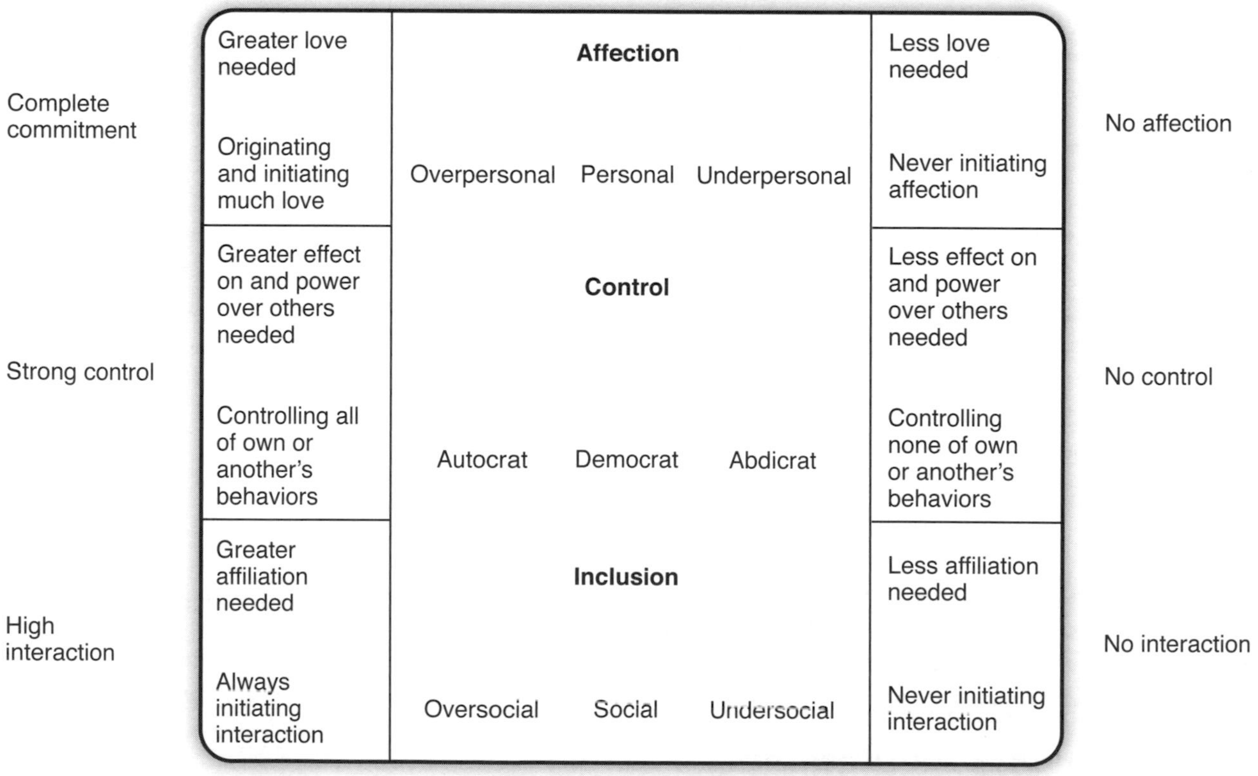

Complete commitment	Greater love needed		**Affection**		Less love needed	No affection
	Originating and initiating much love	Overpersonal	Personal	Underpersonal	Never initiating affection	
Strong control	Greater effect on and power over others needed		**Control**		Less effect on and power over others needed	No control
	Controlling all of own or another's behaviors	Autocrat	Democrat	Abdicrat	Controlling none of own or another's behaviors	
High interaction	Greater affiliation needed		**Inclusion**		Less affiliation needed	No interaction
	Always initiating interaction	Oversocial	Social	Undersocial	Never initiating interaction	

Figure 2.1 Schutz's fundamental interpersonal relationship orientation theory.

than they spend alone. These people are known as *oversocial* group members, as they go out of their way to attract attention to make up for a lack of affiliation. A *social* group member is one whose need for inclusion and affiliation is met by the group. These people are confident working alone or with others in the group. Other members may withdraw or avoid close contact with the group if they feel they are not valued or recognized by the group. These people are known as *undersocial* group members. Although they are associated with the group, their need for affiliation and inclusion is not being met.

Control

We like to feel that we have the power to influence others, the ability to make our own decisions, and the authority to direct our own path. Groups offer individuals the opportunity to meet this need through the chance to control decision making, allocate resources, or take on other leadership roles. Often people who have unfulfilled needs for power take on roles that provide opportunities to take control in groups. This dimension of FIRO is shown in the second row in figure 2.1.

Alternatively, if leadership opportunities are unavailable or are already filled by another group member, people who feel the need for control may disrupt the group process, hold back information or resources, or undermine the group process in an attempt to gain control or power. These people are often called *autocratic* group members. Some people who join groups have lower needs for control than others. These people are usually the followers in the group. They are called *abdicratic* members, particularly if they are hesitant to exert their need for control. Finally, people whose control needs are fulfilled by a group are known as *democratic* members. The need to control or be controlled is a strong motivator for people to join groups.

Affection

The need for intimacy, or the need to experience friendships, close bonds, and positive relationships with other group members, is the last component of Schutz's theory. As with the needs for influence and control, group members may exhibit varying degrees of the need for affection. Overpersonal group members need to connect with every group member on

a level that may seem disingenuous or overbearing. They may also press relationships with other group members despite obvious signs that others are uninterested. Some people's needs for affection are met by the group. These people relate well with other group members, can provide affection when needed, and are equally comfortable in groups where affection is of little importance. These people are called *personal* group members. Underpersonal group members do not feel liked by other group members and may separate or withdraw completely from the group. This dimension of FIRO is shown in the first row of figure 2.1.

Maslow's Hierarchy of Needs

Abraham Maslow's hierarchy of needs (1954) has been used to describe many human behaviors and may also be used to explain why people join groups. There are five levels to Maslow's hierarchy (see figure 2.2):

1. Physiological needs
2. Safety
3. Belongingness
4. Esteem
5. Self-actualization

Maslow believed that people must meet the needs low in the hierarchy in order to address the needs higher up the hierarchy—that is, the basic needs of everyday life such as food and shelter must be met before we can begin to fulfill the need to become the

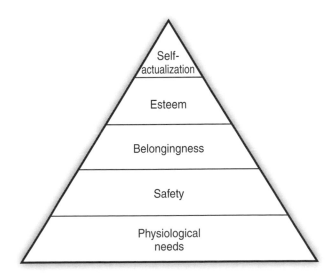

Figure 2.2 Maslow's hierarchy of needs.

best person we can be. All these needs may be met through membership in a group and can help explain why people are drawn to specific groups.

- **Physiological needs.** When we are young, our food, water, and shelter are usually provided by our family. Extended families that include multiple generations help provide these basic needs to group members.

- **Safety.** People may join groups to fulfill the need for security and to protect themselves from physical, mental, or emotional harm. Street gangs, neighborhood watch groups, and gated communities are examples of groups that form to meet the need for safety.

- **Belongingness.** Belongingness relates directly to Schutz's need for affiliation. People like to feel that they are part of something larger than themselves. Individuals join book clubs, sport leagues, and online communities to fill the need to belong. As we grow older, we increasingly look outside the family to peer groups to fill this need. This phenomenon may be seen in the increased need for recreation, leisure, and experiential education programming for youths and adolescents, particularly programming designed with group interaction in mind. Teenagers must deal with developing a sense of identity away from their family,

and recreation, leisure, and experiential education programs may offer an important opportunity for them to explore new and different identities. The need to belong is especially strong for this age group.

- **Esteem.** Groups help people with their esteem by providing them with the chance to feel important and respected. People feel they are valued by others when they are part of a group. Group positions, such as president, as well as recognition given by groups help fulfill esteem needs. If an individual is the sole group member who excels at a task that she believes important, and others recognize that ability, esteem needs will be met. On the other hand, if there are others in the group who perform equally well or better on the task, or if there is little or no recognition, then esteem needs may not be met.

- **Self-actualization.** Groups can help individuals fulfill the need of self-actualization, or obtaining full personal potential. People join groups because they see an opportunity to become all they are capable of becoming, even though self-actualization is an individual process. For example, people might join a running club because they see it as a means of reaching their full capability as a runner. We meet self-actualization needs through group membership because groups allow us to reach our full potential.

Toolbox Tips

Here are six techniques you can use to find out what needs have motivated people to join your group:

1. Include an open-ended question on registration forms that asks why people have signed up for a particular activity.

2. Conduct an expectations session early in the group's life span. Encourage people to share what they hope to get out of the group experience. Ask them to speak about things they need as well as things they don't need.

3. Observe individual behavior in the group. What gets people excited? How do they contribute? About what are they passionate? Use these clues to deduce the needs people may have.

4. Hold debriefing sessions before, during, and after key group events. During the debriefing, encourage people to share how their needs have been met. These sessions may change or shape individual needs.

5. Meet formally or informally with individual group members to find out what their needs are and if they are being met.

6. Keep track of attendance at group events. People come to the activities that meet their needs.

Why should you understand Schutz's FIRO theory and Maslow's hierarchy of needs? As a leader, you can try to determine why people are motivated to join your group and then create conditions to maximize their experience. For example, you might suspect that someone has a strong need for control, as this person tries to influence group decisions to such an extent that he actually disrupts the decision-making process. You can suggest that this person be assigned a formal position in order to fulfill his need for control and to make decision making more efficient. You can also compare individual needs for belonging with the rest of the group's need. Longtime group members might not feel the same need for belonging that someone who just joined the group feels. As a leader, you can suggest that the established group members go out of their way to welcome new group members and to initiate them to the workings of the group. In the long run, this practice will help the group reach its full potential!

Factors of Attraction

As the Director of Special Events in charge of planning the Waterfront Extravaganza, you might have a guess as to why each attendee has come to the first meeting of the steering committee: The group will help these people do something they couldn't do on their own. Most of us cannot build a house or play basketball against a team of five alone. We need others to feel accepted and to feel like we're contributing to a greater good.

We are attracted to groups both by what the group can do as a whole and by the individuals who are already members of that group. Interpersonal attraction plays a substantial role in group development. It helps determine which individuals are drawn to a group as well as how established members go about recruiting new members (Forsyth 1999). Many of us have been drawn to a group because of someone we know in that group or have invited a friend to join a group we have already joined. We do this because of interpersonal attraction. There are both external and internal forces that make groups attractive to people:

- **Physical attractiveness.** Often, we become interested in groups that include people who are physically attractive to us. Attractiveness influences men

more than women, particularly in North America. People want to be with those who they see as physically beautiful. Physical attraction is a factor in the early stages of becoming interested in a group, but its influence declines over time (Beebe and Masterson 2000).

- **Proximity.** People are attracted to other people and to groups that they encounter regularly. One way of meeting people regularly is by being in close proximity to them. Imagine that a friend gives you her season tickets to the orchestra for the final performance of the season. There is a good chance the people with season tickets sitting around your friend's seats will ask you what happened to your friend or ask you why you are sitting in her seats. Continuous exposure to people encourages us to develop a positive idea of these people, and seeing them regularly over time may lead to the sense that a group exists solely because of this exposure. Other examples of the effects of proximity and exposure include groups of people who share school spirit, live in the same dormitory, sit in the same seats in class every day, and have the same academic major. At a university, an individual who majors in outdoor recreation, parks, and tourism is referred to as a *rec'r* from the moment that person registers for courses in the program. This inevitably creates positive feelings toward the whole group of outdoor recreation, parks, and tourism majors. People who are outside of the regular contact or close proximity experienced by these majors tend to think of those who are inside as being members of that group. With the increased application of technology to communication, the term *proximity* doesn't necessarily denote physical closeness anymore—rather, it refers to closeness created by repeated interaction and shared experience (Forsyth 1999).

- **Similarity.** Most people like others who are similar to them, particularly if the others share similar values, beliefs, cultures, political viewpoints, or interests. Why do we like others who are similar to us? First, we use other people as a means of comparison. If another person holds the same political beliefs we do, our viewpoint is validated as correct. Second, we find it easier to understand and be understood by people who are like us. Third, we feel a connection with other people once we've determined there are similarities between us. For example, you might feel an immediate liking for someone who plays the same sports you do. This shared interest suggests, on a superficial level, that you may have other things in common and that this similarity might minimize future conflicts. Fourth and finally, we can avoid cognitive dissonance by interacting with others who are most like us; that is, we won't have to spend unnecessary psychological energy in rectifying differences.

- **Complementarity.** There is some truth to the old saying that opposites attract. Just as we are attracted to people who are similar to us, we are also attracted to people who have qualities that differ from ours. This is particularly true if those qualities complement our own abilities. Which has more influence over whether a person joins a group—similarity or complementarity? Researchers have found evidence that supports both viewpoints (Forsyth 1999). The strongest groups may be made up of people who are both similar and complementary to one another. For example, people who need to receive affection might be attracted to a group that has members who need to give affection. Similarity doesn't always mean that group members will be compatible with one another.

- **Cost-benefit analysis.** Have you ever considered a group to be a drag and felt like you were putting more effort into that group than you were getting out of it? If so, you most likely have weighed the costs of group membership against the benefits of being in that group. We generally prefer groups that provide us with the maximum benefit for the least cost. In recreation, leisure, and experiential education settings, benefits may include the opportunity to participate in a favorite activity, make friends, and increase skill levels. Costs may include time, money, irritation with other group members, and lost opportunity to do other things. For example, you might think you can't go out to dinner because you have to go to volleyball practice. We benefit not only from what the group does but also from who the other group members are.

Most people consider the costs and benefits of a group before they join it. However, people will be more motivated to join a particular group if they are able to compare its costs and benefits with those of other groups. In essence, people comparison shop for groups just as they would for a new car or household appliance. We are more likely to join and be satisfied with a group when we gain the most from

being in that group for the least cost, particularly if no other group can match or provide more benefits for the same level or for less cost (Thibaut and Kelley 1959). For example, the local politician who joined the Waterfront Extravaganza steering committee has decided she may get the most public exposure by being involved with this group rather than the alternative groups available. We continuously weigh the benefits with the costs of group membership, particularly when we discover a viable substitution exists.

- **Welcoming environment.** We like others who say or show their attraction to us. This attraction may be indicated through invitations to participate with the group or compliments on skill level or appearance. The same holds true for people who indicate that they don't like us—we tend to not like them in return. This form of interpersonal attraction is a strong reason why many people become involved in groups.

There are many reasons why people join groups. Some motivators, such as the need for inclusion, control, or self-actualization, come from within individuals. Coupling these internal needs with external factors, such as proximity, similarity, and complementarity, provides a good overview of what draws people to different groups.

GROUP DEVELOPMENT

Have you ever wondered why some groups are so effective at what they do while others are caught in never-ending turmoil? Just as we as individuals develop, groups also develop. Most groups go through distinct stages as they move through their life span. A group that is newly formed experiences challenges and successes that differ from those a group that has been together for a longer time experiences. There are more than a hundred theories that describe how groups develop over time. These theories can be categorized into three main types: sequential stage theories, recurring phase theories, and equilibrium theories (Forsyth 1999).

Although the different models vary in the number of stages through which a group progresses, they are similar in their descriptions of the interpersonal dimensions that categorize the stages. Generally, there is some sort of confusion, decision making, or agreement that must occur in each stage before the group can progress to the next. Often, these processes

Working through conflict usually improves group functioning.

are categorized as conflict. This conflict may occur among all members of the group, between one or two members, or between one member and the rest of the group. Although the term *conflict* is used to describe these uneasy points in a group's existence, working through the conflict usually results in better group functioning. Conflict resolution allows the group to agree on norms, roles, and values and helps the group determine its course of action. This course of action is usually acceptable to all group members, as they have worked through the issues surrounding the conflict and have come to terms with it on a personal level.

Researchers have developed several theories to describe how groups form, work through conflict, accomplish tasks, and ultimately disband. Understanding how a group develops as well as the individual member's experience in the development process will assist you in constructing effective leadership strategies, accomplishing the task at hand efficiently, and providing a positive experience for everyone involved.

Sequential Stage Theories

Sequential stage theories, also known as *successive stage theories,* predict that groups progress through a set number of stages in a specific order. Some theo-

ries focus more on the journey the individual makes as the group develops. Richard Moreland and John Levine (1988) define different levels of membership for the individual: prospective member, new member, full member, marginal member, and ex-member. As individuals move through these different categories of membership, they focus on different group functions and different group members. A prospective member is most concerned with determining whether the group is attractive and with weighing the costs and benefits that joining the group might provide. Marginal members are concerned with their legacy in the group and with transitioning smoothly out of the group. Moreland and Levine's model is helpful in describing the socialization process, which will be discussed later in this chapter.

Two of the best known sequential stage theories are those proposed by Bruce Tuckman (1965) and B. Aubrey Fisher (1970). These theories correspond roughly and describe a group's life span by identifying the unique stages each group experiences.

Tuckman's Stages of Group Development

Tuckman (1965) listed five stages through which a group progresses: forming, storming, norming, performing, and adjourning. These stages are predictable, and each requires some focus on the task and the relationship functions of the group.

• **Forming.** The forming stage is characterized by the attempts of individual group members to determine who else is in the group and to figure out what their role might be in the group. Generally at this stage people are guarded in their interactions with others, as the group has not yet established operating procedures or norms. People do not want to be embarrassed or break any social rules, so they remain superficial in their interaction with others. However, as time progresses, people develop relationships with other group members through sharing information when they feel comfortable. Individuals also synthesize the information they receive from others in an effort to determine the potential norms and roles. The Waterfront Extravaganza committee described at the opening of this chapter is in the forming stage—the people who have arrived for the first meeting are engaged in the processes of this stage. The forming stage can require a considerable amount of energy from the members as they converse, share, and reflect.

• **Storming.** The storming stage is characterized by tension surrounding the development of group goals, roles, norms, and decision making. The nature of the group's conflict may relate to whether the group has a readily identifiable leader. If the group doesn't have a leader, tension will exist among the people vying for a leadership position and other roles in the group. If a group does have a leader, conflict may arise from challenges to the leader's authority or decisions. Some group members may create conflict by withdrawing to the periphery of the group and away from the leader. Other behaviors you might see during this stage include defensiveness, jealousy, and distrust of the process.

As a group negotiates roles, norms, and other group functions, conflict will subside. Most groups benefit from working through conflict, as it helps develop a common understanding of the group's task and relationship functions. This is often the point when mutuality of concern is cemented for a group. Groups that have worked through conflict are stronger in the long run, as they have developed decision-making patterns, built communication strategies, and created stronger bonds among group members. However, conflict during this stage can also destroy a group or prevent it from moving ahead with its real purpose.

In an effort to steer clear of conflict, some groups try to avoid the storming stage altogether. Inevitably, this comes back to haunt them later, because these groups do not have the tools or interpersonal procedures to successfully handle conflicts that may arise.

• **Norming.** The norming stage is marked by the stabilization of interpersonal relationships among the group members. Group norms have developed that outline acceptable behaviors for decision making, interaction, and communication. Support and trust for other group members as well as for group processes have solidified. Group members are committed to the group and its functioning. During this stage, the group turns its focus to accomplishing the task at hand. Although disagreements may arise, the group has an agreed-upon structure in which to operate. The group is more organized for the same reasons. People know where they stand, are comfortable with the group as a whole, and are ready to move on with the work of the group.

• **Performing.** The performing stage is best described as the time when the group hits its stride—the group gets its work done, the members relate to each other well, and the group operates effectively and efficiently. Generally, a group must mature to reach the performing stage. Researchers have found that only a small number of groups actually reach the performing stage and that the groups that do reach this stage generally do so after a lengthy storming and norming process (Forsyth 1999). These groups have the necessary structure and operating procedures to perform, and members are comfortable enough with the others to work toward the goals and objectives of the group. For example, a relatively new group that is rushing to set up camp in a rainstorm may not operate as effectively as a group that has been together for a while. The new group must take time to identify tasks and to figure out which members' skills are best suited for task completion. All the while these group members are getting cold and wet. A group that has been established jumps into action without having to think about what to do as a group. The group members all know who has the skills to complete tasks, and these individuals go to work on behalf of the group with little or no direction. Groups that never reach the performing stage are those that cannot agree upon norms, roles, goals, or objectives. This inability may be due to lack of leadership, poor communication, high member turnover, or perceived shortage of resources. Although time is crucial to reaching the performing stage, it is not the sole factor in ensuring a successful journey to this stage.

- **Adjourning.** When a group is finished with its work or its members decide its purpose is no longer useful, the group has reached the adjourning stage. Adjourning occurs when the group no longer exists and members go their separate ways. This stage of group development may also be marked by conflict. The type of conflict that appears may depend on how the group has reached its end. Has the group fulfilled its purpose? Or has the group disbanded because it cannot function in a meaningful way? Once the Waterfront Extravaganza steering committee has successfully completed the special event, its members may feel sad and reluctant to end the group. Individuals may have come to count on others in the group for support and friendship. The group may have given members direction in life.

Conflict may also arise when groups are forced to break up unexpectedly. Individuals may turn on other group members as a way to place blame for the group's failure. Others may withdraw from the group once the costs of associating with it outweigh the benefits. Whatever the reason for a group's ending, you should recognize and come to terms with why the group has reached the adjourning stage. As a professional, you can help people transition out of group life by planning celebrations, debriefing sessions, methods of evaluation, and opportunities for members to become involved with other groups.

Fisher's Phases of Group Development

Fisher (1970) developed a theory similar to that of Tuckman. Fisher's model focuses on groups that are formed primarily to make decisions. Fisher suggested that there are four phases of group development: orientation, conflict, emergence, and reinforcement. As you will see, each of these roughly corresponds with one of Tuckman's stages.

- **Orientation.** The orientation phase is similar to Tuckman's forming stage. The main issues that group members address in this stage are the nature of the decision to be made and the interpersonal relationships that exist among group members. During the orientation phase, group members try to feel out others' opinions on matters related to the group's task.

- **Conflict.** The conflict phase is characterized by debate and discussion about the merits of the topic.

During the emergence phase, group members listen to others' viewpoints.

People defend different positions around the subject. Opinions are expressed. Possible solutions to the problem are suggested for the first time. This phase corresponds with the storming stage of Tuckman.

• **Emergence.** The emergence phase is marked by a determined approach to finding a solution to the problem. Group members collaborate to make the best decision. Individuals compromise their position and listen to others' viewpoints in an effort to uncover a good solution. Tuckman's norming stage is related to this phase.

• **Reinforcement.** In the reinforcement phase, a decision is agreed upon. Group members defend and implement the outcome of their deliberations. This phase is like Tuckman's performance stage.

As you can see, Fisher's description of group development is like Tuckman's in many ways. Fisher's model describes groups whose primary function is to make decisions, which is one specific task on which a group focuses. Thus, Fisher's model more adequately depicts groups involved in decision making, while Tuckman's model is more generic. Tuckman's model can be used to describe groups that exist for many reasons. Other researchers have built upon these theories in an attempt to explain how groups develop over time. Many of these modified theories use the same elements Tuckman and Fisher use but also use a recurring or cyclical approach to group development.

Johnson and Johnson's Group Development Theory

Another sequential stage theory of group development takes into account the fact that most recreation and leisure professionals are the designated leader of their group. This theory was developed by David Johnson and Frank Johnson (2003), who have written extensively on group theory and group skills, especially in education settings. Having a designated leader influences the stages a group goes through, because the leader's role is already determined, and the leader may direct each stage of development based on what he feels is most important for the group. Johnson and Johnson's model has seven stages:

1. Defining and structuring procedures
2. Conforming to procedures and getting acquainted

3. Recognizing mutuality and building trust
4. Rebelling and differentiating
5. Committing to and taking ownership of goals, procedures, and other members
6. Functioning maturely and productively
7. Terminating

These stages are much like those suggested by Tuckman and Fisher. The main difference is that Johnson and Johnson's stages are viewed from the perspective of the leader, while the stages of Tuckman and Fisher are viewed from the position of the group as a whole.

Sequential stage theories are commonly used to describe group development. However, many groups never reach certain stages or never adjourn. Other theories are used to explain why and how groups cycle back to stages they've already been through. These are called *recurring phase theories*.

Recurring Phase Theories

As implied by their name, recurring phase theories suggest that a group repeatedly experiences a number of stages during its life span. These theories are also called *cyclical theories,* as each stage may be repeated more than once. Although a group may have progressed beyond a certain stage, it may always cycle back to that stage at some point in the future. Some groups never experience stages that other groups go through, and different groups may progress through the stages in different orders. For example, some groups on wilderness backpacking trips go right from the forming stage to the performing stage. The people in these groups often meet one another hours before they set off on their trip, and designated leaders help ensure that group norms and roles are in place. However, as the days go by, the group members might refine these norms and roles as they grow comfortable with one another and the leader. Thus the group experiences the storming phase of group development after bypassing it initially.

Equilibrium Theories

The equilibrium model of group development (Bales 1965) suggests that group members work continuously to maintain balance between the task function and the relationship function of the group. Sometimes the group will focus on the job at hand; at other times, it will have to focus on interpersonal relationships to ensure that the social nature of the group remains intact. The Waterfront Extravaganza steering committee is more concerned with the interpersonal, or relationship, function of the group during its inaugural meeting. People are interested in figuring out where they fit in, what is going to happen, who the others are, and what they are all about. The three interpersonal needs listed earlier in this chapter may also be used to describe issues that groups revisit: As a group develops over time, needs for inclusion, control, and affection are dealt with by both the individual members and the group as a whole.

Often groups react quickly to changes in equilibrium. Theories that describe these fast changes are referred to as *punctuated equilibrium theories.* These changes frequently result from an unforeseen challenge, such as the sudden loss of money from an operating budget. A group faced with this type of challenge will most likely respond rapidly so it may return to a balanced approach to both the task and the relationship functions.

These theories of group development are helpful tools. However, it may be difficult (or nearly impossible) to determine what stage a group is actually in. It takes practice with, and exposure to, many kinds of groups to develop an eye for figuring out a group's stage of development. Despite your best efforts at helping groups navigate through their development, you will discover that there are many unexpected obstacles to overcome.

GROUP FUNCTION

The members of the Waterfront Extravaganza steering committee have chosen to become part of the group for different reasons. They expect the group to help them reach a goal, give them a sense of satisfaction, provide them with a reference point with which to compare themselves, or help them make friends. In turn, the group expects its members to contribute to decision making, communication, and conflict resolution and to help with the work the group must undertake to meet its goals.

As someone working with groups in recreation, leisure, and experiential education settings, you should be aware of the reasons why people join a group. While many people join because of that group's goals,

individual members have unique goals that may differ from those of the group. Additionally, you should be aware of how the group expects its members to behave within the group context. As a professional, you can help the group operate more effectively and avoid negative conflict by understanding these factors.

Group and Individual Goals

Many professionals overlook the individual's experience once that person has joined a group. We often hear, "Put the group before yourself!" This statement has both positive and negative effects on how leaders might deal with an individual's journey through the group experience. Understanding factors that affect the subtle interplay between each individual in the group and the group as a whole will help you create a positive experience for both the individuals and the group.

Group goals are often the main reason why a group exists. The Waterfront Extravaganza steering committee intends to plan and carry out a large special event. Sports teams are intent on winning competitions. A hiking group wants to reach a scenic destination.

Individuals are attracted to groups because they see the group as an opportunity to meet their own goals. Early in a group's life span, individual goals may exert a greater effect on group goals. The founders of a group often interject their individual goals into the purpose of the larger group. However, as time progresses and the group solidifies around its purpose, the group goals supersede individual goals. As new members join the group and bring their individual goals with them, conflict surrounding the purpose may rise. This conflict is normal for group development and will be addressed in the following pages.

One of the most challenging tasks a group faces is figuring out how individual goals and group goals mesh. Establishing mutuality of concern is crucial to a group and is often the cause of conflict and misunderstanding. Successful groups reach their own goals while enabling individual members to reach their goals at the same time. There are several strategies you may use to ensure that this happens. Three strategies are outlined here.

First, identify group and individual goals. This important process will help the group to formulate strategies to meet its goals and help individuals to identify personal goals that might be incompatible with group goals.

Second, as the group works toward its goals, provide time and structure for individuals to meet their goals as well. For example, if one person is interested in developing a particular skill, assign him to a subcommittee directly dealing with that subject or find some other way to involve him that maximizes his chance to improve that skill area.

Third, provide prospective group members with enough information to make an informed decision if that group is for them. Make people aware of the group's purpose, operations (norms), and leadership structure. There is no benefit for the person or the group if neither is able to reach the goals deemed important. Figure 2.3 shows how group and individual needs interact.

Task and Relationship Dimensions

The task dimension of a group relates to the job at hand. Most groups are organized around finishing a task, reaching a goal, or completing some kind of work. The relationship dimension is focused on the interpersonal function of the group—how people get along, interact, and communicate.

Throughout their existence, groups usually devote energy to both the task and the relationship dimensions. Although at certain times one dimension may gain importance over the other, there should always be some energy devoted to both. Otherwise, the group may stall before finishing the job or people may grow frustrated with each other and fail to get along. Most of us have been members of groups in which some

people devoted too much time to the task function and were seen as being bossy and controlling. On the other hand, most of us have also been in groups in which nothing got done because individuals were too involved with talking with others or didn't care about the group's job. It is fairly common for student work groups that are still young in their life span to focus too much on the relationship dimension and to put off paying attention to the task dimension until the night before the assignment is due!

The Waterfront Extravaganza steering committee is meeting to plan and carry out a special event. This is the group's task dimension. To balance this focus and spend some time on the relationship dimension, you might begin by having people introduce themselves and indicate why they are interested in being part of the committee.

Norms

What are some of the rules of behavior that we conform to in everyday life? Generally, we wait until the traffic light turns green to proceed through the intersection. We wait in line at the movies to buy a ticket or get popcorn. We hike an established trail instead of creating a new one a short distance away. Norms are standards or rules that help guide behavior in a group. Norms help determine which behaviors are appropriate and which are inappropriate.

Some norms describe how people regularly behave in a specific situation. These are descriptive norms. People who do not follow this type of norm are viewed as out of the ordinary. Prescriptive norms have more stringent guidelines attached to them. Either you

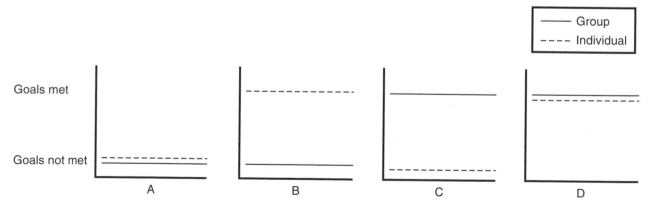

Figure 2.3 Outcomes of interaction of group and individual needs.

abide by the norm or you don't. In general, people who don't follow prescriptive norms are viewed negatively or are evaluated poorly. If a group member doesn't abide by a prescriptive norm, there are usually ramifications. Other group members may punish the individual. For example, the person who has broken that rule might face a monetary fine, be excluded from group activities, or be asked to leave the group. Usually the severity of the punishment reflects how important the norm is for a group.

Identifying Norms

People identify group norms in several different ways. Some norms are really obvious, while others might take a while to figure out. Watching various groups and how they operate can help you establish their norms. Determining how people interact, what processes the group invokes when its members are together, who the leaders and followers are, and what level of behavior is considered acceptable will help you identify norms.

Often norms are listed in a group's handbook, bylaws, or minutes of meetings. These are called *explicit norms*. Usually, they are easy to discern. For example, a sign at a swimming pool might say, "No Running on Deck." Implicit norms might be more difficult to identify. You can usually figure these out by observing group behavior over time. For example, a hiking group might always wait for everyone to arrive in the same spot to start eating lunch. If you were to start eating before everyone was present, you might get a few hard glares or admonishment from other group members. Think about when you walk into a class for the first time. Many students claim their seat for the semester and then feel like someone who sits there in following classes is trespassing on private property!

Developing Norms

New groups develop norms early in their life span, usually during the storming phase. The groups then consolidate and accept these norms during the norming phase. The group's experiences, interactions, successes, and failures during this stage help norms develop. The individuals in the group bring with them their previous experiences with a wide range of other groups. Through that experience, the group members have some sense of norms that have worked for other groups. This process is called *structuration* (Poole, Seibold, and McPhee 1996). Once a norm has been established, it becomes part of the normal operating procedure for the group. In essence, group members have internalized that norm as a social reality.

As a professional, you can assist groups in developing norms or influence which norms a group adopts. There are three ways in which you can help groups establish norms: stating, modeling, and importing. When you tell people how to act or what behaviors are acceptable, you are stating norms. For example, you might tell people how to properly launch a canoe so it is not damaged by rocks in the water. You can model the same behavior by properly launching the canoe every time during a trip. You need not verbally explain what you are doing—by consistently demonstrating the behavior, you are encouraging others to do the same. Finally, you might import norms that are already familiar to people. This is structuration, or using norms that people experience in other situations. For example, you can tell your group that the method for launching a sea kayak is the same as that used for a canoe. You can encourage groups to accept norms that will benefit them by using an appropriate mix of these techniques.

Your words and actions must be consistent. Group members will be confused and lose respect for you as a leader if you don't walk your talk.

Following Norms

Several factors affect how and why people conform to group norms:

- Explicitness or implicitness of the norm
- Punishments for breaking rules or not abiding by the norm
- Feelings of shared responsibility and obligation to follow agreed-upon norms
- Development of group identity
- Individual qualities of group members
- Percentage of others in the group who conform to the norm
- Wish to continue membership in a group
- Status level within the group

Personal characteristics affect an individual's likelihood to comply with norms. Women tend to conform more than men do, but only when they are in direct contact with others. Women also tend to conform more if the context or activity is more traditional in nature. People who come from an ethnic or a cultural background that emphasizes the collective over the individual will abide by norms more frequently. Individuals who have experienced similar norms in other groups will follow norms that are comfortable for them. Individuals who are authoritative conform to norms more often, as do people who have more traditional or conservative values (Forsyth 1999).

Conforming to norms provides both positive and negative consequences for the group. Abiding by norms allows group members to put energy into the task and relationship functions of the group. They don't have to worry about how they have to behave, and they can expect the others to behave in specific ways. However, norms can stifle a group's creativity or create cumbersome operating procedures that get in the way of progress. Norms may lead to conditions that turn away potential new members or create a stagnant environment for existing group members. As previously mentioned, groups often return to the storming and norming phases of group development in an effort to review and revise norms as the group sees fit. Sometimes this revision is the result of new members exerting their influence in the group. More often, it is the need for change and learning from experience that causes the creation of new norms.

Roles

The niches that people create for themselves in a group are referred to as *roles*. These are the parts that people play in group interactions. Roles can relate to the task function, to the relationship function, or to both. Roles determine what behaviors are expected from each group member, give group members direction when participating in an activity or making a decision, and provide structure to regular group activities.

As mentioned, roles may be related to the task function or the relationship function of the group. These are referred to as *socioemotional roles* (Forsyth 1999) or *maintenance roles* (Beebe and Masterson 2000). Some group members may take on individualistic roles, or roles that focus on the self and personal needs instead of the group and group needs—these people may be seen as being selfish, as being lazy, or as riding on the coattails of the rest of the group. Table 2.1 lists 27 roles that individuals assume while working in groups. There are 7 relationship roles that describe how people serve the socioemotional needs of the group, 12 maintenance roles that describe how people serve the task function of the group, and 8 individualistic roles that describe how people focus on their own needs in a group setting.

Some roles are formal—these are the roles associated with positions of perceived importance within a group. Titles such as *leader, team captain,* and so on may be attached to these roles. Informal roles are

Learning Activity

Think about a group you have joined. Write your answers to the following questions on a sheet of paper:

1. What is your standing in the group?
2. Are you a leader or follower?
3. How does the group go about doing what it does?
4. What are the unwritten rules of the group?
5. What happens when a member breaks one of those rules?

Compare your experiences with those of someone else. What advice would you give each other about your groups? What strategies could you use to make changes? Comprehending how groups are structured will help you facilitate recreation and leisure experiences.

Table 2.1   Roles Within Groups

Role	Function
Relationship roles	**Build and maintain group**
Encourager	Offers praise and agrees with contributions of others
Harmonizer	Mediates or reconciles differences and relieves tension
Compromiser	Tries to reach common ground through yielding, admission of error, or disciplining self or others
Gatekeeper or expediter	Regulates communication by keeping channels open or facilitating participation
Standard setter	Sets the bar for the group behavior or evaluates group performance and processes
Group observer or commentator	Records group processes and provides feedback on group performance and processes
Follower	Passively accepts the movement of the group
Task roles	**Facilitate and coordinate group efforts**
Initiator or contributor	Suggests new ideas or ways of group thinking
Information seeker	Asks questions to clarify quality of information
Opinion seeker	Strives to clarify values surrounding group processes or actions
Information giver	Offers facts and personal experiences related to task at hand
Opinion giver	Offers personal views on values surrounding group processes or actions
Elaborator	Describes alternatives by offering rationale for options
Coordinator	Pulls ideas together by clarifying relationships among suggestions
Orienter	Tries to keep group headed in right direction by questioning decisions and solutions to problems
Evaluator or critic	Assesses group outcomes through comparison to standards
Energizer	Calls the group into action
Procedural technician	Attends to the logistics of group functioning such as seating arrangements, copies, and so on
Recorder	Takes notes for the group
Individual roles	**Fulfill needs of individual members**
Aggressor	Negatively affects group processes by deflating status of others, joking excessively, and so on
Blocker	Resists group decisions and actions
Recognition seeker	Calls attention to self through bragging or talking about personal achievements
Self-confessor	Uses group to talk about personal ideologies not related to group
Playboy or playgirl	Displays lack of engagement with group through inappropriate behaviors
Dominator	Manipulates group or members in an attempt to assert authority
Help seeker	Tries to gain sympathy from other group members
Special interest pleader	Advocates for a particular issue without regard for other points of view

Adapted from Benne and Sheats 1948.

those that group members create as needed or ad hoc. These roles usually are contextually and situationally dependent.

Role Diversity

Most groups operate effectively when there is a balance between their task function and their relationship or socioemotional function. When a member occupying one of these roles moves to the forefront of group activity, another member with a complementary role may also step up to balance the need for both the task and the relationship functions. You can observe this by watching a group of your friends decide what movie to see. Usually one person directs the decision-making process, others horse around and crack jokes, and still others sit back and wait for a decision to be made. In the end, an amicable agreement is reached through the subtle interplay of role behaviors and function. It is to the group's advantage to have people fill a wide range of roles. If some roles are not filled, or if several people take on the same role, the group will function ineffectively: Conflict may arise, key tasks may go undone, or the group may stagnate as it fails to make progress.

Role Differentiation

Some people are elected or appointed to a position, while others fall naturally into a role with which they are comfortable. In many recreation, leisure, and experiential education groups, roles are negotiated subtly among group members based on the needs, skills, and strengths that each member brings to the group. Often roles are determined during the storming and norming stages of group development. New group members might look for open roles that they may occupy or might be assigned roles by existing group members despite their preference. Regardless of how someone assumes a role, the process by which roles are taken is called *role differentiation* (Forsyth 1999).

Role Ambiguity

What happens when a group member isn't quite sure of her role or of the behaviors associated with that role? Role ambiguity may result from the lack of information or feedback given to the member assuming the role; lack of resources; lack of purpose, goals, and objectives; or lack of experience in similar situations. New group members, or existing members who take on new roles, may experience role ambiguity if they do not receive appropriate explanation of what is expected of them. Some groups minimize role ambiguity by having written job descriptions, mentoring programs, big-sister and big-brother partnerships, or informal advisement of role responsibilities.

Role Conflict

Role conflict may occur if the requirements of one role are incompatible with the requirements of another role. This type of role conflict is called *interrole conflict*. Another type of role conflict is known as *intrarole conflict*. This conflict exists when the requirements of a single role are incompatible. For example, in your role as an outdoor adventure leader you might be asked to train a new leader. You share the responsibilities for leading the trip and develop a good working relationship with this person, but once you return from the trip, you must evaluate this person's performance. You've become friends, but you must provide an honest evaluation of the person's ability as a leader. This may cause conflicted feelings due to the role expectations of you as a trainer and you as an evaluator. Role conflict can be reduced the same way as role ambiguity is resolved. Written job descriptions, ongoing feedback, and briefing sessions will help individuals navigate the demands placed on them by the single role or multiple roles they inhabit.

Role Status

Roles often have varying levels of status associated with them. In most groups, status is correlated with the duties associated with a role, with the power a person has, or with the group members' perceptions of a person (Johnson and Johnson 2003). The leader is afforded certain rights and privileges based on the status associated with that role. There are also responsibilities associated with positions. A belayer in rock climbing is given a comfortable place from which to belay (manage the rope to arrest a climber's fall) but has the responsibility of constantly attending to the rope and climber. Most groups establish some type of role hierarchy and develop strategies and operating procedures that reflect the status associated with each of these positions.

Learning Activity

You're out paddling with your sea kayaking club for a five-day trip. You volunteered to help organize the experience and have found that people are getting along well and you are on schedule to reach your campsite for the night. As you look around, you see that each group member has occupied some niche in the group. Because you helped organize the trip and help facilitate most of the group's decisions, you are considered the leader.

Rachel is familiar with the area and likes to use her new Global Positioning System unit (an electronic instrument that uses satellites to pinpoint a person's location), and so she's become the group's navigator. Rachel also likes to sing songs around the campfire, so people look to her for evening entertainment. Judd loves to cook and is an avid bird-watcher. He's also done lots of reading on the cultural history of the area. Other group members look forward to Judd's gourmet meals at night, and they continuously ask Judd to name birds they see along the paddling route. However, he is a practical joker and sometimes takes things too far. Logan is new to sea kayaking and to camping. She is loud and doesn't help out much with camp chores. Logan isn't afraid to point out others who she thinks aren't pulling their weight. Rod always seems to be debating someone. He likes a good conversation, and he often plays the devil's advocate. He's a strong paddler and has taught some beginner paddlers how to rescue themselves if their kayak tips over.

Form groups of five. Have each person assume one of the roles just described and then play out the following scene: You're arriving at camp after a long, windy day of sea kayaking. It is starting to rain. Your group lands on the beach and. . . . After you've finished your role-play, discuss the following questions with your group:

1. What roles did each group member fill?
2. Were these roles complementary, or did they cause friction among group members?
3. What were the positive and negative aspects of each role? Are they always positive or negative?
4. What could you do as the leader to take advantage of the strengths of each person's role?

Socialization

Individuals who join a group don't just disappear into the collective mass of members. They experience different levels of engagement in the group over time and may experience stages similar to those the group as a whole experiences. A person's individual journey through group membership is called *group socialization*. Recreation and leisure professionals will be doing themselves, the group, and individual members a favor by keeping an eye on the individual's experience in a group context.

As mentioned earlier, when we are considering joining a group, we evaluate the cost as well as the gain of being associated with that group. A result of that evaluation is our level of commitment to the group, which will change over time (Moreland and Levine 1982). While the individual is evaluating the group,

the group is also evaluating the individual. If the group has a positive evaluation of the member, it will work to keep that person. If the evaluation is negative, the group may force the person out or discourage the person from continuing as a member. Moreland and Levine's (1982) model of group socialization is similar to the model of group formation previously discussed in this chapter. The five stages of group socialization are the following:

1. Investigation
2. Socialization
3. Maintenance
4. Resocialization
5. Remembrance

Figure 2.4 depicts a typical journey through group socialization. At each stage, an individual

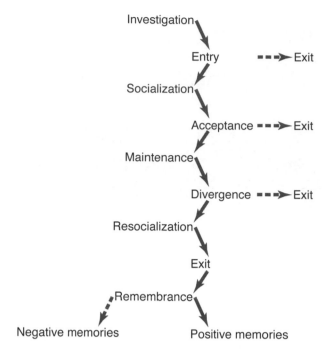

Dashed arrows indicate negative socialization experiences, which most likely cause a person to leave a group.

Solid arrows indicate positive socialization experiences, which most likely cause a person to remain with a group.

Figure 2.4   Stages of socialization.

chooses to leave or remain with the group. Over time, that person's needs and role within the group change. If the person's needs aren't being met, the person exits the group. Upon leaving, she will remember the group either positively or negatively, depending on her overall experience. Each of these stages is discussed in detail in the following sections.

Investigation

The investigation stage is marked by an individual identifying a group to join. A prospective member evaluates the costs and benefits of a number of groups and then determines which group will best enable her to reach her goals or meet her needs. Groups try to entice new members to join and assess the costs and benefits of having a particular person join the group. Once an invitation to join has been extended

to an individual and she decides to accept, the transition to the socialization phase takes place. This transition is called *entry* into a group. The investigation phase is similar to the forming phase of group development.

Socialization

During the socialization phase, a group incorporates the new member and reshapes roles and group procedures to meet the individual's needs. This process is called *accommodation*. Meanwhile, the individual assimilates the group's operating procedures, norms, standards, and means of communication. When this process is complete, the new member is accepted into the group as a full member. However, this process may be compromised if either the existing members or the new members cause the other to perceive them in a negative way (similar to the storming and norming phases in group development). For example, a group of swimming instructors has been teaching a program for the past five summers. Each of the instructors has always taught a specific level of swimming. Then a new instructor joins the group. This instructor has worked at a different facility for three years and challenges the traditions of the existing group by suggesting that the instructors mix up who teaches what class. The new instructor might be ostracized by the rest of the group if he is perceived as being too opinionated or as forcing others to change. On the other hand, the new instructor might think the others have formed an inaccessible good old boys' and girls' club.

Maintenance

The maintenance phase of socialization is marked by continued accommodation and assimilation by both individuals and group members. The group as a whole is working together well and is accomplishing both its task functions and its relationship functions. This phase is like the performing stage of group development. However, there is a constant evaluation of costs, benefits, and value of roles on both the individual and group level. When an individual questions her commitment to the group, or the group questions an individual's value to the collective, a transition to the resocialization phase takes place. This point is called *divergence*.

Toolbox Tips

Individual members come and go at various times during a group's life span. The stage of development that the group is in might make it difficult for an individual to become a full member or for existing members to leave the group on a good note. Here are some ideas to smooth an individual's transition into or out of a group, no matter what stage of development the group is experiencing.

- Set up a buddy system so longtime group members may mentor new members and help them acclimate to group norms, roles, and operating procedures.

- Provide written materials and other information describing how the group works.

- Before a new member arrives, announce that a new person is coming and encourage the group to take time to welcome the new member.

- Get the new member involved in the group in a meaningful way as soon as possible. Don't let new members sit in the background for too long.

- Discourage cliques from forming. Encourage inclusiveness, not exclusiveness!

- Speak with longtime group members who are questioning their involvement with the group—be a sounding board for them. Provide pros and cons about their staying or leaving.

- Encourage current group members to maintain contact with former group members—have a reunion or celebration for the group!

Resocialization

The resocialization phase is much like the socialization phase. The individual and group reevaluate each other and assimilate or accommodate once again. Two outcomes are possible at this point: Either the group member and group come to an agreement and recommit to each other (convergence) or the individual and group part ways. This second point of divergence leads to the individual exiting the group and is akin to the adjourning phase of group development.

Remembrance

During the remembrance stage of socialization, people review and relive their experience in the group, both as an individual and as a member of the collective. If an individual is viewed positively by group members, that person's memory may live on in group history and tradition. If not, that person may be talked about in negative tones and erased from collective memory.

SUMMARY

Understanding what motivates people to join groups is crucial when working with all types of groups in recreation, leisure, and experiential education settings. You can help people transition into full membership by recognizing what may have motivated them to join. You can also compare these motivations to where your group stands as a whole. Perhaps the reason a person is looking to join the group isn't compatible with the stage the group is at in its life span.

Recreation and leisure professionals benefit from knowing what makes groups attractive to individuals as well as what makes individuals attractive to groups. You can market group features that will draw interested people to the group. Attractive group qualities might be based on required skill level, location, ability to participate with others such as family members or singles, or age.

There are many models that describe how groups develop. The most commonly used model is Tuckman's, which includes five stages: forming, storming, norming, performing, and adjourning. Being aware of these phases will help you design lessons and activities and facilitate a positive experience for your group. You can better manage individuals' transitions into and out of the group by knowing the group's stage of development. Professionals often face the difficult task of working with groups that have a very fluid and dynamic membership. Understanding that groups might skip over or repeat certain stages will help you in creating positive recreation, leisure, and experiential education experiences.

Remember the individual's process of entering and leaving a group, as group members come and go at various stages in the group life span. Developing strategies such as assigning a buddy to new members or confronting exclusive cliques of longtime members will help individuals transition into and out of a recreation and leisure group. Good professionals will have sound programming, facilitation, and leadership skills that will allow them to confront any difficulties they encounter with individuals entering and leaving groups as well as with the different stages of a group's life span.

Groups create operating rules, or norms, for themselves. Many recreation, leisure, and experiential education activities have norms in place, such as rules and regulations associated with specific sports. There may also be laws that set norms for participant behavior. Understanding a group's norms and how those norms came about allows professionals to revise norms that don't seem inclusive or supportive of what the group is about. You can also relate norms to prospective or new members so they can be prepared for how the group operates and gain full membership more quickly.

Much like norms, roles provide guidelines for individual behaviors in groups. Depending on the recreation, leisure, and experiential education activity, many roles are already determined. Examples of roles include the point guard in basketball, the dealer in card games, the stern paddler in flat-water canoeing, and the treasurer in the Waterfront Extravaganza committee. A clear understanding of the expectations for each role in the group will prevent misunderstandings and help your group accomplish the task at hand while maintaining positive relationships. If individu-

als become dissatisfied with their roles, perhaps it is time for the group to focus on the relationship function instead of the task function. Once these issues have been resolved, focus may return to what needs to be done.

RESOURCES

Bales, R.F. 1965. The equilibrium problem in small groups. In *Small groups: Studies in social interaction,* ed. A.P. Hare, E.F. Borgatta, and R.F. Bales, 450-56. New York: Knopf.

Beebe, S.A., and J.T. Masterson. 2000. *Communicating in small groups: Principles and practices.* 6th ed. New York: Longman.

Fisher, B.A. 1970. Decision emergence: Phases in group decision making. *Speech Monography* 37:53-66.

Forsyth, D. 1999. *Group dynamics.* 3rd ed. Belmont, CA: Wadsworth.

Johnson, D.W., and F.P. Johnson. 2003. *Joining together: Group theory and group skills.* 8th ed. Boston: Pearson Education.

Maslow, A. 1954. *Motivation and personality.* New York: Harper & Row.

Moreland, R., and J. Levine. 1982. Socialization in small groups: Temporal changes in individual-group relations. *Advances in Experimental Social Psychology* 15:137-92.

Moreland, R., and J. Levine. 1988. Group dynamics over time: Development and socialization in small groups. In *The social psychology of time,* ed. J. McGrath, 151-81. Newbury Park, CA: Sage.

Poole, M.S., D.R. Seibold, and R.D. McPhee. 1996. A structurational approach to theory building in group decision-making research. In *Communication and group decision making.* 2nd ed., ed. R.Y. Hirokawa and M.S. Poole, 114-46. Beverly Hills, CA: Sage.

Schutz, W. 1958. *FIRO: A three-dimensional theory of interpersonal behavior.* New York: Reinhart & Co.

Thibaut, J., and H. Kelley. 1959. *The social psychology of groups.* New York: Wiley.

Tuckman, B.W. 1965. Developmental sequences in small groups. *Psychological Bulletin* 63:384-99.

CHAPTER

3

The Conscious Group

Raul enrolled in a course called *Group Dynamics and Facilitation* offered as part of the recreation degree program he was studying in university. On the first day of class, the instructor intrigued him right away when she said that her purpose was to help her students see groups in a new light. Raul noticed that she didn't say that she wanted to show her students how to be better leaders, to get groups to be more productive, or to help group members get along. So in what way did she want them to see groups differently? After all, aren't groups all about getting things done? Isn't the point of being part of a group to accomplish things that we can't achieve by ourselves?

When Raul asked the instructor why these goals seemed to be missing from her purpose, she thanked him for making an insightful observation and explained that while some of those things were certainly goals she held for her students, she believed that there was a fundamental piece missing from the usual discussions on group dynamics. She promised she would elaborate in the classes to follow, and Raul wondered what was ahead.

The instructor gave them a strange assignment on that first day. In groups, they were to use the final 10 minutes of class to develop a presentation topic for the next class. They were to work only from what they managed to develop in class and could not talk to each other about it once class was over.

When the class met again, the presentations proved to be both funny and frustrating. There was no time to prepare fully, and the resulting problems gave rise to a range of reactions from different students. Some were visibly anxious that their presentations were less than polished. Others looked like they couldn't care less, and still others saw their presentation as an opportunity to practice improv.

Once the presentations finished, the instructor began a discussion about the assignment and its effects on the students. A variety of responses were offered: Some students thought it was a lot of fun, some were confused, and some asked angrily what such an assignment could possibly accomplish. After encouraging the students to speak their minds and listening to them, the instructor simply asked, "How on earth could you all have such different reactions to the same experience?" She then began to discuss the value of working toward becoming a conscious group.

The instructor explained that organized recreational groups generally include personal growth as part of their mandate and that experiences in recreational group activities can have similar or different meanings for the individuals who experience them. Little wonder, then, that experiential education theories, which maintain that personal growth comes from quality experiences, dominate recreational leadership teaching and practice.

Furthermore, in group dynamics, quality experiences require interaction that develops a shared understanding of group members' experiences. Group members who are conscious of this process are likely to create better interpersonal interactions and thereby instill a more positive group dynamic.

In this chapter, we explore the what, why, and how of developing conscious groups in recreation and leisure experiences. Ultimately, conscious groups are about growing toward respect in and for a shared experience.

PERSONAL GROWTH IN RECREATION GROUPS

Pure enjoyment of an activity is inadequate to describe quality recreational pursuits. Research has indicated that an increase in life quality and well-being through personal growth is very often associated with organized recreational groups. In fact, this element of experience within a recreational group is so entrenched that it has become a fundamental part of what is taught in college and university recreation programs worldwide. Many recreation and leisure service providers recognize that personal growth is a social good, and they have not only developed programs around this benefit but also started marketing it as part of the experience they deliver. For many involved in the field, recreation should not only provide an activity to take up a person's time, but also contribute to the health and well-being of the person and the community. One pointed example of how closely connected recreation and personal growth have become is the spread of therapeutic recreation courses and programs. Programs for youths at risk and persons with disabilities have boomed in recent years. The link between recreation and personal growth is now well established.

In Western societies, most people have come to expect some personal growth and lasting increase in quality of life from their participation in recreation. This is precisely the type of group that this book addresses. While leaders of any group may find the "conscious group" approach developed here helpful, we are most interested in providing a framework for the positive evolution of groups that identify personal growth as an inherent component of their purpose. We refer to this as *purposeful recreation*—that is, recreation that seeks to contribute positively to the self, others, and the community.

Achieving personal growth in group settings requires the group to focus at least some of its activity and energy on this area. Sometimes the group may be aware of this, but not always. Group leaders, for example, may allow for the discovery of some aspect of personal growth without divulging their plans in advance. Sometimes group activities may be fun or challenging and completely absorb the group members as they try to achieve what they see as success. The leader, on the other hand, may want to use the activity for another, more social, purpose. A common example of this is giving newly formed groups a series of initiative tasks. These are generally fun tasks that present a problem that frequently requires creativity and almost always requires the group members to work together in order to solve it. The ultimate goal of the initiative task, from the leader's perspective, has more to do with group members learning to cooperate than it does with finding a solution. In these activities, the group members need to make the connection that the point of the exercise has more to do with team building and group dynamics than the task itself.

A key commonality in purposeful recreation is that the group members grow personally, and it is so

© iStockphoto/Mark Rose

Ultimately, group members need to understand that activities are more about team building than just having fun.

much better if they become aware of this growth and how it is happening. Making the entire group aware that positive personal and interpersonal growth is part of a group's purpose can enhance group dynamics and the overall outcome of group process. If group members are mature and understand that personal growth is central to their group's purpose, ultimately they could take on the responsibility for their own continued growth. Such a committed, self-aware collection of people can accomplish great things, and these people are well on their way to being a conscious group.

A conscious group, then, is one that recognizes that the personal growth of its members is a main focus besides any other goals or productivity objectives it may have. Members of a conscious group seek to learn and grow from their experiences, strive to better themselves and their relationships with others within the group (and preferably beyond the group as well), and are aware that this personal growth component is part of what they hope to achieve.

EXPERIENCE AND MEANING

Recall Raul's revelation about students in his class experiencing the assignment in different ways. Experiences are subjective—their meaning depends on an individual's interpretation of what has happened. Acknowledging that experience is subjective can help us understand group dynamics because it allows us to ask how to meet people's diverse needs and perspectives. When participants directly address what the experience means to the other group members, they are able to see each other's needs and the meanings they attach to the same activities and events. In other words, in group settings, working toward a shared understanding of what an activity or event means to each of the participants will likely enrich each person's own experience, enhancing the enjoyment of it and the learning taken from it.

Experiences are indeed diverse and result from the relationship between the individual (e.g., the individual's personality, cultural background, gender, mood, and other personal factors) and the context (the physical and social environment in which the activity takes place). All sorts of factors affect how people interpret their experiences. Many conditions will be common to group members, such as the physical environment and shared cultural understanding. On the other hand, quite a few conditions will be unique to each individual. This blend of common and unique aspects that make up each group member's experience explains some of what happens in the development of subjective meaning that can be generated by people who, on the surface at least, are experiencing the same activity. Some meaning will be common to all or most participants, and some will belong to only one individual.

If you've ever been part of a group that has talked about an event it has participated in, you may be able to recall how group members experienced the same occurrences differently. Imagine that during a one-day ski trip you took with a group of students last winter in a densely wooded area, your group became lost despite attempts to navigate with map and compass. There were concerted efforts to become found again, and positive thinking was expressed that the group must be headed in the right direction. All morning there were discussions about where you might be, and the level of frustration rose for almost everyone at the prospect of not being in control of the situation. Just before lunch, the student leading at the time noticed ski tracks ahead. After some investigative work, you all deduced that the tracks were your own: the group had circled around and ended up almost exactly at the place you had started. Everyone decided to have lunch right there and discuss the options.

While the talk among the students ranged from how you could have become so turned around to how frustrated many people felt, Sara gave everyone some insight into her own experience of the morning's events, one that was quite different from the rest of the group. She had noticed from the map that you were in no real danger, as the area you were traveling in was bounded by roads on two sides; she also knew that if worse came to worse, the group could simply retrace its tracks to find the way back (the beauty of traveling in freshly fallen snow). With that mind-set, Sara had simply let the morning unfold and was overjoyed to be out on such a glorious day. The frustration felt by the rest of the group had not infected Sara at all. As a result of Sara's reflection, your group's afternoon was less stressful, and several others noted later that a highlight of their day was realizing that there was no real need to feel frustrated. Sara had provided a perspective that helped the rest of you to see your shared experience in a different light.

Providing a different perspective is not the only outcome of sharing your view of an experience. You may also find that your thoughts and feelings are similar to those of others, even if you were under the impression that you were the only one thinking and feeling that way. In fact, often two or more group members are sharing similar thoughts and feelings. For example, it's quite possible that someone else in your ski group—let's call him *Ben*—was feeling the same way as Sara but didn't speak up for fear of making the rest of the group members more frustrated or even angry at him because of a perception that he didn't care about being lost. When Sara voiced her opinion at lunch, Ben would have felt a wave of relief that someone else had a view similar to his; he would have felt validated.

Recognizing experiences as individualized as well as shared creates as many opportunities as it does barriers. An approach to group dynamics that negotiates those individual experiences is a viable option. It is advantageous for members of a group to be exposed to the other members' interpretations of an experience. It broadens their horizons and not only assists them in seeing the world through the eyes of others but also gives them opportunities to compare and evaluate perspectives. People may receive validation from other members, but they may also be presented with new and beneficial ideas. In the scenario with Sara

and the skiing group, it was not necessary (nor would it always be appropriate) for the rest of your group to adopt Sara's experience, but her thoughts certainly gave the rest of you something to think about. Some people may have left that day thinking that they had a brand new approach in their perspectives toolbox, while Sara, and certainly Ben, may have learned how empowering it is to feel validated by someone else sharing a similar view.

You can begin to see how a group sets itself on the path to becoming a conscious one. Sara helped the rest of you learn something about yourselves and others that day. You all grew personally from her insight; it challenged or affirmed your way of thinking and therefore your experience. Sara's sharing not only altered your afternoon but also quite possibly changed future experiences of this nature for the better because of what the group learned from reflecting on her input.

However, the events of this day did not automatically make your ski group a conscious group. The learning was accidental, and you were not necessarily committed to personal growth as part of what you were out to discover that day. Learning and personal growth do not have to be strictly planned, but they do have to be *planned for*. In other words, allowing the learning to happen needs to be made a priority,

Learning Activity

At Camp Northstar, a group is preparing for a canoe trip. The group will be spending a week away and will encounter the typical geography seen on canoe trips: big and small lakes, rivers (including rapids), and portages—some easy, some long and difficult. In thinking about what they hope for and expect from the trip, the campers share similarities but also have significant differences as well. Two campers are looking forward to learning more about technical white-water skills, while another is dreading that part of the trip. A few are looking for some downtime and relaxation. One camper wants to push herself and test her limits. Still another is anticipating a feeling of independence, two more are simply interested in wilderness living, and one is not sure what he wants from the trip.

Frustration could certainly result as you try to meet everyone's needs—especially those personal goals or expectations at odds—in a setting that legitimizes each person's wish for an enjoyable time on a canoe trip. Whether or not the campers enjoy the trip is contingent on the trip meeting their expectations. More than likely the social relationships in the group will be affected by individuals' perceptions of how well the trip is meeting their preconceptions. Is it possible to facilitate a trip that will create different experiences and satisfy expectations? How might you develop a shared understanding of what the canoe trip will be like before you go?

which often requires setting aside a specific time and space for learning to occur. The process of group members seeing the value of the learning to their own lives and witnessing the positive changes that result is what makes the group conscious.

EXPERIENTIAL EDUCATION AND GROUP DYNAMICS

A great deal of what influences, or even guides, experiences in the recreational field is a concept called *experiential education.* While experiential education evolved primarily as a theory of education, it relates easily to the field of recreation in that a great deal of learning makes up recreational experiences, especially those of conscious groups. Whether a person wishes to take up a new recreational activity or refine already accomplished techniques, learning will have to take place. And in the arena of group dynamics, learning is a constant if mutual respect, open communication, personal growth, and group consonance are to be achieved and maintained. Group members will need to learn continually about others and themselves in order to contribute to a smoothly functioning unit.

There has been some debate about what exactly experiential education is, and the debate is still active today. In his book *Experience and Education,* a watershed text for educational reform, John Dewey wrote that "all genuine learning comes about through experience" (1938, 25). Dewey rejected imposed learning, sometimes referred to as *didactic learning,* in which a teacher gives information and it is assumed that students then learn the material. Dewey argued for an educational philosophy that engages the whole person, one that students could relate to through experience. While some have defined experiential education as learning by doing (which is one of the reasons it has been attractive to people involved in recreation), more recent efforts to describe the complexities of experiential learning have realized that it involves more than simply being active. This understanding reflects Dewey's thoughts:

> The belief that all genuine education comes about through experience does not mean that all experiences are genuinely or equally educative. Experience and education cannot be directly equated to each other. For some experiences are *mis-educative. Any experience is mis-educative that has the effect of arresting or distorting the growth of further experience. An experience may be such as to engender callousness; it may produce lack of sensitivity and of responsiveness. Then the possibilities of having richer experience in the future are restricted. (25-26)*

Dewey regarded experiences as continuous, one building on the next, and took the view that there is an element of quality to a person's experiences. Mis-educative experiences provide a poor foundation for further positive growth, while quality experiences not only engage the learner in the immediate lesson but also facilitate further interest, creative responses, and learning.

Experiential Learning Models

Neill (2004) outlined nine models, constructed by various theorists, that have attempted to describe how learning happens in experiential education. Neill grouped the models according to how many stages they involved. Let's take a look at the various stages. Models with 1 to 3 stages are generally straightforward, while more explanation is needed for models with 4, 5, or 6 stages.

One-Stage Model

The simplest form of experiential learning, the one-stage model, involves only experience. In the earlier days of Outward Bound in North America, some instructors made a call to "let the mountains speak for themselves." These instructors believed that interpreting an outdoor experience was unnecessary because the act of traveling in and living among the mountains was enough to create positive change for people in their courses.

Two- and Three-Stage Models

In the two-stage model, participants are encouraged to reflect on the completed event or activity. Presumably the reflection will lead to change, a step that the three-stage model makes more explicit. The three-stage model calls for group members to plan for future experiences based on the reflection done with the current one (see figure 3.1).

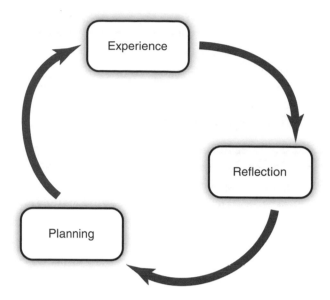

Figure 3.1 Three-stage experiential learning model.

Kolb's Four-Stage Model

The best known four-stage model of experiential learning is Kolb's (1984) experiential learning cycle. Kolb's model breaks the reflection process of the three-stage model into two parts: reflective observation and abstract conceptualization. Reflective observation asks participants to reflect on their experience, perhaps by describing it or answering questions that help create meaning. In abstract conceptualization, participants use other abstract thoughts to arrive at conclusions that will allow them to transfer the learning to areas of life not related directly to the experience they had. Thus, the whole cycle involves a concrete experience followed by reflective observation and abstract conceptualization and finished with active experimentation to apply new ideas and principles to other situations.

Joplin's Five-Stage Model

In developing a model to portray the components of experiential education, Laura Joplin (1995) followed Dewey in describing all learning as experiential. Learners must feel personal interaction with what they are learning. In other words, learners must feel engaged by the information or insights they are processing; the learning must mean something to the learner. Joplin's five-stage model (see figure 3.2) illustrates how the components of an experience come together in a cyclical fashion to create meaningful learning.

- **Stage 1: Focus.** The first stage of the cycle, focus, is the preparation phase and is used to orient the participants to the upcoming task. Ideally, a focusing action leaves ample room for participants to develop their own interpretations about what is

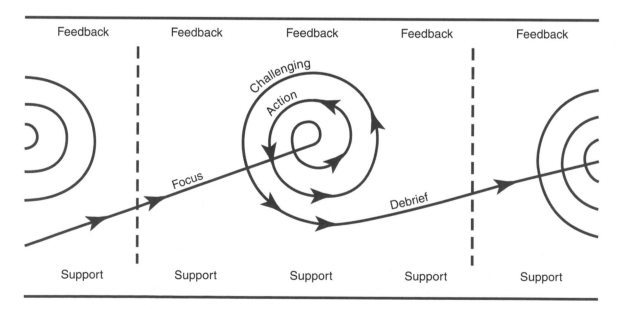

Figure 3.2 Joplin's five-stage experiential learning model.

Reprinted, by permission, from L. Joplin, 1995, On defining experiential education. In *The theory of experiential education* (Boulder, CO: Association for Experiential Education), 16.

going to happen and to bring their own meaning to the experience. Whatever the message delivered in the focusing action, the goal is to spark interest in participants and to begin to engage them in the upcoming activity. Telling the Northstar campers a story about a canoeing adventure is one way of focusing them for their upcoming trip. The story could describe how satisfying hard work can be, demonstrate how its characters discover something about themselves, show how wilderness canoeing is a great way to connect with nature, or highlight the adventure and fun of canoeing. Focus can be indirect, such as when the counselor reads a story, or direct, such as when the counselor simply asks her campers to voice their expectations of the next few days.

• **Stage 2: Challenging action.** Challenging action is at the center of the model. During this stage, participants find themselves in situations that require actions from them that are not simply a reconstruction of things they have done before and require new skills or problem solving. For example, for anyone who is an only child, sharing a tent with other campers requires learning new social skills and solving the problems that arise from losing control over personal space. The implication is that a significant part of the responsibility for learning is held by the participant. Of course, assigning tasks that have a reasonable chance of success is also important. The camp counselor who requires his campers to paddle from dawn to dusk each day in order to complete an extremely demanding route runs the risk of turning his campers off canoe tripping for a long time if they have other legitimate goals that are not met while on the trip.

• **Stages 3 and 4: Support and feedback.** Support and feedback provide the background in which the participants negotiate their activity. Engendering support—ideally among all members of a group—allows individuals to feel that they exist in a safe and caring environment and can therefore risk failure without being ostracized or judged. In addition, participants can feel that their successes are shared and celebrated. Properly constructed feedback supplies information that increases either the individual's or the group's opportunities for success. A simple example of physical feedback is giving corrective suggestions for a camper's white-water technique. Other, less objective forms of feedback include praising someone for his awareness of others' feelings or suggesting to a swift-handed camper that this time he let someone else be the first to choose from the neatly arranged plates of dessert.

• **Stage 5: Debrief.** The debriefing stage is when the learning is made conscious. While debriefing can take a variety of forms (e.g., discussions or closing activities that stimulate reflection), Joplin, like many experiential educators, insists that it must include some element that is made public. Without input from others in the group, individuals will miss the opportunity to contextualize their own learning—to further their understanding of how they and others overlap and differ in their construction of the personal meaning and lessons they will take away from any given experience.

Six-Stage Model

In a modification of Priest's (1990) judgment model, Priest and Gass (1997) developed the experiential learning and judgment paradigm, a formulation of experiential learning that includes Dewey's emphasis on judgment as a key component in an experiential learning cycle. The paradigm contains the following six stages:

1. Experience
2. Induce
3. Generalize
4. Deduce
5. Apply
6. Evaluate

This six-stage model breaks the reflection phase of the other models into three distinct stages: induce, generalize, and deduce. Priest and Gass describe this portion of the learning cycle, which immediately follows the experience, in this way:

Second, you subject these specific experiences to inductive reflection, moving from the specific to the general. Third, you form generalized concepts and store them in memory (either long- or short-term) as a map of connected concepts. When faced with uncertainty, your brain searches these memory maps for relevant concepts. Fourth, you subject these retrieved concepts to deductive reflection, moving from the general back to the specific. (1997, 155)

With some additions, the story of Raul's experience told at the beginning of this chapter is an example of how this part of the Priest and Gass model works. The presentation assignment was an experience, after which students were invited to discuss their observations of individuals' reactions to the assignment. The professor's lecture used that discussion to develop abstract concepts that helped Raul connect his previous ideas with ones that were newer to him. For instance, Raul was able to connect how the subjective nature of experience can explain why he and other group members viewed the assignment so differently. In addition, he was able to imagine that working toward conscious groups can enhance personal growth. In deductive reflection, Raul might use the general concepts and connections he has made in class to work toward a specific solution he might be looking for in working with a group of troubled youths.

The fifth stage of the Priest and Gass model (apply) is similar to Kolb's active experimentation in that the learner puts into practice what she has learned from the earlier stages of the cycle. Priest and Gass added the sixth stage (evaluate) to formalize the importance of assessing how well the learning works when it is put into practice.

Reflection is what connects one experience to improved future experiences.

Reflection

One of the keys to connecting experiential education and group dynamics rests with the stages that have been described as reflection, debriefing, or processing. In all except the one-stage model, reflection is what connects one experience to improved future experiences. While leaders concerned with group dynamics must ensure that the initial and intermediate stages of a group's involvement in an activity are high quality, it is not enough to then simply assume that the experience can speak for itself or that each group member has undergone a similar experience. Simpson, Miller, and Bocher (2006) define processing as "a planned activity designed to give meaning to the action" (18). In answering the question, "Why process?", these authors suggest the following:

> The most common reason for processing is to make clear to all participants the lessons of a specific activity. Some lessons are self-evident to 80% of the participants, and processing reveals those lessons to the 20% who did not discern them on their own. Other lessons of an action are subtle, and just about all of the participants need a processing session to appreciate the implications. In these instances, processing brings to light the less obvious lessons of an experience. (18)

Learning the lessons of an experience may also involve gaining insight into the meaning that others attach to the experience. Gaining insight into the meaning of other people's experiences can be a powerful tool in group dynamics.

If you were to spend time talking with the Northstar campers after their canoe trip, you would find that while there are many similarities in how they view their personal experience of the trip, there are also significant differences. From the small, almost unimportant differences, such as not liking the same meals, to the larger, more meaningful disagreements, such as feeling that the trip was too difficult or too easy, not everyone will—or even should—have had the same experience. Often, participants will not even be aware that their individual experiences varied from

Corey Rich/Aurora Photos

Learning Activity

To test these ideas within your own experiences, discuss with others some of the successes and failures you've experienced around interpersonal relationships in groups you've been part of. Analyze what it was that contributed to the success or failure of interactions among group members. Were your groups conscious of their purposes? Do you think the members had similar or different experiences of the same events? Were there attempts to understand individual experiences? Was this understanding used to modify the group to enhance group members' awareness of each other's subjective experiences?

those of others in the group until the meanings of certain events are explored.

Therein lies the key to developing a conscious group: creating conditions in which group members can understand each other better and thus develop empathy and caring for others. Although it is not always necessary or desirable to facilitate reflection (sometimes the lessons are painfully obvious, the timing is not right, or the group members feel processing fatigue), reflection is needed in many situations to foster a shared understanding of experience. If personal growth is individual change that enhances a person's understanding of and connections to self, others, and the wider world, it is difficult to conclude that people can achieve their highest levels of understanding and connection without input from and communication with others.

If important meanings are allowed to remain unexplored, the consequences for group development, group dynamics, and personal growth can be severe. For example, if some group members had been expecting to learn white water on the trip but did not get to, they could harbor considerable bitterness or even resentment against the people they perceive to be responsible for this failure. Interestingly, the interpretation of an experience can become rather complex. In the white-water example, it could be that the expectation to learn white water was not expressed or even a part of the trip objectives. However, it could also be that the intention to run white water was thwarted by environmental conditions (the river was flooded or too low), overall group competence (the rapids encountered were too difficult for all members to run safely), or changing priorities (falling behind schedule and the need to reach the end point of the trip left no time for white-water instruction). Reflection gives group members the opportunity to clarify intentions

and misunderstandings. It allows people to realign the actual events of an experience with what they were hoping would happen when they started out, and perhaps get some perspective from hindsight.

Although reflection is an important component of becoming a conscious group, it is not the intention of this book to detail debriefing or processing and the accompanying techniques. There are many fine resources that do much greater justice to the topic, several of which can be found in the reference list at the end of the chapter.

If we look at group dynamics in recreation from the perspective of experiential education, two main ideas emerge. First, in recreation fields, personal growth is not just a by-product of being in a group—very often it is part of the reason why the group exists. As Dewey asserted, not all experiences are of good quality, and recognizing this makes a recreational group's purpose as much about the personal development of the group members as about the activity the group revolves around. Second, group members who are aware of their own and others' experiences (and the meanings those experiences hold for them) are more likely to understand each other, respect each other, and help each other realize individual goals and expectations. In other words, the conscious group—one that is aware of and attends to the meanings of its members' experiences—has an advantage when it comes to creating productive, healthy, and growth-oriented relationships.

SUMMARY

This chapter provided connecting ideas to make the case that interpersonal dynamics in recreational groups can benefit from an experiential education approach. In the recreation field, personal growth of group members is integral to a group's purpose. This chapter also argued that members of a conscious group form stronger and healthier relationships and that experiential education provides a framework for this to take place.

RESOURCES

Dewey, J. 1938. *Experience and education.* New York: Macmillan.

Joplin, L. 1995. On defining experiential education. In *The theory of experiential education,* ed. K. Warren, M. Sakofs, and J. Hunt Jr., 15-22. Dubuque, Iowa: Kendall/Hunt.

Knapp, C. 1993. Lasting lessons: A teacher's guide to reflecting on experience. Charleston, WV: ERIC.

Kolb, D. 1984. *Experiential learning: Experience as the source of learning and development.* Englewood Cliffs, NJ: Prentice Hall.

Neill, J. 2004. Experiential learning cycles: Overview of 9 experiential learning cycle models. http://wilderdom.com/experiential/elc/ExperientialLearningCycle.htm.

Priest, S. 1990. Everything you always wanted to know about judgment, but were afraid to ask. *Journal of Adventure Education and Outdoor Leadership* 7(3): 5-12.

Priest, S., and M. Gass. 1997. *Effective leadership in adventure programming.* Champaign, IL: Human Kinetics.

Simpson, S., D. Miller, and B. Bocher. 2006. *The processing pinnacle: An educator's guide to better processing.* Oklahoma City: Wood 'N' Barnes.

Sugerman, D., K. Doherty, D. Garvey, and M. Gass. 2000. *Reflective learning: Theory and practice.* Dubuque, Iowa: Kendall/Hunt.

Part II

Developing the Conscious Group

With part I having laid the theoretical foundation of a conscious group, part II focuses on the information needed to develop groups in this direction. In understanding what a conscious group looks like, you might ask, "What should we consider in getting there?" Chapters 4 through 10 answer that question.

Chapter 4 takes a detailed look at the relationships existing among purpose, goals, objectives, and expectations. It defines these terms, outlines the importance of articulating them, and provides direction on how to develop them with group members. Chapter 5 examines moral development and discusses how it may be used to create more emotionally and ethically mature groups. A central role of groups is to establish decision-making processes. Chapter 6 presents this important element of group life, providing a variety of decision-making techniques groups can explore and potentially use to suit their own unique set of circumstances. Chapter 7 outlines how power and conflict can affect group functioning both positively and negatively and provides strategies for framing as well as managing and transforming conflict so as to produce optimal results. Understanding how gender may affect interactions among group members is a key issue in group dynamics, especially in the context of recreation and leisure. Chapter 8 explores the concept of gender in group development and function, reviewing the creation of gendered individuals, examining gender roles in groups, and exploring gender and leadership. Based on the assumption that people who read this book are leaders or are interested in leadership, chapter 9 presents basic leadership theories and then applies the notion of leadership to facilitating a recreation group. The final chapter in part II, chapter 10, looks at factors affecting groups that are external to the individual personalities within the groups. Chapter 10 explores the way physical environmental factors (such as temperature and noise level) and social environmental characteristics (such as personal space and territoriality) affect groups.

4

Purpose, Goals, Objectives, and Expectations

As a new program director for a summer camp, Luc was excited for the start of the season. The staff had just come through an intense week of training, and only a few days remained until all the young faces would arrive. All of the counselors were in planning mode, preparing program activities and trips for the cabin groups they would soon meet.

As Luc wandered around the dining hall, checking on individuals and small clusters of people busily creating the fun and learning of the next few weeks, he was a little surprised to see a group of counselors having a very difficult time planning the route and activities for a multicabin day trip for the oldest campers (15- and 16-year-olds). The discussion had become heated, and Luc approached in time to hear Dylan say that they should make it a hard day of paddling. Almost instantly, Eban pointed out that such a trip would not allow for much else beyond paddling, and he was very keen to pass on his knowledge of natural history. Then Bethany and Carmen expressed impatience for learning the "names of plants and bugs" and made the case for a day filled with games, cookouts, and catching a few rays. In the meantime, Astrid attempted to make everyone happy by suggesting that they do a little of everything. At first, the other counselors considered Astrid's appeal for compromise,

but after a little more discussion they all concluded that they wouldn't be able to fit all of the ideas into one day and that some of the activity proposals were in fact in opposition to each other.

Luc agreed that they wouldn't be able to cover everything, but fortunately for this planning team, he was able to recognize the group's main problem. His background with group goal setting allowed Luc to see that the counselors were attempting to plan the content of the day without fully understanding (or at least agreeing on) what the day should be about. Luc knows that activities are a means to an end, and he saw that the counselors had skipped the vital step of asking what they wanted the day to achieve for their campers. He proceeded to give them a quick lesson on purpose, goals, objectives, and expectations and explained how the counselors could go about setting them for the day trip.

Ten minutes after Luc left the group, he went back to check on the counselors and saw with some satisfaction that although they had to take a step back in their planning process, they were now on track and creating activities based on a much better understanding of what the day should be about. Luc made a mental note to make some adjustments to the next year's staff training session on setting goals and objectives.

DEFINING TERMS

Defining the group purpose, goals, objectives, and expectations is a mainstay of organizing groups and their activities. Interestingly, however, if you browse the Internet or flip through an assortment of dictionaries to gain an understanding of these terms, you

might come away even more confused than you were when you started. Many dictionaries, for example, treat the words *goals* and *objectives* interchangeably, often using one word to define the other. The terms used in specialized fields such as recreation do not always mesh well with the way the same words are used in everyday language. Thus it is important for you to know the meaning of terms as they are used within your chosen field.

Even within the recreation context—in which purpose, goals, objectives, and expectations are embedded in what it means to facilitate groups—practitioners do not always distinguish these words. In the worst cases, groups never identify their purpose, goals, objectives, or expectations. However, it is also confusing when leaders lump these ideas together, and participants sometimes find themselves trying to identify their *goalsandexpectations* or their *goalsandobjectives*. If you want your groups to have a better feeling of what they are about, what they are supposed to do, and how they might go about doing it, it will help to understand the meanings of these terms and the relationships among them. Let's look at how mission statements, statements of purpose, goals, objectives, and expectations can be described in useful ways that will not only distinguish these terms from each other but also clarify how they are connected.

Purpose

It is necessary to be clear on what a purpose is speaking to. Generally, a statement of purpose describes the core of something—the reason for its existence. However, it may be conceived of differently depending on whether it is written for an organization as a whole or for a particular experience. If it relates to an organization, a statement of purpose usually is associated with taking a philosophical position and often speaks to the organization's values and beliefs. These formulations may include mission statements and vision statements, such as in the case of the Association for Experiential Education (AEE). In describing its reason for existing—its purpose—the AEE moves from the very broad to something more focussed (Association for Experiential Education 2008):

Our Vision

The vision of the Association for Experiential Education is to contribute to making a more just and compassionate world by transforming education.

Our Mission

The mission of the Association for Experiential Education is to develop and promote experien-

tial education. The association is committed to supporting professional development, theoretical advancement and the evaluation of experiential education worldwide.

A closer look at the relationship between vision and mission would reveal that a vision is future oriented and rather general. A vision should be about how the world—or your small corner of it—will be changed as a result of your group's existence. A well-known outdoor clothing and gear company in Canada, Mountain Equipment Co-op (MEC), views a mision statement as being informed by a vision, with both being influenced by an expressed set of values. MEC's mission statement then allows the company to develop a business model that guides their everyday operations. Table 4.1 spells out specifically what each term means to MEC and how each applies to the organization.

The purpose of a group or an organization may or may not be the same as the purpose of a particular experience because the experience may be narrower in focus. The purpose of individual courses or programs within a college, for instance, would almost certainly be more practical than the overall purpose of the college. Nonetheless, whatever it serves, a purpose should speak to the reason why an entity or experience exists—the purpose is an overarching statement of what is to be gained from this existence.

Goals

A goal is also a broad statement, but it should embody intended outcomes. In other words, a goal is a result that is hoped for as a consequence of being involved. Goals can be set by the group leader, by participants, or by both working together. Several examples of goals follow:

- To create a climate of trust and emotional safety in group discussions

- To provide opportunities for personal growth through reflection

- To facilitate the development of leadership skills

- To encourage participants to transfer lessons learned on the trip to their everyday lives at home

Table 4.1 Purpose, Vision, Mission, and Values of Mountain Equipment Co-op

Our purpose	To support people in achieving the benefit of wilderness-oriented recreation.	Our purpose is what we resolve to do.
Our vision	Mountain Equipment Co-op is an innovative, thriving cooperative that inspires excellence in products and services, passion for wilderness experiences, leadership for a just world, and action for a healthy planet.	Our vision is our picture of the future and outlines where we want to go.
Our mission	Mountain Equipment Co-op provides quality products and services for self-propelled wilderness-oriented recreation, such as hiking and mountaineering, at the lowest reasonable price in an informative, respectful manner. We are a member-owned cooperative striving for social and environmental leadership.	Our mission tells us what business we are in, who we serve, and how. It represents the fundamental reason for MEC's existence.
Our values	We conduct ourselves ethically and with integrity. We show respect for others in our words and actions. We act in the spirit of community and cooperation. We respect and protect our natural environment. We strive for personal growth, continual learning, and adventure.	Our values influence our conduct both collectively as an organization and individually as employees, directors, and members of our community. We strive to have our actions reflect these values, demonstrate personal accountability, and be publicly defensible.

From Mountain Equipment Co-op 2008 and Five Winds International 2004.

- To become a more competent swimmer

A goal should contribute to a group's overall purpose, and group leaders should be able to trace an abstract path between the two. The connection may not be immediately obvious. At the very least, a goal should not counter a group's purpose. A goal should be another step along the continuum from abstract to concrete. While it may be difficult to decide, for example, if your vision for contributing to a just society is being realized through your program offerings, it is a little easier to know if your group members have managed to develop an atmosphere of trust and emotional safety during their time together. How you can know to what degree and in what ways you have reached your goal is where objectives come into play.

Objectives

An objective is outcome-based, specific, and, when possible, measurable. A classic educational objective could be written like this: "Students will be able to identify and display at least five positive communication techniques." Being measurable does not have to

mean that percentages or other quantitative assessments must be set and reached. A perfectly acceptable objective can be assessed based on whether an outcome took place. For example, to reach a goal to "provide opportunities for participants to improve group leadership skills," one objective could be written as follows: "Each participant will facilitate a formal debriefing session." Further elements of what should take place in that debriefing session could be added, if desired. The main idea is that it is easy to assess an objective simply as a result of whether it actually happens.

Objectives that involve human interaction and achievement, especially in the recreation field, often are expressed in behavioral terms. In addition, objectives should contribute to identified goals. One way to express the relationship among purpose, goals, and objectives is illustrated in figure 4.1.

Expectations

Although expectations do not fit neatly into the diagram of figure 4.1, addressing expectations, especially

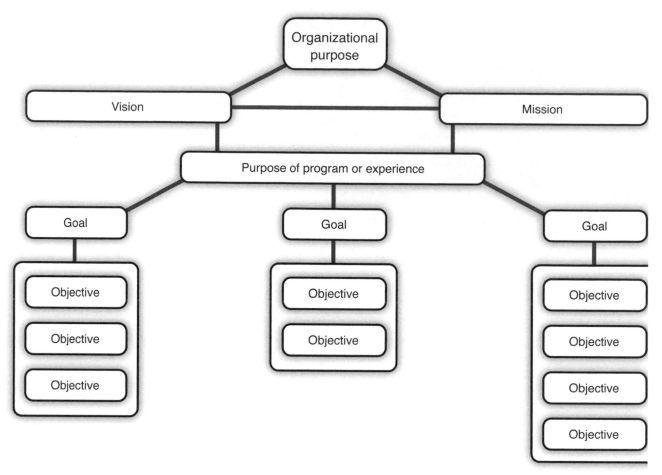

Figure 4.1   Relationships among purpose, goals, and objectives.

on the individual level, is important for groups to avoid fundamental misunderstandings and for group members to affirm their alignment with each other. Expectations relate to goals and objectives in that we strive to meet them, but they are also fundamentally different. An expectation is not something to shoot for or partly achieve; it is something that is so core to a person's assumption of what an experience will contain that its absence signals a failure of that experience for that person. In other words, an expectation is something that must be met for an experience to be considered a success.

Despite how vital expectations may be for people, not all of them can or should be met. Saying this may seem a paradox since we've already said that expectations are so important to those who hold them that an experience can't be considered a success without the expectations being met. Within this apparent paradox lies the value of group members exploring and discussing their expectations.

Not all expectations are reasonable, and even a valid expectation may not be accounted for in a planned experience. The assumptions people make about what should take place vary widely from person to person, from group to group, and from situation to situation. Taking the time to clarify what expectations people hold allows for either the expectations or the experience to be adjusted. It is much better to find out in advance that one of your group members is expecting to progress from a nonswimmer to a medal contender in the next Olympic Games as a result of taking your introduction to swimming class. Similarly, the same course may need some tweaking if a participant expects to put her face in the water, but you are not planning to have anyone get in the pool. These are extreme examples, perhaps, but even subtle discrepancies can significantly damage a group and its functioning.

When a group member expresses an expectation that is validated by other group members and the group leader, he will be more aligned with the rest of the group, more comfortable with his own participation, and more self-aware of what he needs (and what others need) from the experience. Clarifying and refining expectations not only makes clear for everyone all of the valid needs that must be met, but also helps ensure these needs are all realized.

CLARIFYING PURPOSE, GOALS, OBJECTIVES, AND EXPECTATIONS

Once you know what the terms *purpose, goals, objectives,* and *expectations* mean and how they relate to each other, your next question might be: How can I set the purpose, goals, objectives, and expectations with my group? This part of the chapter will focus on this task. In doing so, it addresses setting goals, objectives, and expectations at the level of the group and not at the level of the organization. If your group operates under the umbrella of an organization, you will need to be aware of the organization's statements of purpose, mission, and vision in order to provide direction for your specific group's activities. The organization's statements will provide an excellent place to start.

Instructors and group leaders, working as individuals or as teams, may set out everything in advance. School teachers and leaders of young children are examples of positions that demand this kind of approach. With many other groups, however, setting goals, objectives, and expectations collaboratively is more rewarding. The advantage of collaborative goal setting is that it creates agreement among group members—agreement not only on what the goals should be but also on the fact that they are worth pursuing. With this agreement in place, group members are much more likely to work actively toward reaching the goals. While this chapter aims to help group facilitators to work collaboratively with their groups to set goals, objectives, and expectations, the basic techniques outlined for this process will also be helpful for facilitators who set goals, objectives, and expectations in advance or without input from group members.

Before getting started, be clear with your group members about the process they are about to undertake. Make sure they understand your rationale for their involvement. Then define the terms and their relationships among one another. Doing this could involve something as simple as a quick discussion to clarify the concepts that are outlined earlier in this chapter.

Purpose

In setting the purpose for either an organization or an experience, ask why the organization or experience exists and what the associated values and beliefs are. For example, in the scenario at the beginning of this chapter, Luc reminded the counselors that they needed to ask themselves the reason why they were programming a day of getting together. What was it about this day that would make it important? In really general terms, the group of counselors had to agree on what the day was *for.* What was the main value of the planned day? After discussing it for a while, the counselors realized that the day was about building a sense of community. The multicabin event was providing an opportunity to address community building more effectively than it could be addressed in the programs the counselors could develop for individual cabin groups. Imagine that the counselors are working at your camp and came to that conclusion because you, as the program director, reacquainted them with the camp's vision and mission, and Carmen noticed that written into the mission statement was a commitment to building community among campers and staff. From that point forward, the counselors were able to evaluate all of the activity ideas in terms of whether they contributed to the overall purpose of the day. Even better, with the counselors' realization of the day's purpose, a major component of what the camp hoped to achieve as an organization was more consciously—and therefore probably more effectively—accomplished.

In the opening scenario, Luc's mental note to change staff training the next year incorporated the idea that ensuring what happened with this group of counselors would happen with other planning groups meant rethinking the order of the planning process. If each planning group would identify the camp's mission statement *before* trying to decide on specific activities, the mission would have a better likelihood of being represented in the activities, and the decisions regarding the activities and how to run them would be easier for the staff.

Goals and Expectations

In articulating goals, objectives, and expectations, objectives are the last of the three to be done. Because objectives are concrete ways to reach goals, you will first want to know what it is you want to accomplish. Either goals or expectations can be generated first, or they can be developed concurrently. However you generate them, you should discuss both before moving on to objectives.

In addition, goals and expectations should be compared or at least talked about in relation to each other early on in the process. The discussion of one will probably affect the other, and they may exist in different categories for different people. For example, one student might say that he has a goal of getting 80 percent as an overall grade in his university course. Invariably, another student will say that she expects to get at least 80 percent. For her, anything less would jeopardize her scholarship and would be a failure. How these two individuals picture their involvement in the course could be quite different. At the same time, attaining 80 percent as either a goal or an expectation is valid depending on the context.

One way to go about setting and delineating goals and expectations for a group that is not yet aware of the distinction between the two is to brainstorm two lists side by side. One list answers the question of what group members would *like* to see happen, while the

Reaching your goal can be very satisfying.

other answers the question of what group members think *must* happen. At the conclusion of the exercise, the group facilitator could introduce the concepts of goals and expectations and match them to their respective lists. At this point, the list of goals (what the group would like to see happen) is ready to be categorized and prioritized.

Categorization can take on a variety of forms. One is the threefold classification of short-, medium-, and long-term. Another might be task and process—that is, goals related to what the group wants to accomplish and those related to the maintenance

Toolbox Tips

Questions to set goals by include the following:

- Is this the first time we've done this as a group? If not, what did we come up with last time?
- Do we know the main purpose of our group? Why do we exist? (Answers to these questions may be provided by the larger organization.)
- What are all the things we would we like to see happen in the short term? Medium term? Long term?
- Of all the ideas generated from the previous questions, which are the most important to us?
- Do the short- and medium-term goals build toward the long-term goals?
- What are the problems we face? What can be done to get around them or minimize them?
- What forces are working in our favor? How can we optimize these?

of the group. Some goals might even be both. Goal priorities can be set by discussing which ones are most important for various group members. The group should end up with a prioritized list of goals to work toward and a list of outcomes that are mandatory (i.e., expectations).

Remember that not all goals and expectations should be met or are capable of being met. Any list of expectations developed by a group should be vetted so that the group members who hold them know whether they are reasonable or need adjusting. A long list of expectations, unless they are easily fulfilled, is a red flag, as is any expectation lacking a visible path to its realization.

Goal setting is more effective when the goals are realistic. Goals that are set too high may cause someone to give up prematurely; conversely, goals that are set too low may cause that person to feel unchallenged and lose interest. However, while setting realistic yet challenging goals is productive in most situations, the balance between challenge and achievability should be tailored to the group. Group facilitators may wish to consider the following when trying to match goals to the group:

- Set more easily attainable goals for groups that need to experience success.

- Set higher goals for groups motivated by challenge.

- Set a mixture of goals for a mixed group.

In the scenario at the beginning of the chapter, the group of counselors planning the programming for the day might have identified the following goals:

- To promote feelings of connectedness and belonging with other campers and staff members

- To promote a friendly, welcoming, and emotionally safe atmosphere

- To foster an appreciation for the synergy of diversity

- To learn cooperative social skills

Objectives

Once a group has identified its goals, objectives need to be set in order to map out a path to achieving those goals. For each goal, articulate a series of measurable tasks or actions that, when taken together, will ensure that the goal is reached. Each objective should relate directly to attaining some part of the corresponding goal. Peter Drucker's (1954) management by objectives (MBO) introduced the extremely popular SMART acronym as a method for setting and assessing objectives. According to the SMART approach, objectives should be the following:

- **Specific (well defined, concrete, and detailed).** Specificity is at the heart of what an objective is meant to be. The outcomes sought in an objective should be precise.

- **Measurable (able to be assessed by tangible results).** There should be a tangible way to determine when the objective is met.

- **Achievable (attainable).** Group members should be set up for success. Objectives can be challenging when it is appropriate for group development, but setting the bar too high will contribute to a feeling of being defeated.

- **Realistic (reasonable—not just possible—given the resources and limitations of the group).** The context the group is operating in needs to be accounted for. An objective that is achievable for one group may not be achievable for all groups. The limitations that affect a particular group may be greater than those of other groups you have worked with. Limitations need to be considered when developing objectives.

- **Time related (can be completed within a set time frame).** Participants need an appropriate amount of time to complete their objectives. If there is insufficient time to meet the objectives, group members may become frustrated even when progressing adequately. Conversely, motivation and a sense of challenge can be compromised if there is no limit on time.

For the counselors in the chapter's opening scenario, a series of objectives for one of their goals might look like this:

Goal: To promote feelings of connectedness and belonging with other campers and staff members

Objective 1: Staff will facilitate at least two icebreaker games when all campers have assembled for the day.

Objective 2: Each staff member and camper will learn the names of at least five other campers before lunch.

Objective 3: Campers will develop a skit to entertain the rest of the camp at the evening campfire.

Objective 4: Campers will be able to sing the "Seniors' Section Song" by the end of the day.

Goals, objectives, and expectations should be reviewed periodically. Circumstances and group members change, making it necessary for groups to reevaluate the accuracy of the map to their destination.

SUMMARY

Understanding the meanings of and relationships among purpose, goals, objectives, and expectations can result in greater effectiveness for groups. This chapter outlined a hierarchy that moves from overarching and vague statements that embody a group's or an organization's purpose to more specific goals and then to very concrete and tangible objectives that spell out the path for reaching the related goal. This chapter also suggested a process for setting goals, objectives, and expectations and recommended questions to ask and an order in which to explore these concepts with the group in order to strengthen the setting of each.

RESOURCES

Association for Experiential Education. 2008. About AEE. http://aee.org/customer/ pages.php?pageid=24.

Drucker, P. 1954. *The practice of management.* New York: Harper & Row.

Five Winds International. 2004. "Environmental Sustainability Case Study: Mountain Equipment Co-op's Green Building Approach." http://www.fivewinds.com/publications/publications.cfm

Mountain Equipment Co-op. 2008. "Social and Environmental Responsibility at MEC." http://zonecours.hec.ca/documents ?A2005-1-570260.S132-108A2005Mountain EquipmentCoop.ppt

CHAPTER

5

Moral Issues in Groups

Marketa was on a weeklong group cycling trip that followed a historic route taken by early settlers moving west across the country. She had chosen this trip because her family has roots in the mass migration that led so many people from one side of the country to the other. Both of her grandparents had died a few years earlier, and she remembered her grandfather telling her stories of being a little boy in that sea of humanity moving west.

Family history was becoming more important to Marketa, and she had developed a need to understand more of where she came from and of what life was like for those who had such an influence on her own life but were lost to her across the span of time. Marketa was an avid cyclist, and so the cycling trip was the perfect opportunity to see a little of the country her ancestors saw and try to imagine it through their eyes—or so she thought.

On the morning of the third day, the tour leaders announced that they were behind schedule and would have to push a little harder to get back on track. The rest of the group seemed to be fine with this, and although Marketa was unsettled by the announcement (she had loved stopping at the roadside pullouts to take in the scenic views and read the interpretive plaques about the history of the area), she thought that if she was the only one to feel this way she should avoid rocking the boat. After all, she was sure that they would still stop at the important places.

That day the leaders set a blistering pace and stopped less frequently, pushing the group as promised to try and make up time. When the group members pulled into the night's campsite, they were told that it had been a good day and that one more like it should get them back on schedule. But Marketa was beginning to get frustrated. The trip—her trip—was being sacrificed for the sake of making up time. Couldn't these people see that the really valuable experience was not reaching a destination campground each afternoon? Still, she kept this to herself because no one else seemed upset about it.

The next day proved to be more of the same, and Marketa became increasingly frustrated each time they passed another historic marker. She found herself getting angry and dwelling on what each one might have told her about the landscape they were traveling in and how it could have affected her ancestors. At lunch, she decided to say something. With everyone seated at a couple of picnic tables pulled together, Marketa summoned her courage and asked if they were at a point where they could start easing up a bit and taking in the sights again. She even thought she saw at least two of the tired faces perk up at her question, but the others deflated somewhat when one of the leaders said they could reevaluate how they were doing when they reached the designated campsite later that afternoon. Marketa asked the group members directly if they felt that the change in pace over the past two days was what they wanted. The same two people who brightened up at her initial question said that it would be nice to return to a more leisurely pace, but they also said they didn't want to slow down the group. A few others mentioned that they were OK with pushing on for the rest of the day and then reassessing in the evening. A few more went further, with one person saying, "There are only so many boring interpretive signs I want to read in a day."

Sensing that he needed to do something to help the participants who desired to connect with the history of their route, one of the leaders offered to tell the group a little about what they would be cycling past in the afternoon. One description made Marketa sit straight up. She recognized it from a journal entry her great-great grandfather had made about a memory of a campfire on a migration trek. That night so long ago, camped just short of a low mountain pass with a view that was pretty but insignificant, a young man who was traveling to a place he couldn't know what held for him met his future bride, Marketa's great-great grandmother. The place took on such meaning for the young man that he later wrote everything he could remember about it.

It was all too much for Marketa. She wanted to walk away, but she stayed as her eyes welled with tears. Even though she did not know some of her group members well, she felt that in order to see this place and give it the time it deserved from her, she would have to explain what it meant to her. Through a voice filled with emotion, Marketa told them the story of her great-great grandfather and how the upcoming overlook could be what he saw as a young man meeting his future wife. The effect on every other group member was instant. There was a unanimous decision to stop at the overlook and to spend as long as Marketa needed to be there. What Marketa found interesting was not only that her story garnered such strong support for making the stop but also that it catalyzed a change within the group. That night the cyclists shared stories of their families around the campfire. Afterward Marketa felt more connected to the people she was sharing this trip with; they even traveled more as a group and less as a collection of individuals.

Few resources on group dynamics feature discussions of values, ethics, and morals. It may be that these issues are left out because they are sensitive. How, for example, can ethics and values be included in group processes without creating biases or possibly offending someone's deeply held personal beliefs? These are indeed treacherous waters to navigate, but could it be just as dangerous to stay out of them? What risks are being taken by a group when its members avoid or remain ignorant of each other's values and moral positions? Will the values that each person holds never enter the picture as the group members attempt to work together and make decisions? More likely, these values will enter the picture and conflict will occur but will be more difficult to resolve because of the lack of understanding about what is motivating people's positions on certain issues.

Of course, this isn't to say that group leaders should simply gather the group together for an outpouring of everyone's values. There are at least two considerations in deciding whether an exploration of values and ethics is worthwhile for your group.

1. Are values and ethics relevant to your group's purpose? While values and ethics are embedded in almost everything humans do, it's not necessary to discuss or examine them in everything we do. For example, if you are leading a small volunteer group for a local swim club, the purpose of which is to develop an organizational plan (what events will take place when and where) for an upcoming swim meet, there is not much to be gained from asking everyone to discuss their deeply held beliefs at the first meeting! In fact, inappropriate discussions of values can be counterproductive to the group's goals and potentially harmful to some members.

On the other hand, if close relationships and personal growth as a result of deeper interpersonal understanding are part of your group's purpose, it may

Discussing values and ethics might be valuable in a conscious group.

be important to be aware of the role values and ethics play in the interactions of your group. In addition, a conscious group might facilitate such growth more easily if there is a general desire among members to understand and respect each other's values and ethical stances.

2. Is the group ready? Some group members may not be ready for discussions on values and ethics. Group leaders will have to be wary if the group members are not mature enough to discuss values with respect or are uncommitted to such a process. As you will see later in the chapter, moral development does not occur readily if value positions are imposed on individuals as mere cognitive elements or if group members are not open to reflecting on the internal moral conflicts that are created when people are exposed to new and different concepts of what is good and bad. Group members must be developmentally ready and active in their own self-questioning in order for changes to be genuine and lasting. Moral growth can occur even without these conditions, but it is important to encourage discussions in which individuals do not feel that their own values or ethical systems are being challenged directly. In other words, a person's moral development may not be helped along if you make that person's behavior a subject of group discussion. Abstract and hypothetical scenarios can be helpful for situations in which you plan to enhance the moral reasoning of group members.

DEFINITIONS

There is a great deal of overlap in the use of the words *values, ethics,* and *morals,* probably because these terms depend on each other for understanding. At this point in the chapter, it will help to develop some sense of what each of these words means.

• **Values** are a person's fundamental beliefs about what is important in life. This statement requires two points of elaboration. First, values are steeped in belief. They are theoretical in the sense that they are not really provable; adopting them requires an act of faith. Second, values are filled with emotion. Taken together, these emotion-filled beliefs form the foundation for establishing an ethical stance.

• **Ethics,** also called *moral philosophy,* is one of the five major branches of study in philosophy. Generally, the study of ethics attempts to understand the nature

of morality. Specifically, the study of ethics deals with questioning and systematizing ideas of right and wrong. Some of the big questions philosophers grapple with include the following:

• What is the good life?

• What makes some behaviors right and others wrong?

• Are there universal right and wrong actions, or are ethical criteria a matter of personal choice?

Generally, the study of ethics is divided into three categories: metaethics, which explores where ethical principles come from and what they mean; normative ethics, which involves deciding on moral standards of conduct; and applied ethics, which involves investigating specific moral issues that social groups face. Current examples of North American issues in applied ethics include euthanasia, gay marriage, abortion, and animal rights. Applied ethics tends to rely on the other two categories for its basis of examination of specific issues.

• **Morals,** like ethics, have to do with right and wrong. Morality can be seen as a code of conduct that is based on a collection of beliefs. Morals can be put forward by an individual, a group, or a society, although the larger the collection of people, the less specific the moral code must be in order to accommodate differing moral perceptions about what is good and bad, right and wrong.

MORAL DEVELOPMENT

The growth of morality in humans appears to match other types of growth, such as intellectual growth and even the physical growth of arms and legs. Given social stimulation, humans develop and mature morally, much like we develop intellectually or physically. A significant amount of work has gone into researching how humans develop morally, and the insights of three of the most well-known figures in moral development theory will help you as a group leader comprehend your groups' interactions when moral issues are at play.

Jean Piaget

Although he saw his work as mainly relating to epistemology, Jean Piaget is a large figure in the area of developmental psychology. Epistemology is defined as the study of the nature, sources, and legitimacy of knowledge. Epistemologists ask questions such as, "Are you sure you know what you think you know?" and "How do you know what you think you know?" Epistemology deals with the knowledge that we all think is true and the ways in which we come to understand what we think is true. His work on moral development from the 1920s until shortly before his death in 1980 paved the way for a number of theorists and continues to influence developmental psychology and epistemology today.

Early in his career, while scoring children's intelligence tests, Piaget noticed that younger children consistently answer certain questions wrong. His curiosity led him to question why such a distinction could exist and be tied so closely to a child's age. Piaget developed the following two stages of moral reasoning for children.

- **Heteronomous stage.** This stage is characterized by egocentrism, in which children are unable to see the world from the perspectives of others. For example, in one experiment Piaget introduced a model of three mountains of various sizes to children and asked them to pick out a picture of what someone on the opposite side of the table would see. Children under six consistently chose photographs of what they *themselves* saw. In combination with a second influence in this stage, namely the unidirectional relationship with adults, heteronomous moral reasoning is marked by a belief that consequence automatically follows actions (especially wrongdoing). Thus, during this stage rules and authority are paramount.

- **Autonomous stage.** As children mature, they acquire the ability to assess the rules and laws of their social lives to see if those rules create inequity. In the autonomous stage, children are able to see the world from their own perspective as well as from that of others. This leads to a moral standpoint that takes reciprocity and fairness into account. Children in an autonomous stage of moral reasoning are able to view the intent as well as the letter of a law or rule.

Lawrence Kohlberg

Intrigued by Piaget and John Dewey, Lawrence Kohlberg spent most of his career developing and testing his framework for moral development. Kohlberg expanded on Piaget's two-stage model, creating six stages within three levels (see table 5.1).

Table 5.1 Kohlberg's Stages of Moral Development

Level	Stage
Preconventional morality	1: Punishment and obedience
	2: Instrumentalism and exchange
Conventional morality	3: Conformity
	4: Law and order
Postconventional morality	5: Social contract
	6: Principled conscience

To set the stage for a discussion of Kohlberg's stages, let's consider Kohlberg's proposal of the Heinz dilemma. A woman with cancer is near death, but her husband, Heinz, learns of a new treatment that could save her. The local druggist who developed the medication sells it for $2,000 U.S., ten times the cost of producing the drug. Heinz tries to raise the money by borrowing from friends and pursuing all other legal options, but he is able to raise only $1,000 U.S. Heinz approaches the druggist to try and persuade him to sell the drug for a reduced cost or allow Heinz to pay the balance at a later date. The druggist refuses, saying that he developed the medication and he will profit from it. In desperation, Heinz breaks into the pharmacy one night and steals the medication.

Engage a small group of people in a discussion of the Heinz dilemma and you will quickly find that there does not seem to be just one answer to what is right. Kohlberg was interested in this phenomenon, and he proposed the following three levels of moral development, each comprising two stages, to explain how our moral reasoning becomes more sophisticated as we mature.

Preconventional Morality

At this level of moral development, people act within socially accepted norms. However, they do not process the reasons for doing so outside of deference to authority (and the consequences for defying authority) and self-interest.

Stage 1: Punishment and Obedience

In Kohlberg's first stage, children cannot see beyond what is imposed by law and authority. This stage is similar to Piaget's heteronomous stage, in which morality is fixed by external forces. Children in this stage indicate that Heinz was wrong to steal, but their attempts to explain why are limited to a reiteration of the externally imposed law: "It's against the law to steal."

Stage 2: Instrumentalism and Exchange

Kohlberg's second stage is marked by decisions of self-interest. Individuals recognize that differences in moral perception may occur (for example, Heinz and the druggist have different perceptions) but believe Heinz should make his decisions based on what is best for him. While the ultimate decision may vary, the rationale is tied to what is best for the individual in question. For instance, one person could argue that Heinz should not have stolen the medication because he was risking jail time, while another could say that he was justified in stealing because he needs his wife to help him look after the family. Both responses are based on what is good for Heinz.

Conventional Morality

At this level, individuals display moral reasoning that is predominant in society. Hence, their morality is conventional.

Stage 3: Conformity

Stage 3 moralists attribute more weight to the qualities associated with good behavior in close relationships. For example, concern for others and empathy might influence individuals in this stage to feel compassion for Heinz. Someone in stage 3 might reason that Heinz's intentions were good and that he should not get into trouble because he was trying to save a person's life.

Stage 4: Law and Order

Stage 3 moral reasoning is based on close relationships, ones formed with family and good friends. Individuals with stage 4 moral reasoning are able to broaden this perspective to include the wider community and society as a whole. People in stage 4 consider what might happen to social order if the structure of laws is relegated to relativistic justifications such as the ones given in stage 3. People in stage 4 also work from a sense of duty and responsibility to social cohesion. The result of stage 4 is similar to

that of stage 1 (i.e., that Heinz should not break the law), but whereas the child in stage 1 cannot explain a moral stance beyond a willingness to follow authority, the person in stage 4 adopts a position that accounts for social connections that is well beyond stage 1. A person in stage 4 who decides to punish Heinz might argue that while it is unfortunate that his wife is suffering, it is a greater danger to the social fabric of a nation to allow him to disregard the law. Thus people should obey the law even when there might be compelling reasons to not do so. The social chaos that might result from such a precedent is unpalatable to stage 4 reasoning.

Postconventional Morality

Kohlberg believed that most people do not reach the third level of moral development. At this level, people are concerned for the functioning of society, but they do not confuse efficiency with justice.

Stage 5: Social Contract

A genuine concern for the welfare of others and a recognition that some moral principles may oppose each other collide at stage 5. For instance, a person reasoning in stage 5 might indicate that while it is not desirable for Heinz to have broken the law, the circumstances of his desperation should be taken into account. Such a position could find Heinz guilty but let him off with a suspended sentence. Individuals in stage 5 ask themselves what a good society should look like. Looking beyond the rules and associated morals of their society, these people begin to examine what a society should value.

Stage 6: Principled Conscience

Stage 6 is sometimes referred to as a *theoretical stage* because researchers could not find enough people operating consistently within this type of moral reasoning. In this stage, people attempt to define universal principles that lead to justice. Kohlberg maintained that in order for us to achieve justice, we must view the situation objectively from each person's perspective. Stage 6 moralists would take each character's viewpoint and weigh it against the moral principles at play. They would also attempt to put the characters in each other's shoes. So, in the story of Heinz, the druggist, and Heinz's wife, each person must be invited to view the world from the perspective of the others. Undergoing this process requires treating everyone involved with equal respect and seeking justice for all.

Kohlberg believed that people must progress through the stages in order, moving one stage at a time. For example, an individual cannot jump from stage 2 to stage 4 without passing through stage 3. Kohlberg also believed that progressing through the stages is the result of neither genetics nor social processes. While socialization can provide the background for development, progress must result from our own thinking about moral issues. Debates with family, friends, and colleagues provide the raw material for challenging current positions. The conflict a person faces when confronted with new ideas motivates that person to develop more inclusive and comprehensive moral views.

The notion that we cannot teach people the cognitive aspects of moral development and then expect them to operate at a higher level has significant implications for facilitators and group leaders. Kohlberg found that when it comes to inducing long-term change, it is less effective for an authority figure, say an adult leading a group of children, to supply moral reasoning at the stage beyond the one from which the children are operating. The group members must be active in their own development in order for change to be persistent and pronounced. In other words, group members must engage in discussion, preferably with peers, and then have the opportunity to process the conflicts that were presented to them during the discussion. For group leaders, this means that it is far more effective to present a moral challenge and then act only as a moderator and facilitator as the group examines the challenge. During a morally based discussion within a group setting, leaders should consider providing input through paraphrasing, clarification, furnishing factual information, and asking provocative questions that are one stage ahead of that of the group members.

For instance, imagine that a person who is a competent swimmer is out for a stroll in the evening. She witnesses another person who cannot swim fall off a pier and into the deep water below. The nonswimmer, a teenage boy, appears to be in serious trouble and likely to drown if he is not saved. The competent swimmer decides to not help him because she is worried she might catch a cold if she gets wet in the chilly air. Now imagine the discussion the members of a group might have when asked if the woman has an obligation to save the boy. One group member might say that it's obvious that the woman has an obligation to save the boy and that she will probably go to jail for murder if she doesn't help him. If another group member doesn't bring it up first, the leader could offer up the information that it is not against the law for an observer to refuse to help someone in distress if the observer isn't the cause and isn't in a position of responsibility for the distressed individual. This suggestion sets up a conflict for the group member. He may still believe it is wrong for the woman to refuse to help but now cannot justify why it is wrong within his current moral framework. The group leader could then offer help in the form of synthesis and paraphrasing. The leader might say, for example, "Though you now know it's not against the law to refrain from helping, I can see that you still feel it is wrong. Is there something more at stake here than just what the law says?"

Toolbox Tips

- Be patient. Moral development requires maturity and takes time and reflection. Change will last longer and be more meaningful if group members reach conclusions themselves.

- Be sensitive and respectful. People have deeply held beliefs and values. Unless the beliefs are harmful, group members should be made to feel that it's OK to hold all sorts of beliefs. Exploring beliefs can help group members to clarify and strengthen those beliefs for themselves.

- Be open. If you are willing to discuss the values of others, you should be open to exploring your own as well.

Learning Activity

Working in a small group, create a scenario that presents a moral dilemma in a recreation setting. Discuss how members of the "typical" group you work with day to day might react to the scenario you develop. What questions can you generate to help your "typical" group members evolve in their moral reasoning?

Carol Gilligan

Kohlberg's initial research suggested that, on average, girls do not develop as high a sense of moral reasoning as boys develop. In her well-known book, *In a Different Voice: Psychological Theory and Women's Development* (1982), Carol Gilligan critiqued Kohlberg's framework as favoring boys because its scoring method focuses on principles of justice and downplays moral principles centered on relationships, an orientation girls are more responsive to.

In a moral orientation that is based on justice, the emphasis is on equality, objectivity, and universal principles. Gilligan proposed that a morality steeped in cultivating relationships and caring for others is perhaps connected but distinct from a justice view of morality. A morality of caring, or what came to be known as an *ethic of care,* is not easily explained, but it can be described as being in a relationship with another person (or persons) in which you genuinely care about the other person's welfare. Noddings (1984) distinguished between *caring for,* which denotes a face-to-face relationship with another person, and *caring about,* which means having concern for the welfare of another person you don't know personally. Gilligan and other moral theorists saw the care view of morality as not turning away from someone in need.

Subsequent research has shown that both boys and girls operate from a justice view and a care view as opposed to operating from one or the other. The work of researchers such as Gilligan has added a dimension to the assessment of what constitutes advanced morality.

Ultimately, Kohlberg did adjust his scoring method as a result of Gilligan's critique, with the result that boys and girls now score evenly.

If we were to apply the element of caring to an advanced stage of moral reasoning in Kohlberg's model, we might ask what could be the implications for using this kind of moral reasoning in society at large. Is it even possible to implement caring on the level of social interaction? Are there other ways to incorporate a care view into the Heinz dilemma?

It might be decided that Heinz's wife be given the medication because life must be valued more than property. This decision could be arrived at because presumably the druggist could sympathize with being in her situation and would not be able to ignore her obvious need. At the same time, the druggist deserves something for his efforts, and respect for his situation requires fair compensation. At issue is what constitutes fair compensation, and one solution to the dilemma is the argument that fairness is not achieved by sameness. In other words, if all that Heinz is able to raise for a necessary medication is $1,000 U.S., he should not have to pay as much as a richer person should have to pay. In fact, the richer person may be required to pay more than the standard $2,000 U.S. in order to create fairness for the druggist. In this way, caring for each person involved does not imply that they be treated exactly the same way.

An ethic of care involves genuine concern for others.

© iStockphoto/Juan Monino

APPLYING MORAL THEORY

At the end of this section, you will find some moral dilemmas you can discuss with your group. These dilemmas draw on the theory presented in this chapter and will help you put some of what you may find in group situations into perspective. First, however, a brief exploration of normative ethics is required in order to set the stage for discussing the dilemmas. Recall that normative ethics involves deciding on standards of moral conduct. In other words, normative ethics provides an individual the structure for making moral decisions; it establishes the principles that a person applies to a particular situation. In normative ethics, there are three broad theories: consequentialism, deontology, and virtue ethics.

Consequentialism

As implied by the name, consequentialist theories are those that focus on the consequences of actions in moral matters. The goal is to arrive at the result that creates the most good for the most number of people affected by the action. For example, consider the dilemma presented by the popular question, "If you could travel back in time, would you kill Adolf Hitler before he came to power if you had the opportunity to do so?" A consequentialist would be swayed by the argument that a preemptive assassination of Hitler might prevent millions of unnecessary deaths. The chance to save millions of innocent lives therefore warrants the killing of one person, even if that one person has not yet done anything wrong.

Deontology

In opposition to consequentialism is deontology. Deontological ethics maintains that the basis for good moral decision making rests with adhering to duty and to the rights of individuals. It is wrong to give superior status to the consequences of our actions. Proponents of deontology argue that under some circumstances, innocent people could be harmed by a consequentialist moral system. Deontological ethicists believe that there are unassailable universal truths and fundamental natural rights held by all. Accordingly, it is our duty to safeguard these rights and act consistently with universal truths. In fact, the famous German philosopher Immanuel Kant argued that we must always tell the truth, even if harm is the result. Predictably, consequentialist moral theorists object, contending that the universal truths and unassailable rights championed by deontologists are never universal and are open to subjective interpretation.

Virtue Ethics

Whereas the previous two approaches focus on actions and consequences, virtue ethics is concerned with the character of the person making the decision. The goal in virtue ethics is the pursuit of a virtuous life. Virtues are those parts of the personality that are inherently good and must be nurtured. Classic virtues include courage, wisdom, temperance, chastity, and prudence. The criticisms leveled at virtue ethics are similar to those of deontology, namely that the virtues upheld by one person or social group may not be the same as those upheld by another and therefore are open to interpretation. In most Western cultures, for example, the virtue of women and girls being submissive does not hold the same value it once did.

MORAL REASONING EXERCISES

In groups, discuss the following moral dilemmas. Determine the best course of action for each situation and answer the accompanying questions. As you work with each scenario, keep in mind the theory presented throughout the chapter.

Scenario 1

Imagine that you are Winston Churchill, Britain's prime minister during World War II. The year is 1941 and the war is going badly. Britain has suffered heavy defeats and has had to withdraw and regroup. Nazi Germany occupies much of Europe. The one piece of good news is that your cryptographers (code specialists) have broken the German code and the information is proving to be reliable. Through applying the code to intercepted messages, your intelligence officers have discovered that the Germans are planning to bomb Coventry, a small town in southern England. If you evacuate the town, you could save hundreds—perhaps thousands—of lives, but it would become clear to the German forces that you know the code, and they would change it immediately. Coventry is not an extremely strategic point, and it has taken months already to break the code. If your intelligence officers could discover more information about troop movements, you could make more decisive strikes, which might help to end the war sooner, also saving lives. What do you do?

Questions

1. Which of the normative theories best fits your response? Explain how you know this.

2. Think of other moral dilemmas you've faced recently. Was your approach to them similar to the system you used to solve the scenario? If so, you may be aligned with a specific system for making moral decisions. If not, why do you think you reason differently from one moral decision to another?

3. Can you think of why you might reason the way you do in your moral decision making?

Scenario 2

Working for a leadership development organization, you are the leader of a weekend team development course. You are debriefing your latest group just before it packs up to head home. The group consists of corporate administrators and managers from a relatively well-known company out of New York City. Their boss, the president and CEO of the company, sent them on this course to "smooth out some of the conflict at head office." The weekend was spent introducing different exercises and initiative tasks, and as the leader you consider it a failure. The people on the course were not concerned for others and did not have any interest in learning to display mutual respect. The exercises took much longer to complete with this group than they did with any other group you've led before, and many of the initiative tasks were treated as competitive games to be won rather than as challenges to be solved through teamwork. Most of the interpersonal interaction was selfish, and the group members seemed to expect you to do more than your share of the camp chores that everyone is supposed to participate in. In fact, in your opinion, these group members were downright lazy. The group became known among your fellow staff members as *The Group From Hell.*

Now, in the final debriefing, the members are expressing only wonderfully positive remembrances of the weekend. They not only failed to learn about interpersonal communication and teamwork but also

are unaware that they did poorly as a group; they all think their performance was just fine. You are trying to tactfully challenge this assumption by asking debriefing questions such as, "What do you think could have gone better this past weekend?" But rather than accepting responsibility for any shortcomings of the weekend, the group members are now attempting to blame your leadership and are drawing attention to trivial matters. For example, one member has said, "Well, instead of taking 45 minutes for our lunches, we should have cut that down to 30 so we could have had extra time for the sessions and exercises." You have already gone through the process of questioning the group on how you could have done better as a leader, and you know for certain that the significant problems of the weekend were not your fault. You have talked over many of the events of the weekend with your supervisor, and she has told you that this is the most challenging group she's ever seen. However, in this debriefing session they are not taking ownership for their shortcomings and mistakes. As the debriefing leader, how far should you go in getting the message across that they did not do well?

Questions

1. What is the moral dilemma you face in this scenario?

2. What are the choices you have in your actions?

3. Who is affected by what you decide to do?

4. What are the likely consequences of each choice?

Scenario 3

Aaliyah is a 14-year-old girl who lives with her brother and mother in a single-parent household. Her mother promised her that she could go to a special rock concert coming to their town if she saved enough money from babysitting to buy a ticket. She managed to save the $50 U.S. the ticket cost plus another $20 U.S. for spending money at the concert. The week before the concert, Aaliyah's mother changed her mind and told Aaliyah to spend the money on school supplies. Aaliyah was disappointed and angry with her mother and decided to go to the concert anyway. She bought a ticket and told her mother that she had been able to save only the $20. That Saturday she told her mother that she was spending the day with a friend and then went to the concert. A week passed without her mother finding out. Aaliyah then told her older brother, Shea, that she had gone to the performance and had lied to her mother about it. Shea wonders whether he should tell their mother what Aaliyah did.

Questions
1. Prepare moral responses that match Kohlberg's stages 1 through 4.
2. What would you do in this situation? Why?
3. What stage of reasoning is your response according to Kohlberg?

SUMMARY

Values, ethics, and morality are not always discussed in the context of group dynamics because of the sensitive nature of these types of issues. However, if the conditions within the group are right (e.g., a shared understanding of group members' values is relevant to the purpose of the group and the group members are ready for respectful discussion), an exploration of values and ethics can enhance the functioning of a conscious group and contribute to the moral development of its members.

This chapter discussed the contributions to moral development theory made by Jean Piaget, Lawrence Kohlberg, and Carol Gilligan and explained the three main theories of normative ethics: consequentialism, deontology, and virtue ethics. Throughout the chapter, several scenarios were presented in order to demonstrate the application of the theories and to assist you in assessing your own moral development and ethical stances. These scenarios may also provide creative resources for you to use in approaching the potential moral development of the groups you work with.

RESOURCES

Gilligan, C. 1982. *In a different voice: Psychological theory and women's development.* Cambridge, MA: Harvard University Press.

Kohlberg, L. 1981. *Essays on moral development, vol. I: The philosophy of moral development.* San Francisco, CA: Harper & Row.

Noddings, N. 1984. *Caring, a feminine approach to ethics & moral education.* Berkeley, CA: University of California Press.

Piaget, J. 1955. The child's construction of reality. London: Routledge & Kegan Paul.

Piaget, J. 1995. *Sociological studies.* London: Routledge.

CHAPTER
6

Decision Making and Problem Solving

Ev, Miguel, and Kiko are the leaders for a river paddling trip in the desert southwest of the United States. They are working with a group of 13 that includes people who have physical and cognitive disabilities. They are on day four of an eight-day trip, and the group is working well together. In the middle of the night, Ev is shaken awake by one of the participants. The participant tells her that Pierre, a man with a traumatic brain injury, is not in his tent. Ev does a quick search around the camp and can't find any sign of Pierre, so she wakes up the other leaders and fills them in on the situation. Kiko asks if they should consult with the rest of the group about a plan of action, but Miguel argues they are much better off making a decision on their own and shouldn't involve the rest of the group in the process. What should the leaders do—involve the rest of the group in the decision making process or make the decision on their own?

The leaders of this trip are faced with a tough decision. They undoubtedly need the help of the rest of the group for the search process, but should they consult the group in creating the search plan? What happens if the leaders don't ask the group and one of the participants knows that Pierre liked the pictographs a short hike away and perhaps wanted to see them in the moonlight? Maybe the group will take too long deciding which course of action makes the most sense. Perhaps Ev should make a decision on her own, as she is the head leader for this trip. Does she have the information required to make a sound decision?

Professionals make decisions and solve problems daily. Some of these decisions and problems are easy to deal with, while others require considerable thought and resources. Sometimes leaders make decisions and solve problems themselves. However, when working with groups, these tasks are often taken on by the group as a whole.

This chapter explores methods for decision making and problem solving, identifies the pros and cons of these methods, and provides strategies for working with groups to effectively and efficiently make decisions and solve problems.

ADVANTAGES OF GROUP DECISION MAKING

Most people like to have several options to choose from when shopping for a new car, researching recreation and leisure programs, or looking over the selections at a restaurant. Decision making that is undertaken by more than one person allows a diversity of choices. In essence, a group can create a menu of potential decisions—a group can create many more options than most individuals can create on their

Groups often make better decisions than individuals make.

own. Studies have found several reasons why groups usually make better decisions than individuals make. These include the collective nature of information gathering and processing, social facilitation, and risk taking or group polarization. However, there are also weaknesses that accompany group decision making. These include withholding of information, issues with discussion, and groupthink.

Collective Information Gathering and Processing

One of the greatest assets a group has in the decision-making process is the gathering of each member's experience, knowledge, and skill level. Like individuals, groups gather information and think about potential decisions. However, groups differ from individuals by adding a social component to the decision-making process. The social component usually takes the form of a discussion or debate. For example, think about some friends who are going rock climbing for the day. They have the choice of several different locations where they can climb. Most likely the group will spend a few minutes deciding where to go. The individual group members think about the alternatives by themselves and then discuss the alternatives with the others to come up with a decision. What makes this exchange a powerful factor of group decision making? The interaction among

group members allows individuals to come up with reasons, factors, ideas, or suggestions that they would not have reached on their own. This phenomenon is called *process gain* (Johnson and Johnson 2003). A potential downfall of process gain is that it can produce so many alternatives that the group becomes bogged down and can't make a timely decision.

Group decision making is also strengthened by the memory of the group as a whole. This memory is referred to as *collective memory*. A group's collective memory includes its methods of processing information, histories, stories, special occurrences, successes, and failures as well as each member's recollection of what has worked and not worked for the group. A group's collective memory allows the group to recall past events more accurately. One individual may provide insights that prompt others to remember specifics about an earlier group decision or situation. This process is enhanced when groups assign specific group members information to be recalled in the future. This transactive memory system (Forsyth 1999) is a primary reason why groups are better at making decisions than individuals are. However, groups may forget past decisions and experiences that didn't work well for them. If these are not recalled through collective memory or the transactive memory system, a group may be destined for failure by repeating mistakes it has made in the past.

Finally, the collective nature of groups allows for better collection and processing of information. Usually, groups are better equipped to analyze choices and recognize potential consequences than individuals are. Groups can recognize and discard poor decisions better than individuals can. In essence, the old saying that two heads are better than one is true!

Social Facilitation

Working with others in a group provides support and assists in decision making. In general, people perform better when in the presence of others—a finding called *social facilitation*. Social facilitation

Learning Activity

Performing in a Group Setting

Observe swimming lessons at a local pool. Watch how the swimmers perform when in a group, when alone, and when watched by others. Discuss the following questions:

1. Do the swimmers appear to perform better when in a group (and relatively anonymous) or when alone and being watched by others?

2. What do you think causes this phenomenon?

3. Have you experienced it before?

4. What are some strategies you might implement as a recreation, leisure, and experiential education professional that might alleviate problems you observed?

allows group members to contribute to the process with little fear of being embarrassed by their suggestions or by failing to perform as they think they should, especially when there is a complex or difficult decision to be made. Generally, people perform well while doing simple things in the presence of others. That changes, however, when the task becomes more difficult—people don't perform as well in these situations. In these cases, people are nervous about underperforming, feel they are competing with others, or fear being embarrassed by not being up to par with others. As individuals narrow their focus to concentrate on what they are doing, they miss important clues as to how to make a successful decision. The social nature of group decision making makes it stronger than individual decision making because the collective and cooperative nature of the group decreases the chance of these issues arising. This allows the group to take full advantage of what each member has to offer and to arrive at a good and timely decision.

Group Polarization

There is strength in numbers, and there is weakness in numbers. As groups work through the decision-making process, the opinions and positions held by individuals are often overwhelmed by social facilitation. Through this process, groups frequently adopt more cautious or more risky positions than those held by the individual members at the outset of the discussion. This phenomenon was originally called *risky shift* but is now called *group polarization* because researchers have found that group decisions can be more cautious (cautious shift) as well as more risky than the average decisions made by the individual group members. Figure 6.1 shows the continuum of group polarization.

The initial positions of both the individual members and the group as a whole provide key information as to whether the ultimate decision is cautious or risky. Individuals and groups tend to adopt more extreme positions as the discussion and the decision-making process evolve. However, the final position will become more cautious if the initial position was cautious or more risky if the initial position was risky. As a recreation, leisure, and experiential education professional, you can promote sound group decisions by noting the positions taken during the early phases of the decision-making process. By reminding the group members of what their original thoughts and feelings were, you can encourage the group to reconsider its decision, especially if you recognize that the decision is too cautious or too risky.

Group polarization is easy to observe when watching groups of children strategize while playing games like capture the flag. Often the team will choose one of two tactics: Most players take a defensive role while one or two individuals take the offensive role or most players take an offensive role while one or two individuals guard the flag. If the game continues as a stalemate, often the strategy turns to the all-out assault on the opponent's flag.

Figure 6.1 Group polarization.

Why does group polarization happen? Think about the different ways in which people are influenced by and influence others in groups. The very essence of what draws people to groups, how groups create norms, how people feel connected to others in the group, and what communication patterns group members use all contribute to group polarization. There are at least four reasons why group polarization occurs:

1. Information exchange. Group members are quick to share common knowledge with the rest of the group. However, individuals who have information not available to the rest of the group might withhold that information to flex a muscle or manipulate the process. Additionally, if individuals have information that is unique or might be viewed as strange or out there, they may choose not to share because they don't want their fellow group members to look down on them or disapprove of their information. New information may also sway group members if it is timely, persuasive, and logical. Finally, people may modify the information that they have to fit within the value structure of the group.

2. Group identification and loyalty. Individuals may go along with cautious or risky decisions because they want to maintain positive relationships with others in the group and maintain group membership. Members who are highly loyal to the group may also go along with the decisions.

Toolbox Tips

Recreation, leisure, and experiential education groups often face decisions that affect the outcome of an experience. How can you be sure that the final decision is neither too cautious nor too risky?

- Allow time for decisions to be made. Groups that have more time are able to consider all of the available information and figure out how the information affects a potential course of action.
- Play the devil's advocate. For example, you might suggest canceling a basketball league when it is one of the most popular summer programs run by your city recreation department.
- Teach the group decision-making techniques such as the "six thinking hats" technique or force field analysis.
- Assign group members roles to which they might not be accustomed. This fresh perspective may temper the group's decisions.
- Make sure your organization has good operating procedures to follow. This helps narrow the scope of decisions that are made.

Risky or cautious decisions aren't necessarily bad decisions. The quality of the decision really depends on the situation and the potential outcomes. It is up to you as the recreation, leisure, and experiential education professional to recognize the potential payoffs and pitfalls of a decision that is either too risky or too cautious. Often the only way to get experience is by trial and error. Learn from both your successes and mistakes!

3. Norms. The norms a group sets for decision making may encourage group polarization, especially if the group has repeated success with the process. Individual group members may feel that they need to support the group's position in order to cast a positive light on themselves. These people tend to become strong supporters of the proposed decision without regard for its risky or cautious nature.

4. Convincing nature of arguments. People are more likely to support potential decisions the more they hear persuasive arguments for the decision. The more these ideas are stated out loud, the more individuals and the group as a whole become convinced about the decision, especially if these ideas are conveyed to people outside the group. Usually people are unwilling to change their position, especially once it has been made public.

Group polarization has both positive and negative consequences on group decision making. By being aware of the factors that contribute to group polarization, professionals can benefit from its positive aspects while avoiding the negative outcomes of a cautious or risky decision.

DISADVANTAGES OF GROUP DECISION MAKING

While group decision making has awesome potential and can yield tremendous outcomes, there are also downfalls to group decisions. As a recreation, leisure, and experiential education professional, you will often have to choose between allowing a group to make a decision and making the decision on your own. Your choice will be easier if you can identify potential weaknesses in group decision making, including selective information sharing, ineffective discussion, and groupthink.

Selective Information Sharing

As mentioned earlier, one of the strengths of group decision making is that it allows group members to pool their collective memories and individual information banks. However, it has been found that groups often focus on information that everyone in the group already knows and that crucial information known to only one or two members often is not brought up (Forsyth 1999). If this crucial information is discussed even at a superficial level, it will affect the decision-making process, but the information must be shared among all group members to have a meaningful influence on the final decision.

Because of group norms and the group's collective experience, information that is known to all members is easier to discuss. It provides common ground and is understood by all. It also allows individual members to feel as though they are in the know and part of the group. Shared information is at the forefront of the group's discussion, and only in the later stages of the decision-making process does information known to only a few group members come up. This delay may hinder effective decision making, as commonly understood information may be the primary source used to make the final decision while information known to individual members is disregarded.

Ineffective Discussions

As most people have encountered at one time or another, engaging in group discussions when making a decision can be a trying experience. There are several reasons why discussion can be trying, most of which are interpersonal or social in nature.

- **Using discussion to avoid decision making.** Many groups use discussion to put off a decision, especially if its outcomes have potentially damaging consequences for the group. Decision making can also be avoided by assigning the process to a subgroup. In a discussion, groups often go with the first alternative for a decision. Members look only at the positive aspects of their decision and ignore the negative aspects. In effect, they artificially strengthen the reasoning and support behind their choice.

- **Going with the first decision.** Sometimes groups choose the first decision that comes to mind, especially if a decision needs to be made quickly. Persuasive group members may encourage the group to implement a particular decision by offering a quick explanation of its merits while not allowing the group time to think about its ramifications. Groups are more likely to go with the first decision if their members tend to go with the flow or fail to participate fully in the decision-making discussions.

- **Social loafing.** Some group members see the group as a way to cut back on their input to the decision-making process. People who take advantage of

---

Toolbox Tips

Encouraging Information Sharing

Here are a few techniques to encourage your group to share information that individual members may know but the entire group may not know.

- **State the decision to be made.** Have each group member write down one piece of information related to the issue at the top of a sheet of paper. Pass the papers to other group members and have them add what they know underneath the original information point. Read the collected information points aloud.

- **Appoint a facilitator.** Have the facilitator spend two minutes summarizing the information that the entire group knows. Allow individual group members 30 seconds to add something new to the information pool. Information already shared may not be repeated.

- **Conduct an information fishbowl.** Select a few group members to sit in a circle and discuss the decision to be made. Have the other group members sit in a larger circle around the smaller circle. When appropriate, the outer members may add information points that are known only to them.

Although these techniques may require additional time and resources to implement, they will enrich the decision-making process and encourage group members to share information known only to them in future decision-making situations.

---

being an individual in a group and don't contribute to their fullest extent are called *social loafers*. They turn the positive aspect of group decision making of two heads are better than one to their advantage. In essence, they hide in the crowd and slack off as a result. Several factors encourage individuals to become social loafers. These include a lack of group cohesion, a lack of outcomes tied to individual inputs, a large group size, a perception that others are social loafing, and a feeling that the decision is unimportant or boring.

- **Free riding.** Related to social loafing is the phenomenon of free riding. Free riding is social loafing to an extreme: An individual member does nothing to support the group process. Free riding is frequent in recreation and leisure groups, especially in those that individuals are forced to join. When free riding, the individual receives the most benefit from the group for the least cost. In response, other group members may be inclined to cut back on their contributions to the discussion in an effort to avoid feelings of being taken advantage of. These people do not want to be suckers, stuck doing all the work for the group. If individual contributions are supported and the group

members all pull their own weight, feelings of being a sucker can be avoided.

- **Succumbing to distractions.** Many distractions can occur during discussions that affect decision making. Individuals may think about other responsibilities, pay too much attention to information they think is interesting, or be unable to process all the information presented in the discussion. Often individuals experience production blocking, in which they miss the opportunity to interject their thought or piece of information because the discussion topic changes before they can speak. This missed opportunity leads them to focus on that thought or piece of information and not on the discussion at hand.

Groupthink

Irving Janus, a social psychologist who was interested in how some groups make disastrous decisions, invented the concept of groupthink (1972). Groupthink is the inclination for concurrence seeking among group members. The desire for agreement overwhelms individual concerns with potential downfalls and encourages support and confidence in a faulty decision. Janus outlined several warning signs that a group might be trapped in groupthink:

- Pressure on those who disagree with the majority or favored opinion

- Mind guards, or group members who block information and opinions that counter the decision

- Stereotyping of those who are outside the group and disagree or provide alternative solutions

- Self-censorship to keep individual doubts and concerns quiet by each group member

- Appearances of invulnerability, or the misconception that the group is making positive progress

- Incorrect justification that the discussion or decision is right, even though a reasoned examination would reveal many flaws

- Illusions of morality in which the group believes their decision is right despite potential ethical issues and consequences

- Appearances of unanimity, or the belief that everyone in the group agrees with the decision when in fact not everyone supports the decision

These symptoms of groupthink might not be easy to spot right away and may not be recognized until after a flawed decision has been made. There are some conditions that make it easier for a group to fall into groupthink. These include isolation from outside information, leadership styles that do not allow for free expression of dissenting opinions, lack of heterogeneity or range of experience and background of group members, high feelings of cohesiveness and close bonds among group members, lack of skills to make complex decisions, and lack of time to make a decision.

Although there are many positive aspects of group decision making, there are potential downfalls as well. By recognizing group factors and processes that contribute to poor decision making, professionals can avoid these situations or suggest alternative strategies to encourage better decision making in their groups. An understanding of the various methods of decision making, when combined with an understanding of the positive and negative aspects of group decisions, will assist professionals in promoting good group decision making. The following section presents several processes that groups have used for making decisions.

SIX-STEP PROCESS FOR MAKING DECISIONS

Ahmed and Kristen are cocaptains of a coed recreational league basketball team. The team is down by two points with three seconds left on the clock in the fourth quarter. The winner of the game moves on to the next round of the play-offs. The team has taken a time-out to decide what to do in the last three seconds. The team's center, Mary, has been successful scoring from close to the basket all night. Ahmed thinks they should get the ball to Mary and go for the tie. Kristen thinks they should go for the win and pass the ball to Brady, who has been sinking three-pointers all night. How will the team figure out which strategy to use?

As individuals, people make hundreds of decisions every day. While working with groups, the number of decisions people make expands exponentially. Both the individual members in the group and the group as a whole are making decisions. Think about the first decision people make each day. That decision probably was influenced by one of the last decisions made the day before—what time to get up! As simple as it may be, choosing what time to wake up immediately affects the rest of an individual's day. If a person decides to get up early, she has time for a cup of coffee and a glance at the newspaper before going to work. If she gets up late, however, she does not have time to read in the newspaper that the bridge she normally crosses on her bike ride to work has just been closed for repairs. So she ends up being late for an important meeting. Even a seemingly straightforward decision like choosing what time to get up follows a general six-step process. This process is outlined in figure 6.2.

Often, the first step in the decision-making process is getting oriented with the decision, while the second step identifies factors surrounding the decision. Through these processes, individuals or groups can determine the nature of the decision, issue, or

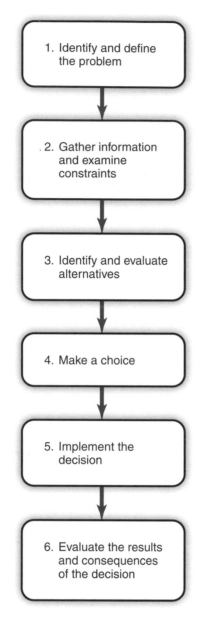

Figure 6.2 Decision-making process

the group needs to get information that is timely and relevant to the decision to be made. The group should consider

- who has an issue,
- what is the issue,
- when the issue is a concern,
- where the issue happens,
- why the issue happens, and
- how the issue came about.

Finally, the group members must buy into the process through discussing the difference between where the group is and where it wants to be. A simple yet effective technique is to conduct a simple cost–benefit analysis of what is known about the issue. The group can identify the costs and benefits associated with the issue and determine how to increase the benefits while minimizing the costs. Through this discussion individuals and the group as a whole become committed to making the decision. Professionals may help groups through this stage of the process by encouraging a reasoned approach to identifying and defining the decision. Many groups move through the first two stages rapidly, and the rush to implement a decision affects the quality and effectiveness of the final outcomes. For Ahmed and Kristen, the cost is losing the game and the benefit is winning and continuing in the play-offs.

The third stage is identifying and evaluating alternative courses of action. Using the clearly defined and articulated issues from the previous stages, the group generates a list of potential decisions. There are four traps that groups might fall into during this stage of the decision-making process:

1. The group might not have the appropriate skills or knowledge to identify or evaluate the alternatives.

2. The group may not have an established way to go about identifying and evaluating different choices.

3. The group may pressure individual members who possess knowledge or skills that would improve the assessment of the alternatives to conform to what the rest of the group is doing.

problem to the best of their ability. At this point, it is in the best interest of the group members to be sure they have adequately defined the decision to be made or problem at hand. Ahmed and Kristen have identified and defined the decision to be made—should they go inside for the tie or shoot the three-pointer for the win?

There are three considerations in these first two stages of the decision-making process. First, the group members need to agree on where they are and where they would like to be. This is the difference between reality and a desired situation. Second,

4. The group may fail to identify all possible alternatives.

Another pitfall is that some alternatives may be discarded early in the process when they should be considered on equal footing with all the choices the group is mulling over. All of these pitfalls may be avoided by proper training, access to information, and good group communication and listening skills. Professionals may help groups avoid pitfalls by providing unbiased leadership, by encouraging open and free debate, by asking outside specialists in the area for help, or by playing the devil's advocate for each of the group's proposed courses of action.

Ahmed and Kristen have identified two alternatives: go inside to Mary or go outside to Brady. There might be other plans of action, but because Mary and Brady have been successful at scoring from their prospective positions, they are the best alternatives from which to choose.

The fourth step in the decision-making process is choosing one of the alternatives to implement and will affect the group's acceptance and support of the final course of action. If the group members feel they have been part of the process and that each individual's opinions have been considered, then the group will be more apt to buy into the final decision. If the group members feel discounted or that individuals have been overlooked or marginalized, they may not support the final course of action. Ahmed and Kristen decide to get the ball to the outside to Brady and go for the win. Some of the team members turn away in disappointment when they hear the decision, while others are excited by the do-or-die events about to take place.

The fifth stage is implementing the decision. This may involve all the group members, selected group members, or one group member. As mentioned earlier, when individuals and groups feel as though they have been part of the decision-making process, they are more likely to implement the decision and perform better in conditions created by the decision. Ahmed and Kristen call for a screen in which Brady gets the ball at the top of the key for a three-point shot.

In the sixth and final stage of the decision-making process, the outcomes of the decision should be evaluated. There are two parts to this process. First, the group should determine whether the decision was implemented the way it was meant to be (or if it wasn't, what made the way in which it was implemented successful or unsuccessful). Second, the group should figure out if the outcomes of the decision were what they were intended to be. For Ahmed and Kristen, the outcome is pretty clear—Brady sinks the three-pointer and the team wins! When evaluating the outcomes, the main question the group should ask is whether the position it landed in as a result of implementing the decided course of action (the actual state) is closer to or farther away from where it wants to be (the desired state). Table 6.1 shows the findings that are possible when evaluating the process and outcomes of a decision.

Ultimately, the group should learn from each of the decisions it makes. If the group is happy with how it went about making and implementing the decision and if the outcomes move the group closer to a state it desires, then the group should continue using that method of decision making in the future. How can a group go about making decisions? The next section introduces several common decision-making techniques.

Table 6.1 Process and Outcome Evaluation

	Outcomes faulted	Outcomes OK
Process OK	The alternative that was selected was not the right choice. The group should generate new alternatives and consider implementing the decision in a similar manner.	The group should recognize the effectiveness of both the process and the outcomes and remember to apply what it has learned from this success to future decisions.
Process faulted	Neither the selected alternative nor the way in which it was implemented was correct. The group should develop new alternatives and strategies to implement its new decision.	The alternative that was selected was the right choice. The method by which it was implemented was not correct. The group should consider a new way to implement its decision.

COMMON METHODS OF GROUP DECISION MAKING

There are several options a group can employ to go about making a decision. Groups use the following methods of decision making: the leaders make the decision, an expert makes the decision, the group uses the average opinions of its members to make the decision, the leaders make the decision after discussing the issue with the group, a minority decides, a majority decides, or the group reaches a consensus about what decision to make. Each of these methods of decision making and problem solving has several strengths and weaknesses, and the different methods require different amounts of resources and time to reach a final decision.

Decision by Leader

If a group uses this technique to make a decision, the designated or recognized leader makes the final choice. The leader does not confer with other group members during the decision-making or problem-solving process. Although decision by leader is quick, only the information and resources available to the leader influence how the decision is made. The advantages of having input from multiple sources (i.e., the other group members) are bypassed, usually for the sake of time. Decision by leader is often used by groups that are organized hierarchically, such as military or business groups. Individual members in groups whose leader makes the decisions often do not support the decisions as readily as they would support decisions they had given input into. If the leader does not do a good job communicating how the decision should be implemented or the problem should be solved, group members may be unable to execute the leader's plan of action. As mentioned earlier, the primary benefit of this method of decision making is that decisions can be made quickly.

Decision by Expert

Groups often turn to experts for input when making a decision or solving a problem. The expert may be a member of the group, or the group may consult a nonmember. A primary strength of engaging an expert who is already a member of the group is the connection the expert has to both the issue and the other group members. The expert who is already a group member usually has an awareness of the group's history, the context of the decision or problem, the strengths and weaknesses of the group's decision-making and problem-solving abilities, and the resources the group has at its disposal. As with decisions made by the leader, decisions made by an expert from within a group may be made relatively quickly. One problem with using an expert from within the group is determining who in the group is best qualified as the expert. Other group members may not support a decision if they do not feel the expert member is truly qualified, particularly if several group members possess similar skills.

Sometimes a group decides to go outside its membership for expert advice. Usually this person is deemed an authority in the appropriate area, and the group gives up its decision-making power to this person. However, the outside expert might not be familiar enough with the group to suggest a course of action the group can complete. Also, group members who do not view the expert as an authority may be reluctant to implement the recommended decision. When deferring to the outside expert, the group also gives up the advantage of having multiple sources of input as well as an awareness of the group's history.

Decision by Average

This method of decision making requires each group member to rank alternatives. Usually a number is used to assign rank. For example, a member's first choice is marked a *1*, the second choice is marked a *2*, and so on. The rankings are then added up and divided by the total number of group members providing input. The decision with the best average is the group's choice. A negative aspect of this method is that it lacks discussion among group members. Extreme responses due to lack of knowledge about the issue may negate the more informed opinions of other group members. The group members may feel that their voices have not been heard, as their opinion is lost in the numbers. Consequently, individual group members may feel the decision was not the best choice and may not work to implement it. Table 6.2 presents two common methods of making decisions by average—the Delphi technique and the nominal group technique.

Table 6.2 Delphi and Nominal Group Techniques

Delphi technique	Nominal group technique

1. Survey is distributed to group members and results are tabulated via mail or e-mail.
2. Tabulated results are sent back to group members for additional comments and clarification..
3. These results are tabulated and further questions are sent out for another review. It is up to the person coordinating this technique to guide future questions, which might address the following:
   a. Factors influencing the decision
   b. Potential solutions
   c. Pros and cons of solutions
4. This process is continued until a clear course of action is evident.
	1. Working alone, group members brainstorm in writing.
	2. Statements are read aloud. This can be done anonymously by shuffling papers with no names on them.
	3. Ideas are discussed with no evaluative comments allowed! The goal is to identify the following:
	   a. Themes
	   b. Ideas
	   c. Potential pitfalls
	   d. Potential positive aspects
	4. Group members rank the items in a secret ballot. The items that come out on top are discussed for possible implementation.

Decision by Leader After Discussion

Under this method, a leader calls a meeting or gathers input from the group. Individual members are able to generate possible solutions and benefit from the opportunity to hear the ideas of others. This technique is effective if the group trusts the leader, particularly if the leader has made successful decisions in the past. Leaders who use this method must exercise good listening skills and ask questions so that they completely understand the alternatives being suggested. However, this technique may create competition among group members as they try to be heard by the leader. If group members do not feel that their voices have been heard, they may disrupt the implementation and successful outcome of the decision-making or problem-solving process. This decision-making method begins to address some of the issues surrounding the technique in which the leader decides without group input.

Decision by Minority

A decision by minority results when less than 50 percent of the group members agree on a course of action. Often when a decision is made by the minority of group members, it is an attempt to push through a decision that is poorly thought out or that benefits those directly involved in the decision. Many times suggestions from the minority are put forth quickly and with little forewarning so that the majority does not have time to consider the ramifications of going along with that decision.

Sometimes decisions by the minority are used to streamline the decision-making process. This technique may be used successfully in a group if members trust each other and have had success in the past. Most often decision by minority takes the form of decisions being made by a committee. If key members of the group, such as experts and those with access to the appropriate knowledge and resources, are included in the committee, this technique can benefit a group as a whole.

Decision by Majority

This is the method of decision making and problem solving that is familiar to most people. In it, at least 50.1 percent of the group members must agree on the course of action or alternative. Usually decision by majority involves a vote of some kind. This process is ingrained so deeply in North American society that most North Americans abide by its outcomes. However, this process does create two subgroups within a larger group—those who got their way and those who didn't. This may become an issue if only a small majority favored the final outcome. Group members whose alternative wasn't chosen may not participate in implementing the decision as fully as they would have if their way had been chosen. These members may band together to disrupt future decision-making and problem-solving processes. As long as the group as a whole creates an atmosphere in which individual members feel they have had their say, this method of decision making can be effective.

Decision by Consensus

Consensus occurs when the group as whole agrees on which decision to implement or method to use to solve a problem. It is the most effective method a group can use to make a decision or solve a problem. Through open and supportive communication, group members can work through the issues surrounding a particular decision or problem and reach a common opinion as to how to proceed. The consensus-building process promotes the effective and efficient use of all the resources the group has available, including collective memory, individual knowledge and experience, and constructive conflict resolution. By the end of the process, group members have shared their own ideas, completely understood others' ideas and the rationale behind them, and agreed to support a particular course of action, even if it is on a trial basis. The primary downfall of using consensus as a decision-making and problem-solving technique is that it requires time. The group must have enough time for its members to state their views, listen to everyone's ideas, debate the merits and disadvantages of each point, and search for the best alternative. Johnson and Johnson (2003, 297) suggest six guidelines for individuals involved in making decisions by consensus:

1. Avoid arguing blindly for your own opinions.
2. Avoid changing your mind.

3. Avoid conflict-reducing procedures.
4. Seek out differences of opinion.
5. Do not assume that someone must win and someone must lose.
6. Discuss underlying assumptions.

Although reaching a consensus is time consuming, the outcomes will be most beneficial to the group in the long run. Through the consensus-building process, group members become more invested in the final decision and the overall group decision-making and problem-solving processes are strengthened.

You now know the common methods of group decision making. Use the Learning Activity on this page as an exercise to explore what each of these common methods is like.

Professionals working with groups will have to make decisions and solve problems on a regular basis. You may find that choosing a particular method of decision making and problem solving is difficult, especially if you are relatively inexperienced at working with groups. The next section discusses some points to consider when selecting a method of decision making and problem solving.

THE LEADER AND DECISION MAKING

Each recreation, leisure, and experiential education practitioner brings different experience, knowledge, and skills to the decision-making and problem-solving process. As you gain more experience working with and within groups, you will develop an understanding of which method of decision making and problem solving will most effectively and efficiently create

Learning Activity

Refer back to the scenario about the basketball team trying to decide which shot to take during the final three seconds of its game. Working in a group of 3 to 5 members, discuss how you would use each of the decision-making and problem-solving methods in this scenario. List the benefits of using each method. List the negative aspects of using each method. Discuss the following: If you were Ahmed and Kristen, what would you do? Why? Is there a specific method of decision making or problem solving that is better suited to this situation? Why? How would the rest of the team feel in that situation?

viable alternatives from which to choose. Time is often a major concern when selecting a method. Other considerations are the ability and experience of both the individual group members and the group as a whole. This next section provides insight into how you may analyze these factors so that you can choose the best method of decision making and problem solving for the groups you lead.

Complexity

Recognizing the relative complexity of a decision or problem helps a leader choose which method of decision making or problem solving to implement. Simple decisions such as when to stop for lunch on a hiking trip involve few variables (it is noon, the group is hungry, the group has access to food), few consequences (if we don't stop for lunch right now, we can stop in 30 minutes and no one will care), and results that are fairly easy to predict (the group members will be hungry if we don't stop and eat, but they can snack until we stop for lunch). Complex decisions such as deciding whether to do a six-mile open-water crossing in a sea kayak on Lake Superior involve more variables (wind, water temperature, motorboat traffic, skill level

of group members), greater consequences (kayak tips over), and less predictable results (the group may or may not make the crossing). Simple decisions may be made in little time, while complex decisions require more thought. Group members may actually resent being involved in simple decisions, as they may perceive group consideration of such trivial matters as a waste of everyone's time. However, group members may also resent being left out of a complex decision, as the outcomes have potentially greater effects on the group.

Another aspect that recreation, leisure, and experiential education practitioners should consider is the potential length of time needed to implement a specific method of decision making and problem solving. Figure 6.3 illustrates the relationship between the quality of a decision-making process (consensus having the highest quality) and the time needed for that process (consensus requiring the most time).

Thinking about the complexity of a decision and the amount of time a particular method of decision making and problem solving requires will assist professionals in determining the best course of action. Choosing the consensus method to work on a complex decision requires more time than a leader

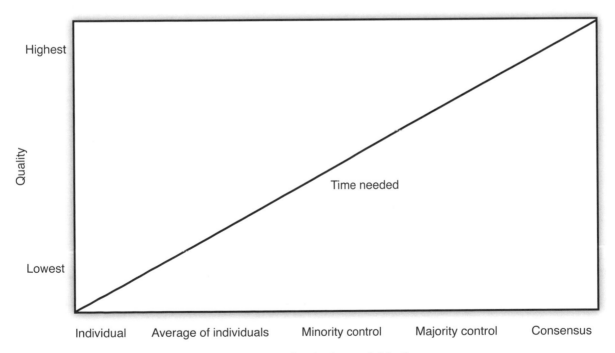

Figure 6.3 Quality of a decision-making process as compared to the time needed for the process.

From Johnson, David W., Frank P. Johnson. Joining Together: Group Therapy and Group Skills, 8/e. Published by Allyn and Bacon, Boston, MA. Copyright © 2003 by Pearson Education. Reprinted by permission of the publisher.

making a simple decision requires. Leaders must be aware of how decision making will influence both the task function and the relationship function of the group, as one or both functions may be affected, and this in turn will affect the overall experience of the group.

Abilities

Recreation, leisure, and experiential education groups will have varying levels of experience and expertise in whatever situation they're in. The leader should be aware of the ability of the group to make decisions and solve problems on its own behalf, particularly if the group is experienced. Generally, if the group members are experienced, group-centered methods (i.e., decision by minority, decision by majority, consensus) are the most effective and efficient. If the group is relatively inexperienced, leader-centered methods (i.e., leader decides, expert decides, decision by average) are the most successful and timely. Figure 6.4 provides a flowchart that describes potential courses of action based on the group's level of ability.

Seeing the Big Picture

One of the most difficult skills for recreation, leisure, and experiential education professionals to develop is the ability to see the big picture. Seeing the big picture is akin to having a crystal ball and being able to predict all of the possible outcomes of the decision-making and problem-solving process. A leader should think of not only the immediate effects a decision will have on the relationship and task functions of a group but also the potential long-term outcomes the decision will have. Situational factors such as who is in the group and environmental considerations such as weather and having access to help if something goes wrong must be considered. Seeing the big picture is not something that can be learned through reading a textbook or attending class. It takes everyday experience to learn this skill!

SUMMARY

Decision making and problem solving are inherent to working with groups. They can be performed either

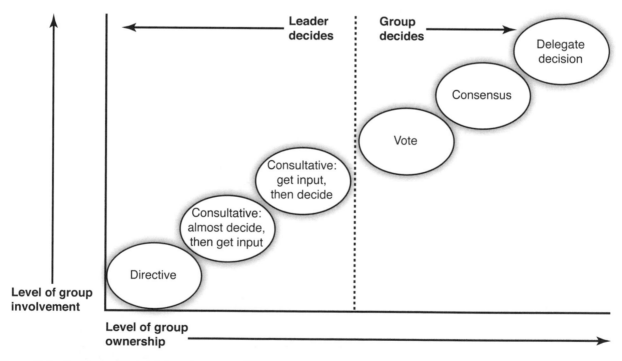

Figure 6.4 Decision-making style based on group ability.

Reprinted, by permission, from NOLS, 2008, *2004 NOLS leadership education notebook* (Lander, WY: The National Outdoor Leadership School), 39.

by individuals or by the group as a whole. There are many positive aspects of involving the entire group in the decision-making and problem-solving process. These include the collective nature of information gathering and processing, social facilitation, and risk taking or group polarization. However, there are accompanying weaknesses as well. These include withholding of information, issues with discussion, and groupthink. Methods of decision making and problem solving that professionals can use include decision by leader, decision by inside or outside expert, decision by average, decision by the leader after discussion, decision by the minority, decision by the majority, and decision by consensus. Depending on the leader, the ability of the group, and the time available, any one of these methods may be implemented. Each of these methods has distinct advantages and disadvantages for both the task and the relationship functions of the group. Professionals should develop their ability to see the big picture, as it will help them assist groups in making the most effective and efficient decisions possible.

RESOURCES

Forsyth, D. 1999. *Group dynamics.* 3rd ed. Belmont, CA: Wadsworth.

Janus, I. 1972. *Victims of groupthink.* Boston: Houghton Mifflin.

Johnson, D.W., and F.P. Johnson. 2003. *Joining together: Group theory and group skills.* 8th ed. Boston: Pearson Education.

CHAPTER

7

Power and Conflict

Konrad and Elizabeth were hired at the same time to work collaboratively on several recreation planning projects for the city's waterfront development initiative. They were told that although they were opposites, they would complement each other well. Early on, Konrad realized that he and Elizabeth were indeed opposites, but they were not complementing each other. To him, she represented almost everything that he did not want to be. She was aggressively outspoken and competitive, and she did not want to share recognition for the accomplishments that they achieved. Often in meetings that the two of them were supposed to run jointly, Elizabeth would interrupt Konrad to explain an idea that he was just about to introduce. Once, Elizabeth surprised him by showing up with an agenda and an information package to hand out to the planning board, even though she and Konrad had talked previously and agreed that the meeting should be an informal exchange of ideas. Konrad found Elizabeth intimidating, and it became increasingly difficult for him to work well with her. He didn't like conflict and began to despise the very thought of having to interact with her. He started referring to her as *Lizardbreath* when he vented to his friends.

Konrad hated fighting with other people—it tied his stomach in knots—and he realized that he needed to do something to change the situation. His first strategy was to overwhelm Elizabeth with kindness, but doing so seemed to make things worse. She told him that she "knew what he was up to" and that his "attempts to make her look bad were not going to work." When he found that he wasn't sleeping well but instead was lying in bed feeling bitter while staring at the ceiling and reliving the events of the day (or the week), Konrad went to his supervisor for help. After a brief meeting with his boss, who told him he was probably worried about nothing and that he should be a man, Konrad's hopes for a solution evaporated. He felt defeated and began to avoid every situation he could that might mean being in the same room with Elizabeth. Eventually, he applied for other jobs and decided to take a temporary position with a local nongovernmental organization that advocated for recreational green spaces. The work was important but not challenging—he was responsible for doing background research on the history of land parcels in the region. On the other hand, he was sleeping well now and he loved the people he worked with. Konrad just hoped that the job would lead to something more permanent and interesting. . . .

Great fiction writers use power and conflict to weave stories of intrigue and to set up moral struggles both between and within characters. Without characters' attempts to exert power over others, or without conflict of some kind, the stories writers tell would be uninteresting. There would be no unfolding drama, no heightening intensity, and no way to keep the reader involved. In order for a story to evolve, its characters must encounter and deal with conditions involving power and conflict. Imagine a novel in which there was no disagreement or suspense about an approaching event, in which people's conversations were about how much they agreed with each other, and in which there was no possibility of a negative outcome. You would not only label the book *boring* but also find the plot lifeless and a little unreal.

Much of the same could be said for real life. Although your everyday social life may not be as theatrical as the lives depicted in novels, your relationships with others are full of issues involving power and conflict, and they couldn't be otherwise. Power and conflict are inevitable when you interact with others for a length of time. In this chapter we describe central characteristics of power and conflict, identify the main sources of each, and discuss strategies to manage or perhaps transform negative consequences into positive ones.

POWER

The use of power is essential in group life. Leaders need to be able to guide their group members in appropriate directions at appropriate times. Simply asserting your voice in a meeting is an attempt to exert power. Likewise, arguing for a particular outcome is yet another way to try to exercise power. Generally, the type of power exerted in the context of human interaction is social power. In a social context, power can be described as the ability to influence others, the behaviors of others, or the outcomes of social interaction. In other words, power is the ability to influence other people or the outcomes of events. Interestingly, while it is easier to exert power if the person doing the exerting has the cooperation of those being influenced, cooperation is not absolutely necessary for the exertion of power to be successful. Consider the following well-known experiments undertaken by Stanley Milgram, a researcher who looked into the relationship between obedience to authority and personal conscience.

Milgram's Experiments

In the years that followed World War II, the world struggled to come to terms with the main defense given at so many trials of accused Nazi war criminals: "I was only following orders." Questions were asked about whether it is possible for people to ignore their own conscience and then proceed to harm, torture, or even kill others. Just what kind of moral bankruptcy would have to exist for the Holocaust to take place, with legions of people simply following orders? In a series of experiments that later became known as the *obedience to authority* study, social scientist Stanley Milgram set up a scenario that forced participants

to choose between obeying an authority figure and resisting that authority when they were presented with evidence that they were being asked to cause harm to another person. The original study, described in detail in a later book by Milgram (1974), tested how far the participants would go in delivering an electric shock to another participant before those meting out the punishment called a halt to the proceedings.

In the experiment's design, an individual who volunteered to take part in the study was introduced to an experimenter and another participant. The experimenter wore a lab coat, assumed an air of authority, and assigned roles to the two participants. One would be the teacher and the other the learner. In fact, the roles were predetermined and the learner was actually a member of the study team—called a *confederate*—set to act out a dramatic part. The true study participant was always in the role of the teacher.

The teacher (the subject) watched as the confederate was seated at a table, outfitted with electrodes, and strapped into a chair that was explained as being designed to prevent excessive movement. The teacher was then led to an adjoining room where the experimenter sat at one table and the teacher sat at another. The teacher's station was furnished with wires, and the teacher was told that the wires connected to the learner's table and chair and gave the teacher the ability to shock the learner in the event that the learner provided an incorrect response to the questions asked by the teacher and prepared in advance by the experimenter. The teacher was asked to increase the voltage successively after each incorrect response in an effort to create increased incentive for the learner to give the correct response in the future. Figure 7.1 is a diagrammatic representation of how Milgram's experiments were conducted. The experimenter (E) was positioned behind and slightly off to the side of the teacher/subject (T). The learner (L) was in an adjoining room and not visible to the teacher.

The switches on the teacher's panel were labeled, beginning at "slight shock" and ending at "danger: severe shock," and two additional switches were labeled "XXX." Voltage amounts ranging from 15 to 450 volts were also provided. No shock was ever delivered to the confederate during the experiment, but he acted as though he was being shocked if the teacher activated the switch. During the course of a session, the confederate began to complain, with

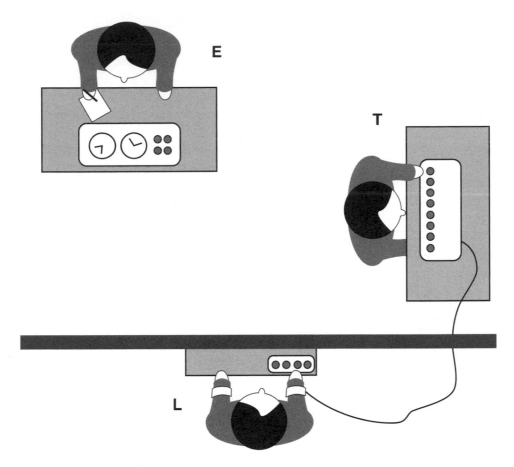

Figure 7.1 Setup for Milgram's experiments.

www.wikipedia.org

his protests becoming more urgent as the "voltage" increased. The confederate sobbed or even feigned unresponsiveness toward the end of the experiment if the teacher kept administering shocks. If the teacher objected to the shocks being delivered to an apparently suffering learner, the experimenter would urge them to continue, stressing that it was essential to continue the experiment.

Before the study began, Milgram predicted that very few subjects would follow through by delivering shocks to the learner at the high-voltage end of the 450-volt panel, but he was surprised to find that 65 percent of the subjects did exactly that and even administered shocks to seemingly unconscious individuals. In addition, *not one* of the subjects stopped before 300 volts. Many of the subjects displayed signs of agitation and discomfort (some quite severe) in carrying out the experimenter's wishes, but assurance and pressure from the experimenter kept most of them obedient.

Surprised by his findings, Milgram conducted further trials to find out if there were conditions that would reduce the experimenter's power over the research subjects. In some experiments, Milgram moved the location from the prestigious Yale University to an off-campus office. In others, he removed the authority figure from the room once the instructions were given to the subject. In still others, a second confederate was added who was introduced as a second teacher. In these trials, the research subjects' compliance declined to 48 percent in the off-campus office scenario and to 20 percent in the other two scenarios. Interestingly, though, when the second teacher was added, almost 70 percent of the subjects failed to stop him when he took over shocking the learner once the true subject had refused to continue.

With today's standards for ethics in research, Milgram's experiments would probably not be allowed to go forward. In fact, these experiments contributed to a discussion on what could be considered ethical for research involving human subjects. Nonetheless, Stanley Milgram's findings have given us a great deal of insight into how many people behave in situations that are directed by a recognized figure of authority.

It could be argued that these studies took place in an era when authority was not questioned. The environmental, civil rights, and peace movements that have not only gained popularity but also transformed much of everyday life since Milgram's time are touted as having changed the relationship between a citizenry and its government and authority figures (at least in democratic countries). However—and this is a sobering realization—there are any number of present-day examples that point to people carrying out unethical actions because of influence from authority figures. One well-known example is the U.S. military's mistreatment of Iraqi detainees at the infamous Abu Ghraib prison. In 2004, with rumors circulating in media circles about torture and humiliation occurring within the prison, a CBS documentary broke the story with pictures of Iraqi prisoners in degrading circumstances. A subsequent investigation found evidence that soldiers were following directions that they said were given by senior military personnel in order to speed up intelligence gathering.

Death at Ipperwash

On September 6, 1995, Dudley George, a First Nations man who was part of a group of protesters occupying Ipperwash Provincial Park in Canada, was shot to death by the Ontario Provincial Police (OPP). The escalating standoff was the result of a land claim made by a local First Nations community attempting to regain title to land that the Canadian government expropriated in 1942 in order to build a military base. More than 50 years later, without a resolution to the land claim, a group of about 30 protesters moved onto the land, building barricades in an attempt to raise the profile of their cause and to protect what they claimed to be an ancient burial site for the Stony Point First Nations.

In late 2005, during an inquiry into the shooting incident, the former attorney general for the province of Ontario testified that the premier at the time, Mike Harris, had made a disparaging remark about the protesters and had made clear his desire for the OPP to remove them. The alleged remark was made at a high-level meeting with cabinet ministers in attendance.

Although the former premier denied the allegation, a senior OPP officer who attended the meeting corroborated the attorney general's impression that Harris and his government believed they had the power to direct the OPP in handling the situation.

Despite the confusing claims and counterclaims regarding the events that led to Dudley George's death in 1995, what remains important is the relationship between the perception of an authority figure's power and the action that often follows. The shooting occurred only hours after the meeting between Harris and his cabinet ministers.

Long-Distance Imposter

A final and stunning example of people being influenced by perceived authority involves a series of bizarre phone calls made to a variety of fast-food outlets and chain restaurants across the United States. Between 1994 and 2004, restaurants reported more than 70 calls in which a man, usually pretending to be a police officer, persuaded restaurant managers and staff into strip-searching coworkers on the premise of the workers having done something wrong. A central theme in the testimonies of why the various restaurant employees complied with the police impersonator was that he was able to convince them that he was who he claimed to be. Incredible as it may seem, the caller convinced managers and assistant managers to strip-search their employees, order them to assume embarrassing positions, and even perform lewd acts. In November 2000 a restaurant manager was convinced to strip in front of a man she was told was a sex offender. She was assured by the caller that undercover officers would intervene if the man made any attempt to accost her. David Stewart, a man using phone cards to call around the country from Panama City, Florida, was eventually arrested; there have been no reports of similar calls since.

These present-day examples of obedience to authority (or perceived authority) tend to validate Milgram's surprising findings. Despite claims that today's society is more skeptical, there are plenty of reasons to believe that power and authority induce obedience, even when the behavior demanded by the authority figure is suspect or even immoral. Why, then, are people able to exert power over others? What are the sources of power that convince many of us to follow the directions of people who hold that power?

Sources of Power

French & Raven (1959) identified five bases of social power: coercive power, reward power, legitimate power, referent power, and expert power. In the mid-1960s, Raven expanded the original list to include informational power. More recently, other scholars have updated and refined the descriptions of French and Raven's typology, adding or subdividing classifications depending on interpretations or applications. However, an understanding of the initial categories is sufficient to gain a working knowledge of power relationships within groups.

Coercive Power

Coercive power is perhaps what is most often associated with the idea of exercising power. It is confrontational and has significant negative connotations. Coercive power involves threatening or punishing others in order to achieve results. Disagreement or failure to comply with demands is met with sanctions designed to intimidate the offending party into conforming or meeting the demand. Coercive power is widespread and practiced on numerous social levels. Parents removing their misbehaving children's TV privileges; church groups threatening excommunication; radical political groups threatening bombings or public violence as retribution; individuals warning their significant others that they will end the relationship unless certain conditions are met; workplace supervisors promising to fire you if you're late just one more time; court judges imposing fines or jail time on those found guilty of breaking the law; and researchers shocking animals to assess their capacity to learn behavior avoidance are just a few examples of coercive power.

It's true that humans are motivated to avoid punishment, so coercive strategies can be effective. However, research has shown that when used as the sole method of gaining compliance, coercion invariably results in fear and negative sentiment toward the one wielding the power. Often, it also inspires rebellion or further antagonism.

Reward Power

The opposite of coercive power is reward power, the ability to provide things that other people need or want in exchange for desired behaviors. Businesses paying wages or salaries to employees, a coach offering a day off from practice if the game is won, a canoe trip leader promising to let the campers sleep in if they paddle an extra few miles today, and customers leaving a tip in exchange for good food and excellent service are all examples of reward power. Often seen as a much more positive approach to motivating people, reward power also has its drawbacks. For example, if a promised reward is not delivered, its withholding may be seen as punishment, even if the intended receiver did not fulfill his obligations.

Legitimate Power

Legitimate power is the authority ascribed to a social position within a group and is the kind of power exerted by the experimenter in Milgram's research. In Milgram's experiments, the person who wore the lab coat took on the persona of a research scientist, a highly respected role in our social structure. Individuals in uniforms, or those who exude confidence and are accompanied by the trappings of a particular job (e.g., a physician wearing a stethoscope and white coat; a uniformed woman stepping out of a police cruiser with a weapon on her hip; a man dressed in black with a white priest's collar carrying a Bible), are given a certain amount of deference simply because they appear at first glance to occupy a position we recognize as carrying some authority. The roles are well established in society to warrant obedience, in part because of our collective acceptance of the responsibility and necessity of these positions.

Legitimate power can be delegated by an established organization, but it can also come from some other recognized process. For instance, leaders may be elected, royalty or tribal chiefs may claim authority by birthright, or people may fill positions by meeting a prescribed set of qualifications. In whatever manner legitimate power is attained in a group, the group members must accept the process in order for the power to be considered rightful. The legitimate authority embedded in recognized social roles is not easily ignored or questioned, even when the authority figures abuse their privileges. As in the case of the long-distance police impersonator, con artists are acutely aware of the tendency in many of us to comply with the demands of an authority figure. You and your colleagues can probably list dozens of scams that you've heard about involving someone pretending to be in a position of authority and duping susceptible people into sending money or giving out credit card numbers or other sensitive information that they would never give to perfect strangers in other situations.

Referent Power

Popularity or charisma is most often used to describe referent power. Within a group, the person who is liked and respected can wield a great deal of influence over others' behaviors and beliefs. One of the reasons why celebrities are sought to speak on behalf of a cause or to appear in media advertising is that they hold referent power. In wanting to be like them, the rest of the population is more likely to buy the products they endorse or take on the values they espouse. When someone holds extreme referent power and is also a recognized leader within a group (legitimate power), that person is said to be a *charismatic leader.*

Popular people have referent power.

Expert Power

We live in an increasingly specialized society. Accompanying the increased specialization are people who are identified as experts within their particular field. Expert power is the type of authority you might enjoy if you are seen as the one with the most knowledge or ability in something. It's easy to acknowledge experts in areas such as breast cancer research or astrophysics, but even within recreation, knowledge and ability can be subdivided into areas requiring expertise not held by the general population. The best snowboard instructors may not have the qualifications to teach Alpine skiing, Telemark skiing, classic cross-country skiing, or Nordic skate skiing. Just that small cross section of related winter activities contains different knowledge sets, and each activity requires a person to possess different qualifications in order to be considered an expert. If you have attained a certification in one or more activities, you probably know how others look to you when they need your knowledge and expertise. Expert power can be confused with legitimate power because often positions are occupied by people who have the credentials needed for a job or task. However, the difference between the two stems from the source of power. While legitimate power is given to people specifically because they occupy a position, expert power is established because a person demonstrates, or is perceived to have, knowledge on a particular topic.

POWER IN GROUPS

Power is not a one-way street. Power is almost always distributed or decentralized, even if it doesn't look that way on the surface. In other words, power is a shared phenomenon, although it's not always shared or distributed equally. For example, when India was considered part of the British Empire in the 1930s, the British controlled all of the social institutions, making laws and policy based on British interests. One law, known simply as the *salt tax,* imposed a tax on the production and sale of all salt in India. The salt tax also made it illegal for individuals to make their own salt. In so doing, the tax not only saddled millions of poor laborers with having to pay for an essential mineral but also outlawed the traditional practice of gathering salt for personal use, even though the salt was easily accessible—and free—for most of the coastal population.

In response, Mohandas Gandhi and his followers invoked the power of peaceful protest, marching 240 miles to the coastal village of Dandi. Upon reaching the sea, thousands of people began making salt, defying the law and ultimately creating a unifying civil protest with salt being made and sold illegally along the coast of India. A number of historians credit the salt march protest and its aftermath as a turning point that dramatically increased the number of Gandhi's supporters and accelerated the push for Indian independence in 1947.

One of the messages that this story highlights is that there are opportunities to exert power in all social situations. Even though an employer has the power to discipline or fire employees, the employees can respond to perceived power abuses by unionizing, organizing work slowdowns and strikes, informing the media or regulatory bodies of unethical practices, and so on. It is rarely the case that those who are in positions seen as less powerful have no options. As the famous philosopher and sociologist Michel Foucault said, "Power is everywhere; not because it embraces everything, but because it comes from everywhere (1978, 93)."

There are many examples of both responsible applications and inappropriate, unethical, or even immoral applications of power. It's probably neither possible nor desirable to eliminate all forms of power and authority in social interactions. Everyone needs organization, structure, and guidance in order to operate effectively in groups. Direction, guidance, goal setting, task accomplishment, and a host of other group activities move forward only by the exercising of power, no matter how subtle or beneficial that power might be. In the best of situations, the exercising of power is an intricate dance in which all partners have access to it and use it to move toward group goals in a positive, self-affirming manner. In this ideal, group members are aware of and sensitive to power dynamics, assessing imbalances and respectfully questioning authority in appropriate ways.

MANAGING CONFLICT

When members of a group exert power, conflict inevitably follows. If the attempt to exert power within a group is also the attempt to influence the group's direction, conflict is unavoidable. It's impossible to imagine that the great numbers of thoughts and ideas expressed within a functioning group won't spark opposing thoughts in one or more group members. Conflict is a natural part of group interaction and development, and it has the potential to be either a positive or a negative force.

In English, the word *conflict* has multiple uses, and the way it is used in group dynamics should not be confused with the ways it is used in other situations. For example, in politics and international relations, conflict often refers to violent, armed struggle, a use that simply doesn't fit when the discussion is centered on groups in recreational settings. Similarly, in psychological terms, an individual can experience personal conflict—sometimes known as *feeling conflicted*—but this is an intrapersonal phenomenon and not overly relevant to the conflict that occurs among group members, namely interpersonal, intragroup conflict.

In group dynamics, the term *conflict* most often refers to disagreement, contradiction, or strife experienced by at least two group members. Conflict can result from any combination of disagreement, contradiction, and strife. For instance, disagreement can exist with or without the frustration and discord you might associate with strife. Friction between members can occur even when there is

Learning Activity

After you finish reading this chapter, keep notes on all your social events for a day (these might include riding the bus to school or carpooling to work, attending class, having lunch with friends, attending committee meetings, coaching your swim class of 8-year-olds, and so on). Identify the situations that involved some type of conflict or the exercising of power. How many situations did you note? Was your inventory surprising to you?

nothing substantial to disagree about. If you've ever seen two people argue solely because they seem to dislike each other, you probably understand how this can happen.

Sources of Conflict

Although scholars and practitioners have identified a variety of conflict dimensions, one basic categorization is a threefold set of dimensions that includes substantive conflict, interpersonal conflict, and procedural conflict.

Procedural Conflict

Procedural conflict reflects disagreement surrounding the methods of group operation. Differences that involve the question of *how* to proceed indicate procedural conflict. Decision making is often at issue in procedural conflict. Even the most informal of groups needs to decide how to decide. If you've ever tried to choose a movie with a group of friends, you've almost surely run into procedural conflict. Do you choose the one that most people want to watch? Do you look for one that no one has seen yet? If one person really doesn't want to watch one of the choices, can she veto it? Does the owner of the VCR or DVD player have more say than anyone else has? These are all questions that deal with how to proceed, and your group needs to agree on a decision-making process before you can address the actual decision in front of you. If the group membership changes (e.g., if you hang out with a different group of friends), the process may also change.

As the structure or function of the group shifts, the decision-making process shifts as well. For instance, a group of policy makers trying to adopt national standards for guide certification in sea kayaking would almost certainly take on a more formal process than that used to pick a movie. There may be basic similarities between the two groups, such as consensus building or simple majority vote, but undoubtedly there would be more subtle process differences that members must adhere to. Procedural conflicts may clarify established procedures, or they may result in the modification of decision-making processes in order to address new situations. Procedural conflict thus has the potential to improve the group's effectiveness.

Substantive Conflict

Sometimes called *task conflict,* substantive conflict arises when there is disagreement about anything related to the group's purpose, goals, or tasks—in other words, its substance. This type of conflict, if it is separated from personal agendas and if the decision-making procedure is stable, can be a productive, positive force in a group's evolution. In resolving substantive conflict, group members debate about the group's goals and direction and about how to best solve problems. Real solutions are the result of pure substantive conflict. In some ways, the creation and resolution of substantive conflict is what groups are all about: coming together to share resources, energy, and ideas in order to accomplish tasks that could not be completed as well by individuals. In your small groups, you should embrace the ideal of pure substantive conflict and welcome its creation because the outcome has the potential to benefit the group and its endeavors.

Groups that avoid conflict, including healthy conflict, tend to stagnate or develop groupthink, a condition in which members conform to their own perception of the group's thinking (see chapter 6). Groupthink discourages critical thinking and can smother creativity. One recent example of harmful groupthink was raised by the U.S. Senate Select Committee on Intelligence 2004's *Report on the U.S. Intelligence Community's Prewar Intelligence Assessments on Iraq.* The report highlighted groupthink as a major contributor to the intelligence community's deficiency in accurately evaluating available intelligence on Iraq's capability regarding weapons of mass destruction (WMD). The likelihood that Iraq possessed such weapons was used by the United States and British governments as a key argument for invading that country. No WMD were ever found.

Imagine that you volunteer to serve on a committee that has recently formed to assess the possibility of integrating the recreational services of two small cities that are growing together because of dramatic migration into the region. The committee comprises representatives from a variety of backgrounds, including members of parents' groups, recreation center staff members, city parks operations managers, summer recreation programmers, city planners, school board members, and law enforcement officials. At the first meeting, these people bring forward many exciting ideas, but some of these ideas conflict. At the end of the meeting, you realize that not all of the proposals brought forward can be accommodated—at least, not in their original form. Your experience from your latest job, a place riddled with political maneuvering and heated arguments that are more fighting over self-interest than they are rational discussion of the issues, worries you about what the second meeting will bring. A few weeks later, at the meeting you've been dreading, you find yourself pleasantly surprised. The group does not shy away from debate, but the ideas are being discussed on their merits and it appears that egos were checked at the door. By the end of the evening, some ideas have been abandoned (but not without fair treatment), others have been modified or improved, and a couple of new ideas have been sparked by the discussion. You leave the second meeting feeling more energized and excited about the whole project than you were before you went in, and you are sure you aren't the only one; the rest of the committee members look exactly how you feel. What is the source of all this synergy and excitement about the possibilities facing your two cities? It's substantive conflict at its best.

Interpersonal Conflict

Variously termed *personal conflict, affective conflict,* or *personality clash,* interpersonal conflict centers on the discordant emotional responses individuals have toward other members of a group. In simple terms, interpersonal conflict arises when people dislike each other and act on that emotion. It's the introduction of interpersonal conflict that makes the whole business of conflict feel uncomfortable. The growing sense that you truly do not like the person sitting across the table has the potential to powerfully—and negatively—affect your interaction with that person and change the entire dynamics of the group in the process. Of course, getting along with someone or liking his personality also affects how you might deal with him. Disliking someone may lead to personal confrontations that are superfluous to the group's goals, such as in the case of making antagonistic remarks. A few years ago in a departmental faculty meeting, one of the professors at the table wished to raise an issue of procedure and began by saying, "I don't wish to hold up the discussion, but. . . ." He

was interrupted by another professor who did not like him, who interjected, "But you will anyway, right?" That kind of antagonism is simply a personal attack and serves only to increase the tension in the room. In all likelihood, the verbal jab also did nothing but encourage the first professor to become entrenched in his position.

Another destructive tactic in approaching interpersonal conflict is to avoid the other person, which has its own negative consequences for the individuals involved and the group dynamics as a whole. Recall the scenario from the beginning of the chapter, in which Konrad sought to avoid conflict by avoiding Elizabeth. His strategy did not work well, and he might have improved the end result by confronting, rather than avoiding, Elizabeth about the things that bothered him.

While having positive feelings for someone else tends to smooth out discussions and makes dealing with other conflicts less heated, group members should be careful of avoidance of conflict with colleagues they like. Avoiding conflict in this way can once again lead to groupthink or even create residual negative feelings that may fester if they go unresolved. The latter can lead to unnecessary interpersonal conflict between two or more formerly amicable group members.

It might seem that the ideal is to keep emotion out of group discussions in order to maintain objectivity. One of the problems with that strategy, however, is that the various types of conflict generally do not exist in isolation. When you experience conflict, you may not be able to separate substantive or procedural discussions from feelings, personal values, culture, and gender roles. In fact, banishing emotional responses may not be appropriate for all groups or even for any groups at all times. What may be more productive is for group members to be aware of the foundations of their own emotional responses and to be sensitive to those of others.

Conflict and Competition

Competition contains the seed for conflict. If a competitive environment exists among group members, conflict will result because in competitive relationships, the competing parties' goals are mutually exclusive. The concept of someone winning a competition is defined by someone else losing. On the other hand, under a cooperative group structure, success for one person can mean success for others.

A well-known and interesting game, called the *prisoners' dilemma,* explores the relationship between competition and cooperation as well as the conflict that may be caused by their interplay. Originally developed by John von Neumann and Oskar Morgenstern in their studies on game theory (see Poundstone 1992), prisoners' dilemma has been used widely for research involving cooperation and competition.

Imagine that two criminals, having been caught after committing a crime, are being interviewed by police in separate rooms. In an effort to gain a confession, the police offer the same deal to both prisoners: "If you confess, we'll drop the charges on you and lock up your partner for 20 years." However, if neither of the partners in crime confesses (if they both clam up), there isn't enough evidence against them for a conviction, and the police will charge them both on a lesser crime that carries a penalty of 2 years in prison. If they both confess independently of one another, both of their sentences will be reduced to 10 years because of their cooperation with the police. Figure 7.2 shows an overview of how the choices that each prisoner faces relate to one another.

Set up this hypothetical situation with two friends to see what they decide to do. Do not let them talk with each other before or during the scenario. Can

you predict what they will choose? What would you choose?

The dilemma for each prisoner is that no matter what the partner does, it makes more sense for each to confess rather than to clam up. As an individual looking out for his own interests, prisoner A gets a better deal by confessing if his partner opts to clam up, and if his partner decides to confess, he saves himself 10 years by also confessing. The irony is that the result of both prisoners following the rational choice of confessing is worse than the result of both following the irrational choice of clamming up. The theory that the dilemma points to is that groups and individuals can face different realities. A group whose members act on rational self-interest (competition) may do less well than a group whose members act contrary to rational self-interest and consider what is best for the group as a whole (cooperation).

Dealing With Conflict

People handle conflict in different ways. If you find that your approach to conflict situations is more or less consistent, your approach is your general conflict strategy. In 1974 Kenneth W. Thomas and Ralph H. Kilmann developed an assessment for conflict situations. Their assessment is predicated on the two basic dimensions of assertiveness and cooperation. They defined assertiveness as the degree to which an individual attempts to fulfill personal needs and desires in a conflict situation. Cooperation was defined as the degree to which an individual attempts to satisfy other people's needs and desires. Using these two dimensions, Thomas and Kilmann created five approaches to conflict:

- **Competing.** The competing individual is motivated by her own interests and has little or no concern for the interests of others. She can be assertive to the point of aggression and comes across as uncooperative. People using this strategy generally adopt a win–lose mentality. A bitter divorce dispute in which both parents fight for full custody of the children exemplifies a competing approach.

- **Avoiding.** This avoiding person is also uncooperative, but his uncooperativeness differs from that of the competing person. An avoider tends to be unassertive because he does not address the issue if he can help it. Avoidance can become extreme if

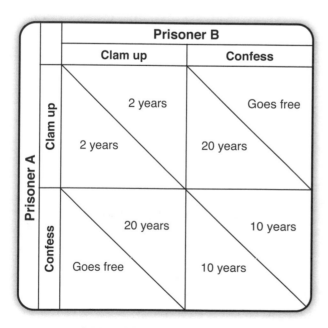

Figure 7.2 Prisoners' dilemma matrix.

there is a high possibility of relationship injury or if the situation feels threatening. When implementing an avoidance strategy, the person may try to bypass an issue or postpone it until a later time.

- **Accommodating.** An accommodating person is not assertive and is quite cooperative with those he is in conflict with. He is more concerned for the interests of other group members than for his own interests and is willing to make sacrifices in order to resolve conflict. This style is appropriate if the person doing the accommodating is in the wrong, but when practiced as a general approach, accommodation can lead to a martyr attitude.

- **Compromising.** The compromiser recognizes both her interests and the interests of others. She seeks the middle ground in resolving disputes, giving up some—but not all—of her initial position in order to obtain agreement. The compromiser is OK with splitting the difference on an issue, especially if it means avoiding power struggles.

- **Collaborating.** The collaborator is both assertive and cooperative and works to satisfy her needs as well as the needs of others. Fulfilling everyone's needs often requires the collaborator to explore an issue in depth and detail in order to identify the fundamental concerns of both parties. The final result is not predetermined in the collaborator's mind, and so she is open to alternative and creative solutions. Collaborators look for win–win scenarios. While collaboration is a very positive approach, the willingness to explore issues in detail may make collaboration time consuming. In addition, if other group members are not equally motivated to being open and self-reflective, collaboration can become frustrating and can deepen or extend the conflict.

Management and Transformation

If you work with a collaborative group, the best approach to conflict is to just let it happen. For members in this group (much like the fictitious committee described earlier) conflict is largely a positive force, contributing to the group's goals and development. Members are emotionally mature enough to discuss ideas on their merits instead of becoming locked into defending a position. They also allow new ideas to develop as a result of their openness and commitment to the task at hand rather than their own egos.

How can groups be moved or move themselves toward a collaborative approach? What can be done if some, or even most, of the members cannot or will not adopt such an approach?

To address the first of these two questions, you should draw on the other chapters in this book to develop strategies for creating a group that values collaborative interaction. This includes encouraging members to become part of a conscious group (see chapter 3). Groups that are aware not only of their goals and tasks but also of the relationship between process and product can recognize more easily that the *approach* to conflict is an important part of the *resolution* of conflict. The quality of the solution reached by the group members will reflect their awareness of themselves and their ability to use that awareness to follow productive and positive strategies.

Until now, we've used the terms *solving problems* or *conflict resolution* in our discussion, but a growing number of theorists today prefer to use the terms *conflict management* or *conflict transformation*. The argument is that these terms encourage a more positive view of conflict and acknowledge its ongoing nature. In contrast to the more familiar term *conflict resolution*, *conflict management* and *conflict transformation* view conflicts as long-term situations that cannot be resolved either completely or quickly. Conflict management seeks to control the negative consequences of conflict and promotes the handling of conflict in calm, equitable, and efficient ways.

Transforming Conflict

Proponents of transformative conflict, such as Lederach (2003), suggest that the term *management* implies the control of people and prefer to think of conflict as affecting everything involved in the initiation of the conflict (individuals, events, and relationships). The transformative approach to conflict promotes change on the personal and systemic levels. Personal transformation involves cultivating awareness, personal growth, and commitment to change in oneself (and others). A significant part of this goal includes acknowledging the emotions that may be tied to conflict, such as frustration, anger, and fear. Once recognized, the emotions need to be addressed so that they become legitimate but not controlling elements of conflict discussions. Systemic transformation refers to increasing justice and equity among group members through the elimination of oppressive structures and behaviors and the fairer distribution of resources.

Conflict management and conflict transformation both seek to maximize the positive potential of conflict while minimizing its negative effects. The biggest differences between the two concepts rest with their philosophical orientations, which in turn influence the strategies employed when putting them into effect. Conflict transformation places considerable importance on values and attempts to incorporate the articulation of these into its approach, while conflict management is more secular and relegates questions of value to a lesser status. You and your group members may want to decide how relevant the articulation of values is to your group's purpose and functioning.

There is no recipe for helping your group to become more conscious of itself and its approach to conflict and to then develop a set of group guidelines to follow. How you go about this will depend on a variety of factors that will be unique to your situation. Perhaps the most important step is to confront the issue and begin to discuss how you and the rest of your group members wish to approach conflict in general. Then you can continue to refine your approach as new situations arise. That said, it is still helpful to have some specific action strategies as part of a conflict tool kit you can draw from in creating your own plan.

Uncooperative Group Members

Sometimes, despite the desire of most group members to be collaborative or to make conflict a conscious part of the group experience, a few individuals will refuse to contribute to that goal. Of course, the first option for working with uncooperative group members is to attempt to convince them to see the wisdom in full group cooperation, outlining the benefits of such an approach. However, there are rare occasions in which some people will simply refuse to work collaboratively with the rest of the group, preferring instead to pursue self-interests whenever possible. The following two strategies are aimed toward these people.

• **Tit for Tat (TFT).** TFT is a recognized strategy in game theory. It was introduced by Anatol Rap-

Toolbox Tips

Following is a list of ideas to begin a brainstorming session with your group members when dealing with conflict or when you know you will be discussing contentious issues. It is not a comprehensive list; add to or modify it as your own circumstances warrant.

- Embrace the positive potential of conflict.
- Set goals.
- Develop communication guidelines for discussions.
- Encourage open, honest, and transparent decision making.
- Avoid ego-based discussions and arguments.
- Encourage the expression of concerns.
- Explore expressed concerns to examine legitimacy.
- Agree to disagree at appropriate times.
- Welcome creativity and alternative solutions.
- Discuss value differences openly and with respect.
- Communicate often and inclusively.
- Be open to being wrong.
- Challenge coercive and overly aggressive behavior.
- Support those who appropriately challenge inappropriate behavior or language.

paport for the prisoners' dilemma game. Discovered to be one of the most effective strategies for reversing or at least minimizing competitive behavior, TFT is based on the concept of reciprocal consequence. There are a few basic rules for implementing TFT:

- Always begin with cooperation, even if you suspect the uncooperative group member (UGM) will compete.
- Respond to competitive behavior with retaliation (i.e., appropriate competitive behavior) as soon as possible following the UGM's initial competitive act.
- Be quick to forgive and move back to cooperative behavior.

The idea behind TFT is to show the other person that while you are willing to cooperate—and cooperation is your first choice—you will not allow negative actions to go unchallenged. The danger of this approach is that outside of game theory, human situations are indeed complex, and you run the risk of protracting and escalating negative conflict, especially if the UGM is willing to go further and longer than you are in retaliatory behavior. In addition, employing this strategy might require you to act outside of your own ethics regarding the treatment of others, an uncomfortable experience for many.

- **Isolating antisocial behavior.** If you marginalize negative behavior, there is a good chance that the UGM will recognize that his influence in the group has decreased substantially. There are a number of ways to isolate antisocial behavior, but by setting out policies and adopting guidelines for acceptable communication and behavior within the group, the rest of the members can establish a foundation from which to challenge unacceptable behavior. There are two important considerations in using this approach successfully: (1) a willingness to consistently challenge the offender and (2) making it clear that it is the behavior and not the individual's overall worth or contribution that is being challenged.

SUMMARY

In this chapter we examined the nature, sources, and effects of social power and group conflict as well as strategies for addressing conflict. We described power as the ability to influence the behavior of others or the outcomes of events. Power is applied more effectively with the cooperation of others, but cooperation is not necessary for exercising power. Power is pervasive, and, as Milgram's experiments demonstrated, authority figures have a surprising degree of influence over people in many situations. Recent examples of the power exerted by people in real or perceived positions of authority show that people are more susceptible to being influenced than we may think they are. Nonetheless, power does not flow in just one direction; almost everyone can exert some degree of power to affect the situations they find themselves in.

Conflict is disagreement, contradiction, or strife experienced by at least two members of a group. It is a natural part of human interaction, and the three basic types of conflict—substantive, procedural, and interpersonal—all have the potential to affect people positively or negatively. Being open and approaching conflict from the perspective of a conscious group can help the group become aware of and then manage or transform negative elements of conflict as well as maximize the positive potential.

RESOURCES

Foucault, M. 1978. *The history of sexuality, vol. I.* London: Penguin.

French, J., and B. Raven. 1959. The bases of social power. In *Studies in social power,* ed. D. Cartwright (150-167. Ann Arbor: University of Michigan Press.

Lederach, J.P. 2003. *The little book of conflict transformation.* Intercourse, PA: Good Books.

Milgram, S. 1974. *Obedience to authority: An experimental view.* New York: HarperCollins.

Poundstone, W. 1992. *Prisoner's dilemma: John von Neumann, game theory, and the puzzle of the bomb.* New York: Doubleday.

Thomas, K. and R. Kilmann. 1974. *Conflict MODE instrument.* Mountain View, CA: Xicom and CPP, Inc.

U.S. Senate Select Committee on Intelligence 2004. *Report on the U.S. Intelligence Community's Prewar Intelligence Assessments on Iraq, July 9, 2004.*

CHAPTER 8

Gender in Group Dynamics

Pat and Chris work for the Center Village Parks and Recreation Department. They colead a programming team that designs, implements, and evaluates the youth recreation programs for the community. Pat and Chris also manage a staff of 20 youth recreation leaders. During their scheduled staff meetings, which occur every other week, Pat focuses on the work that needs to be done, is directive, likes to have the spotlight, and takes up a lot of space in the room. Chris is more concerned with how people are getting along, stresses the community nature of their programming team, and is more expressive when interacting with the group. Most of the youth recreation workers go to Chris when they have questions about how to handle a sticky interpersonal situation with one of the youths in the program. Pat generally fields the questions about the fine points of how a program has been designed to work. Does it surprise you that Chris is a man and Pat is a woman?

Devoting an entire chapter to gender in group dynamics may raise a few eyebrows, particularly for professionals who are used to interacting in mixed-gender groups. As men and women interact daily, many people fail to consider or simply take for granted the effects that gender has on group dynamics. Looking at recreation, leisure, and experiential education programming trends illustrates just how much gender plays a role in how people relate with others and how comfortable individuals are in either single-gender or mixed-gender groups. For example, many service providers are offering more and more women-only courses, programs, trips, and experiences. The explosive growth of health clubs and wilderness trips designed specifically for women is also proof that gender does play a role in group dynamics and in everyday interactions, particularly in recreation, leisure, and experiential education. Gender is important not only from a group dynamics perspective but also from a recreation and leisure behavior perspective. As Kelly and Godbey (1992, 306) note,

"gender continues to be of central importance in both predicting and explaining leisure behavior." Thus, it is important to examine the intersection of gender and group dynamics in recreation, leisure, and experiential education settings.

This chapter discusses how gender influences group dynamics and individual interactions in groups. In doing so, this chapter uses many of the concepts discussed in previous and forthcoming chapters, including leadership, conformity, decision making, communication, conflict management, and power. The chapter starts with a definition of gender and an overview of how gender might affect recreation and leisure behavior. This chapter is based on generalizations about how women and men behave. Regardless of their gender, individuals participating in group settings will bring with them unique characteristics, traits, and behaviors. Recreation, leisure, and experiential education professionals should remember that many people will not exhibit the behaviors listed in this chapter!

GENDER AND SEX

Many people use the terms *gender* and *sex* interchangeably, but there are an increasing number of researchers, social activists, and community members who acknowledge a difference in the ways in which gender and sex are conceptualized. This is particularly important for professionals working with lesbian, gay, bisexual, and transgender (LGBT) individuals, as the intersection of gender and sex becomes more salient when providing service to these individuals.

Sex refers to the biological function of being female or male. Gender refers to the overt appearance and behaviors that society attaches to being male or female. In fact, most people assume that a person is male or female based on looks alone and assume that behavior is dependent on biological sex (Tewksbury and Gagne 1996). People learn gender-specific behaviors through life experience. By observing others, they learn what men are supposed to do and what women are supposed to do. Through this process people also form impressions or stereotypes about what behaviors are acceptable for men and for women. Social role theory (Eagly 1987) suggests that men and women fill specific roles in society and that by filling these roles, they come to anticipate what behaviors are appropriate.

Most people experience this phenomenon as soon as they are born—girls are given pink blankets and boys are given blue blankets. Recreation, leisure, and play activities that boys and girls are encouraged to enjoy often reflect gender-specific behaviors that are condoned by parents and society (Meeks and Mauldin 1990). This process continues through childhood and in many societies culminates during puberty, when "girls become women and boys become men." However, there is often ambiguity in this process, particularly for females. Girls who behave as tomboys are encouraged to do so as children, as the female display of male behaviors tends to be acceptable. After puberty, tomboyish behavior usually is discouraged as being unladylike. When young boys behave in stereotypically female ways, these behaviors are seen as cute or simply ignored. However, once boys enter school, these behaviors are discouraged, as children are viewed as agents of the family, and recreation, leisure, and play behaviors associated with the opposite sex are interpreted as inappropriate (Grossman, O'Connell, and D'Augelli 2002).

In terms of group dynamics in recreation, leisure, and experiential education contexts, it is important to acknowledge that society has a huge effect on how people expect others to behave based on their outward appearance as a woman or as a man. However, it can be misleading to assume that people will behave in a particular way based on their looks in regards to gender. It can also be detrimental in a group setting to prescribe behaviors to one gender or the other, as some men might not behave in ways typically associated with men and some women might not behave in a manner typically associated with women.

Learning Activity

Go to a local playground or school yard. Observe kids playing and record their genders and behaviors. Note if a parent or caregiver corrects any behaviors that aren't stereotypically associated with the child's gender. In groups of 4 to 6 members, discuss the following questions:

- Did the children's behaviors match those prescribed by society? How?
- How were their behaviors encouraged or discouraged?
- In your opinion, how are behaviors encouraged or discouraged as children grow older?
- How does social role theory explain how people behave in recreation, leisure, and experiential education group settings?
- What strategies can you use to help group members recognize that men and women may or may not always exhibit stereotypical gender-specific behaviors?

For some people, distinguishing between gender and sex might not seem worthwhile. However, understanding societal influences on expected gender-specific behaviors strengthens a professional's ability to see beyond stereotypical expectations and look at the behavior of individuals in a group context. This understanding also helps professionals confront stereotypes related to people who are LGBT as well as those related to being a woman or being a man. Professionals will be able to enter group situations with fewer biases and thus will facilitate more efficient and effective group processes and outcomes.

GENDER AND RECREATION BEHAVIOR

While this chapter focuses on gender issues in group dynamics, there is an intersection of recreation and leisure behaviors and experiences that professionals will find useful to understand, particularly when working with groups. This section presents an overview of gender in recreation and leisure behavior and is by no means exhaustive.

Research focusing on women and leisure emerged gradually over the past 20 years (Henderson, Hodges, and Kivel 2002). Early attempts to explain women's leisure focused on the inequalities between women and men. Not surprisingly, women's leisure was shaped by society's expectations of the female gender role—being a stay-at-home mom and taking care of the household. Women's leisure was characterized as being centered on the home, splintered because chores and other obligations did not allow for blocks of uninterrupted recreation, and unstructured (Henderson, Hodges, and Kivel 2002). Women also used recreation and leisure experiences for socializing with others. Perhaps one of the most surprising aspects of how women perceived recreation and leisure was that they did not believe they were entitled to leisure (Shank 1986).

Women's leisure 10 years ago was characterized as one size doesn't fit all (Henderson 1996). As researchers applied different theoretical lenses (most notably a feminist perspective) to the study of women's leisure, it became evident that women's recreation and leisure behaviors and experiences were as varied as each individual. Three main themes emerged that helped explain women's leisure. These included gender and theory, continua of meanings, and diversity (Henderson 1996).

The application of gender theory shed further light on women's recreation and leisure experiences by providing a different lens through which to view women's experiences. The contextual nature of the leisure experience was found to be a key element in describing women's (and men's) leisure. For example, Jackson and Henderson (1995) found that women had more limitations to their leisure than men had and that the differences existed not only between men and women but also among women of various ages and socioeconomic statuses. Women's recreation and leisure experiences were also characterized by the number of roles that women played. These roles were found to be influenced by the expectations of patriarchal society: Women were expected to put men's needs first and as a result often sacrificed their own recreation and leisure (Henderson 1996).

During this time, women's recreation and leisure experiences were also described as continua of meanings (Henderson 1996). As shown in figure 8.1, these continua represent both positive and negative aspects of recreation and leisure for women as well as different conceptualizations of leisure that depend on whether a woman considers leisure from a "self-perspective" or an "other perspective" (Henderson 1996). The meanings along the right side of the figure are associated with the traditional influences of outside forces on women's recreation and leisure. Examples include jobs that have little inherent value for women, activities that suppress women's abilities to express themselves as who they are, and activities that restrain women to stereotypical gender roles. The meanings along the left side of the figure are associated with how recreation and leisure may be used to create socially just conditions for women in society. For example, women should work jobs that are fulfilling and enhance them as individuals. Recreation and leisure experiences should allow women to be empowered to be all they can be and to challenge traditional assumptions about what women can and can't do.

Diversity is the final area that has affected women's recreation and leisure (Henderson 1996). Women who are from minority groups, who have disabilities, and who are aging have greater constraints on their recreation and leisure. It is extremely difficult to characterize the recreation and leisure experiences of women of any specific age, race, sexual orientation,

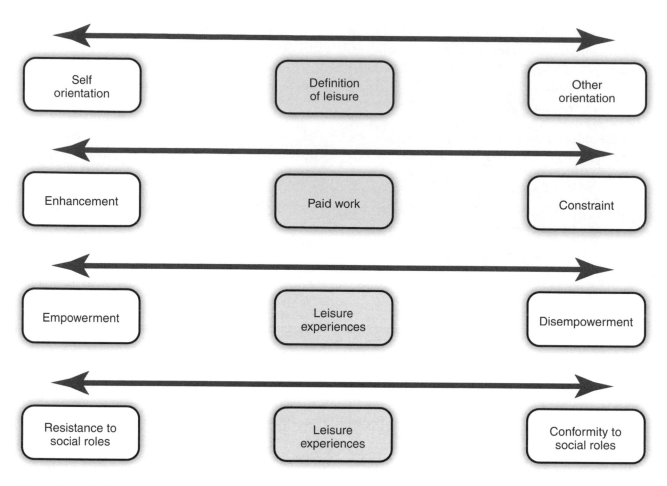

Figure 8.1 Continua of meanings.

or socioeconomic status. It is the intersection of these factors, contextual elements, and the social fabric of society that affects how women have recreation and leisure experiences.

Lately, women's recreation and leisure experiences have been characterized by the cultural ideology that influences behavior (Henderson 1996). Cultural ideologies have helped to describe leisure behaviors not only of women and girls but also of men and boys. Other research has focused on the experiences of women throughout the life span, paying particular attention to teenagers and older women. The leisure experiences of women and girls have been found to be influenced by status and power differentials among different demographic groups as well as by negative aspects of leisure such as gambling and drinking (Henderson 1996).

What does all this have to do with gender and group dynamics? First, as indicated in figure 8.1, there are many parallels between women's experiences in recreation and leisure and their experiences in group settings. Traditionally, most groups have constrained and disempowered women as well as caused women to conform to artificial social roles. Second, it is possible to extend some of the theories on women's recreation and leisure behaviors to group dynamics settings. While these theories might not be a perfect fit or provide a clear picture of every situation, they certainly provide a starting point to further examine how gender plays a role in group dynamics. Perhaps one of the biggest skills a recreation, leisure, and experiential education professional should have is the ability to recognize how an individual has been socialized. Understanding the life contexts that shape an individual is an important step in working with people in a group setting. Savvy professionals remember that one size doesn't fit all, regardless of whether a participant is women or man, young or old, gay or straight, or wealthy or poor. The remainder of this chapter is devoted to examining how gender influences specific facets of group experiences.

GENERALIZATIONS OF GENDER-SPECIFIC BEHAVIORS

While making generalizations about how women and men behave differently in situations specific to group dynamics counters the point made in the previous discussion, women and men in North America have, for the most part, been socialized to behave in different ways in everyday life. First, it is more acceptable for men to be forceful in many facets of group dynamics. Men are more likely to interrupt, assume positions of leadership, take up more physical space, and engage in self-promoting behaviors (Reich and Wood 2003). Second, women tend to be concerned with the relationship function of the group, whereas men are more concerned with the task function. Women are inclined to focus on the interpersonal relationships and social aspects of the group more than men do—women tend to have a group orientation while men tend to have an individual orientation. Women are more apt to focus on the communal aspects of group function, while men focus on themselves. Third and finally, men are often less expressive than women are, and men tend to behave in a manner that will help the group accomplish its task. This kind of behavior is called *instrumental behavior* (Reich and Wood 2003). These generalizations of differences between women and men appear in many of the contexts of group dynamics, particularly leadership.

MEN AND WOMEN IN LEADERSHIP

As just described, men and women tend to take different approaches to group interactions. The same holds true for how they approach leadership. Men tend to focus more on the task function of leadership, and women focus more on the relationship function of leadership. In a review of studies on leadership, Eagly and Johnson (1990) found that women did exhibit more behaviors related to the relationship

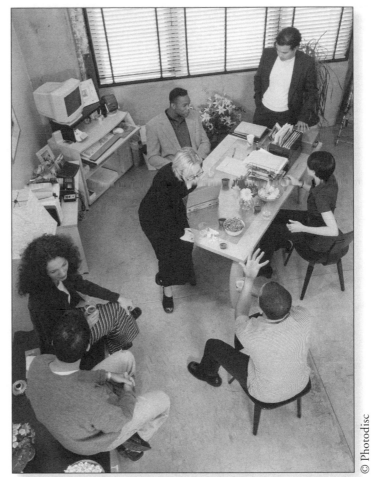

© Photodisc

Women and men approach interactions differently.

function than men did. Good all-around leaders are able to discern when it is time to address the task or time to address the relationship needs of the group.

Every day more and more women are taking leadership roles in the workplace, in recreation settings, in leisure and experiential education settings, and in all aspects of daily life. However, just as gender-role expectations affect women's recreation and leisure experiences, they affect women's leadership experiences. Women are less likely to access positions of leadership, as traditionally men have been the ones in the workplace. This finding is particularly true for high-level positions. The lack of access to leadership positions has been called the *glass ceiling*.

Groups perceive leaders differently depending on the gender of the leader. This is the result of how most people conceptualize leadership, which usually reflects characteristics stereotypically associated with men. Thus, women who are leaders generally start at a disadvantage because stereotypes about women and about being a leader do not correspond with one another. One way this disadvantage manifests itself is through a double standard biased against women. When evaluated on performance, men were assessed more positively than women were even though the women performed equally well (Eagly, Makhijani, and Klonsky 1992). A second way this disadvantage is apparent is that when women assume more masculine leadership traits such as being directive, assertive, or task oriented, they are viewed negatively because their behavior doesn't fit with socialized gender-role expectations. However, when women do not display these behaviors, they are seen as being too soft, too focused on the relationship function of the group, or too ineffective as a leader. In essence, gender-role expectations put women leaders in a lose–lose situation. A third way this disadvantage is evident is that many groups do not perceive female leaders as having legitimate authority to direct the group (Atwater, Carey, and Waldman 2001). Finally, group members are more critical of female leaders whose outward appearance is feminine. Female group members were particularly critical of these leaders (Hackman et al. 1993)!

Interestingly, most people in groups prefer to work with leaders who exhibit traits that are stereotypically associated with women. These include focusing on the communal aspect of the group, displaying good communication and interpersonal skills, recognizing the contributions of group members, and creating a positive group atmosphere. Women tend to use leadership styles that are supportive and collaborative and that capitalize on the strengths of the group. These include transformative and participatory styles of leadership (Eagly, Johannesen-Schmidt, and van Engen 2003). It is surprising then that women get such a bad rap as leaders! Professionals can work toward minimizing gender biases by focusing on what it is to be a good leader instead of focusing on what it is to be a male leader or a female leader.

CONFORMITY

It is a common assumption that women are more apt to conform to group pressure than men are. However, evidence suggests that this is true only in situations in which women are in direct contact with group members and in which they must verbalize their agreement or disagreement. In situations in which people are removed from direct contact with other group members (e.g., on the computer), there is little difference in how women and men conform to the group (Guadagno and Cialdini 2002).

Socialized gender-role expectations may explain why women tend to conform more than men do in

Toolbox Tips

Consider the following suggestions for working in mixed-gender leadership teams:

- Develop a method of addressing interpersonal disagreements that occur before an experience or a program begins. Likewise, create a system at work for handling misunderstandings that occur during a program.
- Communicate, communicate, communicate.
- Celebrate successful programs and leadership experiences!
- Treat feedback as a positive opportunity for growth as individuals and as a leadership team.
- Model a good mix of leadership skills with regards to stereotypical expectations. For example, have a male (or more masculine) partner lead a session on interpersonal relationships and have a female (or more feminine) partner teach portaging.
- Tell the group up front what the leadership expectations are for the group.
- Be aware of dominance, especially when it relates to gender issues and perceptions and leadership.

face-to-face situations. As previously noted, women have been socialized to conform to others' needs, often while sacrificing their own needs. This is particularly true for recreation and leisure experiences, especially those that involve the family. A second reason why women are more apt to conform is that society has afforded them less status. People with less status are more likely to conform. Think about how many people (women and men alike) purchase clothes, CDs, or other products because they are influenced by others to whom they ascribe status. In a related sense, women are somewhat more likely to cooperate than men are, but the difference is marginal at best.

There are differences between women who favor traditional gender roles and those who believe in nontraditional gender roles. As you might expect, the women who ascribe to nontraditional gender roles are less likely to conform. There is no difference in how men and women with nontraditional gender-role constructions conform to a leader's or group's expectations (Bem 1985).

Finally, it appears that the gender of the leader may influence the extent to which people will conform. If the leader is a man, more people, regardless of their gender, will conform to his wishes. If the leader is a woman, people of both genders will show a lesser tendency to conform. While there is little overall difference in how and why men and women conform in group situations, professionals should question why people might be going along with the rest of the group. This is particularly true if the group is in a face-to-face setting and the leader is male. Prudent leaders will make sure everyone's opinion is heard and will encourage an atmosphere of open communication and debate. Remember that conflict often results in better group processes!

DECISION MAKING

As you might recall from chapter 6, there are many stages to the decision-making process. During each of these stages, a leader, individual group members, or the group as a whole facilitates the direction of the group. In recreation, leisure, and experiential education settings, decision making is an ongoing process. Are there differences in how women and men approach the decision-making process and ultimately make a decision? At first, most of us would say "yes!"

based on how we have been socialized to expect women and men to behave.

Most people expect men to make decisions faster, use individualistic decision-making techniques, use directive leadership styles in group decision making, and be more focused on the outcomes than on the process. Women are expected to take longer to make a decision, use collective decision-making techniques, use democratic leadership styles in group decision making, and be more focused on the process than on the outcomes. Research has suggested that men are expected to use directive or analytical approaches to decision making, while women are thought to use conceptual or behavioral styles. However, King (1995) found conflicting evidence suggesting that these styles were reversed.

Other researchers have found that women tend to ask more probing questions before making a final decision (Hawkins and Power 1990). This initially appears counter to the gender-role stereotypes to which most people are socialized. However, these questions could be asked as a means to an end; in an effort to be sure that the final decision meets the needs of the group women may probe more deeply than men do. This could also result from men focusing on the decision itself and not on the actual process of decision making.

Although there appears to be differences in how women and men make decisions, having diversity in a group can improve the quality of the final decision the group makes. Diverse groups tend to avoid decisions that are either too conservative or too risky and avoid common traps such as groupthink (see chapter 6). In recreation, leisure, and experiential education groups, any number of approaches to decision making will work. Although many people are socialized to believe that decisions should be made in a particular way, there are several models of decision making that do not use gender as a factor but instead take into account the skills and experience of the leader, the skills and experience of the group, the environmental conditions of the group, and the potential outcomes of a poor decision.

COMMUNICATION

There are some differences in how women and men communicate. From the perspective of both the message sender and the message receiver, women tend to be better communicators. As stereotypical assumptions about gender suggest, the communication style of women is more supportive and collaborative and about connecting with others, while the communication style of men is individualistic and focused on task completion (Woodward, Rosenfeld, and May 1996).

Women also tend to start the communication process more often than men do, and women offer new topics for conversation on a more regular basis. However, the topics that women begin are more often glossed over or dropped during the communication process. Women are also more likely to notice a shift in the style of communication and are more accepting of this change, particularly in relation to the level of involvement of the person they are communicating with (Burgson, Olney, and Coker 1987).

Women are more accommodating to interruptions than men are, and men interrupt more often than women do (and talk more as well). Men may subconsciously or even consciously use this technique to dominate the other person, regardless of that person's gender. Women interrupt conversations too, but their interruptions are more a sign of support or understanding and often continue the flavor of the conversation, while men's interruptions are often to change the topic or correct the speaker.

Another area of difference in how men and women communicate is how they either promote or apologize for themselves. As you might expect, men tend to promote what they have done or who they are, and women tend to apologize. Women also tend to be more tentative in the communication process. When women do share something of which they are proud, it is usually about someone they are affiliated with, such as their children, spouse, or partner. This promotion is deemed OK, as it is not about the woman herself. These behaviors of men and women are referred to as *self-aggrandizement* and *self-effacement,* respectively (Oyster 2000), and they create a power imbalance in communication that favors men. Most people in North America in particular are socialized to accept these patterns of communication.

When it comes to nonverbal communication such as body language and facial expressions, women do a much better job at interpreting as well as sending nonverbal messages (Andersen 1999). Women also tend to use facial expressions to a greater extent than men do. As most people use nonverbal communication to convey a large portion of their message, women are better equipped to understand the intended message in a communication exchange.

There are several differences in how men and women behave when it comes to gestures, posture, eye contact, and facial expressions that affect communication. In general, women use fewer gestures, use fewer one-handed gestures, tap their hands, and keep their hands down on the arms of the chair. Men use more gestures, including one-handed gestures, move their legs and feet, and tap their feet. Men tend to have more open body positions than women have, sitting with their legs apart and arms farther away from their bodies. When it comes to eye contact, women are more likely to establish eye contact than men are, but they avert their gaze more than men do, as men tend to stare. Finally, in terms of facial expressions, women use more of them and are better at conveying emotions through them. Women also tend to smile more than men do and are more attracted to other people who smile. It is important to understand these subtle differences in how women and men use nonverbal communication. A gesture or facial expression may not mean the same thing from one person to the next, particularly when gender is concerned.

Socialization plays a role in how both women and men use verbal and nonverbal communication. As society grows and gender-related assumptions change, perhaps the differences in how men and women communicate will change as well. Professionals can encourage people to use good communication and listening skills regardless of their gender. Good communication ultimately will help the group reach its goals and objectives.

CONFLICT MANAGEMENT

Stereotypical assumptions lead most people to believe that women use communal styles of conflict management such as negotiation, compromise, and collaboration. These same assumptions lead most people to believe that men use competitive conflict management styles. In general, these assumptions hold true. However, some researchers have found that women are more apt to avoid conflict altogether, as it isn't congruent with their sense of community (Wilmot and Hocker 2001). Women are also more likely to depart from a group when conflict occurs on an ongoing basis.

When arguing occurs, women prefer consensus within the group while men argue from a competitive standpoint (Engleberg and Wynn 2003). Women are more likely to be open to a multitude of viewpoints, whereas men usually see arguments as having only two sides. Generally speaking, women and men also show differences in how and to whom they disclose information. Stereotypically, it is assumed that women are more open and that men are more guarded in sharing personal information (Wilson 2005). In fact, women are more open both to disclosing personal information and feelings and to listening when others disclose this type of information. Women prefer to disclose to other women. Men, however, prefer to self-disclose to women and are more open with women (Wilson 2005).

When it comes down to dealing with conflict, men prefer working through conflict in public, while women prefer to address conflict in private. Women might seem to be better equipped to deal with conflict, as generally their approach is more collaborative and focused on maintaining community within a group. However, women often implement competitive conflict management techniques because these techniques are what North American culture teaches is the best method. The media, movies, and popular fiction encourage people to "fight for their rights" and "never take no for an answer!"

As noted in previous chapters, group cohesion may reduce group conflict. Strategies that professionals might employ to enhance group cohesion, such as emphasizing teamwork, celebrating success, developing an atmosphere of respect and trust, and creating group identity, all relate to female gender construction. However, professionals should implement any conflict management strategy that they feel will work best with that specific group. Sometimes group members need to work together to resolve conflict, sometimes the group needs to be told how to resolve conflict, and sometimes the conflict should be ignored.

POWER

Power is about getting other people to do what you want. Traditionally in group dynamics, men have held more power than women have held. One of the positive characteristics of recreation, leisure, and experiential education activities is that careful program planning and leadership can erase this traditional power imbalance. For example, in challenge course settings, certain group members may be given the power to make decisions or direct others. Leaders and facilitators can ensure that all group members have power and that both men and women have equal influence over others in the group. The leader or facilitator may appoint a woman to a position that traditionally was held by a man.

These suggestions might seem like slapping a bandage on what is a systemic problem in today's society. However, when given the chance, women in positions of power use many of the same strategies that men use to influence others (Grob, Meyers, and Schuh 1997). Many of the types of power (legitimate, referent, expert, reward, and coercive) have connotations related to stereotypical male characteristics. This may help explain why in some situations women are not as readily accepted as leaders. People may be unable to ascribe power to women in leadership

Recreation and leisure activities offer many leadership opportunities for women.

© Chris Giles / Aurora Photos

positions, as they have been socialized to think that only men can have power and therefore only men can be leaders.

STATUS

Status is a person's importance. It can be related to power or a position that has power attached to it, such as president or chairperson. Status may also be awarded to someone who has helped the group reach its goals or to someone who has traits that are admired by others. Status also has connotations of physical prowess and strength. Gender-role stereotypes once again favor men when it comes to deciding which group members have status. Traditionally, men have had more status than women have had (Forsyth 2006), and structures in society have been created and maintained to ensure that men are awarded status. Status generalization is the awarding of status based on characteristics that may or may not be relevant to the situation. For example, people who are doctors, lawyers, or university professors are awarded status based on their profession alone. In a recreation, leisure, and experiential education context, sports often favor men over women. In mixed-gender teams, a man is often the captain or de facto leader of the group. Although things are slowly changing, the media favors men's sports over women's sports. If you tune in to sports on a weekend afternoon in North America, chances are you will see football, basketball, baseball, golf, or soccer—all featuring men.

The language choices of announcers who present sporting events also affect the difference in the status of women and men in sports. Female athletes are often referred to as *girls,* whereas male athletes are referred to as *men.* While this difference in language use might seem inconsequential, it perpetuates the status differences between men and women.

In the past, men's and women's sports were awarded different status levels on college and university campuses. There were more men's teams with better equipment and funding. However, this changed when legislation such as Title IX mandated gender equity in athletics in education systems. The way in which macrostatus is awarded in organized sports does filter down to the ways in which individuals are granted status in society, particularly in recreation, leisure, and experiential education settings, which have close ties to the sporting world.

People with high status in groups generally have greater influence over a group's course of action, feel better about themselves as a result of their status, are listened to more regularly, and participate at a greater level. In order to maximize the positive aspects of diversity in a group, leaders should be aware of the statuses of group members and implement strategies to be sure that everyone participates in the group process. Doing so allows women (and other minority group members) to be active contributors, and this in turn allows the others to accept them for their abilities instead of certain characteristics such as being a woman or belonging to a specific ethnicity.

Leaders and facilitators can encourage women and other minorities to take an active role in group processes that will enable them to gain status in the eyes of other group members. Being active and interested

Learning Activity

Make two columns on a sheet of paper. In the first column, list words and phrases used in sport, recreation, and leisure settings to describe female athletes and participants. In the second column, list words and phrases used to describe male athletes and participants.

Combine everyone's papers into a pile and randomly distribute them among the class members. Share what words others have listed. Answer the following questions:

- How commonly are these words used in your community?
- Are there significant differences in the words listed for females and for males? What are they?
- Why is it important to avoid words that have negative connotations regarding female athletes?
- How can professionals help participants use language that is appropriate?

in the collective is more effective than being passive and individualistic when it comes to gaining status. By encouraging others to listen to low-status group members (which traditionally have been women), a recreation, leisure, and experiential education professional can capitalize on the strengths of every group member. Ensuring that women and men have equal status in a group also enhances cohesion and sense of community, as having status increases self-esteem. Creating situations in which group members possess relatively equal levels of status (regardless of gender) allows group members to focus on doing what the group is together to do.

TASK SOLUTIONS

Groups work together to solve problems and complete tasks. In the recreation, leisure, and experiential education world, most groups generate solutions and complete tasks every time they meet. What strategy will get the runner from third base to home plate? What inbound play needs to happen to score the winning basket? How will the group get from one end of a canoe portage to the other? Playing a game as a team or moving through the wilderness as a group is, in essence, a problem that needs to be solved or a task that needs to be completed. Are there differences in how women and men go about solving problems and completing tasks?

Just as individuals prefer working on certain jobs or completing certain tasks, women and men perform better on different jobs and tasks. Generally, the tasks women and men prefer correspond with gender-role stereotypes, a finding that is a common theme for this chapter. Women tend to do better when the relationship or social function is more important than the task function or mechanical side of task solution and completion. Men tend to perform better on tasks that stereotypically fit with men's interests—tasks that require more focus on the nuts and bolts of solving the problem and less focus on the relationship function or social side of group work (Wood, Polek, and Arken 1985).

The difference in how women and men approach task completion is nominal at best, particularly as the gender gap in this area has closed dramatically. Employers are requiring workers to have well-rounded skill packages and to be able to solve problems as well as get along with others in the workplace. This is par-

ticularly true in recreation, leisure, and experiential education settings, as face-to-face interactions with diverse groups of people is the meat and potatoes of the profession, whether the professional is providing direct service to participants or collaborating with coworkers, board members, special interest groups, and politicians. While individuals might prefer either the task function or the relationship function, they must have adequate skills in both areas to succeed in today's world.

SUMMARY

Women and men have been socialized to believe that people of different gender should behave in certain ways. This socialization affects how individuals expect others to behave as well as shapes individual behavior. People who grew up in different areas of the world, during different eras, and with varying levels of education will behave in diverse ways and will expect varied behaviors from others. This is called *social role theory* (Eagly 1987). Social role theory has emerged as a common theme in this chapter to help describe differences in women's and men's behavior in recreation, leisure, and experiential education groups. While many readers of this book might have yet to experience gender-role stereotypes or might believe that these stereotypes have been diminished, they only have to observe interactions among people of different generations, cultures, and even parts of North America to see that many of these traditional role expectations are perpetuated today.

The research related to gender and recreation and leisure behaviors indicates that these role expectations affect women's recreation and leisure. There is also ample evidence that leadership style, conformity to group expectations, decision-making style, communication style, conflict management techniques, power, status, and task solution are different for women and men. Often these differences are influenced by social role theory.

Professionals should take away six key points from this chapter:

1. Individuals have been socialized to expect different behaviors based on overt demographic characteristics of others.

2. People's behaviors are influenced by how they were raised and how they were socialized.

3. Recognizing differences in individual behavior in group members enables practitioners to confront biases and stereotypes before they become issues for the group.

4. Celebrating the differences women and men bring to a group capitalizes on the many benefits diversity creates.

5. Recreation, leisure, and experiential education programs and activities are a great platform for addressing stereotypical assumptions regarding behavior of women and men.

6. Although the differences between expectations for women and expectations for men have narrowed, there is still room for growth and acceptance of gender differences in today's world.

Many people, especially in their role as a professional, are nervous about confronting stereotypical biases and gender-role assumptions. Don't be shy about educating others on the benefits of different approaches to various facets of working with groups. As Plato said, "the beginning is the most important part of the work!" (Gookin 2003, 60).

RESOURCES

Andersen, P.A. 1999. *Nonverbal communication: Forms and functions.* Mountain View, CA: Mayfield.

Atwater, L.E., J.A. Carey, and D.A. Waldman. 2001. Gender and discipline in the workplace: Wait until your father gets home. *Journal of Management* 27:537-66.

Bem, S.L. 1985. Androgeny and gender schema theory: A conceptual and empirical integration. *Nebraska Symposium on Motivation* 32:179-226.

Burgson, J.K., C.A. Olney, and R.A. Coker. 1987. The effects of communication characteristics on patterns of reciprocity and compensation. *Journal of Nonverbal Behavior* 11:140-65.

Eagly, A. 1987. *Sex differences in social behavior: A social-role interpretation.* Mahway, NJ: Erlbaum.

Eagly, A., M.C. Johannesen-Schmidt, and M.L. van Engen. 2003. Transformational, transactional, and laissez-faire leadership styles: A meta-analysis comparing women and men. *Psychological Bulletin* 129:569-91.

Eagly, A., and B.T. Johnson. 1990. Gender and leadership style: A meta-analysis. *Psychological Bulletin* 108:233-56.

Eagly, A., M.G. Makhijani, and B.G. Klonsky. 1992. Gender and the evaluation of leaders: A meta-analysis. *Psychological Bulletin* 111:3-22.

Engleberg, I., and D. Wynn. 2003. *Working in groups: Communication principles and strategies.* 3rd ed. Boston: Houghton Mifflin.

Forsyth, D. 2006. *Group dynamics.* 4th ed. Belmont, CA: Thomson Wadsworth.

Gookin, J., ed. 2003. *NOLS wilderness wisdom: Quotes for inspirational exploration.* Mechanicsburg, PA: Stackpole Books.

Grob, L.M., R. Meyers, and R. Schuh. 1997. Powerful/powerless language use in group interactions: Sex differences or similarities? *Communication Quarterly* 45:282-303.

Grossman, A.H., T.S. O'Connell, and A.R. D'Augelli. 2002. Leisure and recreational 'girl-boy' activities—studying the unique challenges provided by transgendered young people. Paper presented at the Leisure Studies Association.

Guadagno, R.E., and R.B. Cialdini. 2002. Online persuasion: An examination of gender differences in computer-mediated interpersonal influence. *Group Dynamics* 6:38-51.

Hackman, M.Z., M.J. Hillis, T.J. Paterson, and A.H. Furness. 1993. Leaders' gender role as a correlate of subordinates' perceptions of effectiveness and satisfaction. *Perception and Motor Skills* 77:671-4.

Hawkins, K., and C.B. Power. 1990. Gender differences in questions asked during small decision making group discussions. *Small Group Research* 30:235-56.

Henderson, K.A. 1996. One size doesn't fit all: The meanings of women's leisure. *Journal of Leisure Research* 28(3): 139-54.

Henderson, K.A., S. Hodges, and B.D. Kivel. 2002. Context and dialogue in research on women and leisure. *Journal of Leisure Research* 34(3): 253-71.

Jackson, E.L., and K.A. Henderson. 1995. Gender-based analysis of leisure constraints. *Leisure Sciences* 17:31-51.

Kelly, J.R., and G. Godbey. 1992. *The sociology of leisure.* State College, PA: Venture Publishing.

King, C.S. 1995. Sex-role identity and decision styles: How gender helps explain the paucity of women at the top. In *Gender power, leadership and governance,* ed. G. Duerst-Lahti and R.M. Kelly, 67-92. Ann Arbor, MI: University of Michigan Press.

Meeks, C.B., and T. Mauldin. 1990. Children's time in structured and unstructured leisure activities. *Lifestyles: Family and Economic Issues* 11(13): 257-81.

Oyster, C.K. 2000. *Groups: A user's guide.* Boston: McGraw-Hill.

Reich, N.M., and J.T. Wood. 2003. Sex, gender and communication in small groups. In *Small group communication: Theory and practice.* 8th ed., ed. R.Y. Hirokawa, R.S. Cathcart, L.A. Samovar, and L.D. Henman, 218-19. Los Angeles: Roxbury Publishing.

Shank, J. 1986. An exploration of leisure in the lives of dual-career women. *Journal of Leisure Research* 18:300-19.

Tewksbury, R., and P. Gagne. 1996. Transgenderists: Products of non-normative intersections of sex, gender, and sexuality. *The Journal of Men's Studies* 5(2): 105-13.

Wilmot, W.W., and J.L. Hocker. 2001. *Interpersonal conflict.* 6th ed. New York: McGraw-Hill.

Wilson, G. 2005. *Groups in context: Leadership and participation in small groups.* 7th ed. Boston: McGraw-Hill.

Wood, W., D. Polek, and C. Arken. 1985. Sex differences in group task performance. *Journal of Personality and Social Psychology* 48:63-71.

Woodward, M.S., L.B. Rosenfeld, and S.K. May. 1996. Sex differences in social support in sororities and fraternities. *Journal of Applied Communication Research* 24:260.

CHAPTER

9

Group Leadership

Aileen had been looking forward to Saturday for at least a week now. No stress, no problems from school or work would follow her on this day! A friend of the family owned a sailboat, and Aileen's mom had arranged for her and several friends to be crew for a day. The weather was perfect. Aileen didn't have any real sailing experience, but that felt like a positive development to her because she imagined that having no knowledge meant that no one would give her any responsibility. The last thing Aileen wanted this weekend was any responsibility. Her image of the day included relaxing on a boat with some great friends and letting the wind and sails do the peaceful work of moving them around the lake.

The first problem occurred shortly after the phone rang in the morning. It was Sami, one of the friends who would be crewing with her. His news was that he was not feeling well and wouldn't be able to join them. Aileen felt sorry for Sami, but a more immediate issue was that Sami had been planning to drive Aileen and four other friends to the marina. Sami sounded ill and Aileen kept him on the phone only long enough to ask if he had called anyone else or if there was another plan she should know about. Sami apologized, but the answer to both of her questions was no.

Aileen wondered why Sami had called her. She didn't have access to a vehicle this weekend and wouldn't be able to pick up the others. Still, she had to let the others know what was happening and try to arrange a ride to the marina in the next half hour. Aileen phoned the others and after a few calls back

and forth managed to organize an alternative ride schedule with Kyle, whose girlfriend Rose had a car and was willing to drive. Unfortunately, Rose's car was small and she couldn't take everyone at one time. "Riiiiiight," Aileen thought. "That was why Sami was driving originally: He had a minivan."

Aileen worked out what she thought was an efficient way to pick everyone up from Rose's house and do it all in two shifts. She called Rose to confirm the plan and then called the rest of her friends to let them know what to expect. They all made it with a few minutes to spare. Rose took their thanks graciously and headed home with a promise to pick them up again at the end of the day. Aileen found the boat and her mom's friend, Bruce, and introduced him to her friends—his new crew for the day. After a quick tour of the sailboat, Bruce pulled out a nautical chart and said they could decide where to go for the day. To the south was a great beach they could anchor at for lunch, to the east was an island with a rustic sauna and a jumping rock, and to the west was an ancient and historically significant pictograph site at the base of a 200-foot (60-meter) cliff.

Bruce told them he had a few more things to get ready on deck and would return in a few minutes to hear their decision. When Bruce disappeared through the companionway, Aileen looked up from the chart to see all four of her friends looking at her expectantly. She knew the expressions on their faces meant that they wanted her to start them off and lead the process that would result in a decision. So far, Aileen's day had been far from free of responsibility.

Leadership is an important and inescapable component of a group's structure and function. Even in the most egalitarian groups, leaders emerge or are appointed temporarily as a result of some passing need. There are no known cultures that do not include leadership as part of their social organization. In fact, if you stop for a moment to ask who this book is written for, you'll realize that it's aimed at people who either are leaders or will be leaders in the recreation field. Much of the study of group dynamics is aimed at group leaders so that they may help their group members function better. As a leader of a group, it will be up to you to implement what you learn about group dynamics with the groups you lead. Just like Aileen's friends, people in groups often find themselves looking to a leader to initiate action, solve problems, or just begin the conversation.

WHAT IS LEADERSHIP?

Leadership is a mysterious thing. There is no recipe you can follow that will ensure you become a great leader of people. There are no two groups whose members behave the same way or appreciate the same type of leadership. There are as many styles of leadership as there are leaders. There are also almost as many theories on leadership as there are leadership theorists. Finding a useful, concise definition of leadership is probably impossible if you wish to include all the situations in which leadership is found.

Leadership has been defined by a person's ability to inspire, motivate, influence, manipulate, or even coerce others into doing something the person wants done. It has also been described as an aptitude for synthesizing and communicating what the group members want but cannot articulate on their own. Effective leadership has been attributed to both physical and mental traits, including height or physical attractiveness, intelligence, forcefulness of personality, charisma, integrity and moral fiber, and compassion. While the Western world traditionally has viewed leadership as being contained within a person consistently located front and center in a group, some cultures take a different view. In some Eastern traditions, for example, leaders are encouraged to work from within the group. One version of Lao Tsu's famous quote illustrates this: "A leader is best when people barely know he exists. And of that leader, when his work is done, the people will

say 'We did this ourselves.'" For an excellent contemporary treatment of this type of approach, see Steven Simpson's (2003) book *The Leader Who is Hardly Known*.

Despite the efforts put into researching leadership, it remains a complex concept, an art as much as a science, demanding to be reconsidered and reworked virtually every time it is employed. Contemporary recreation professionals must realize that the understanding of what it means to be a leader is subject to changes, exceptions to the rules, and subtle perceptions that are open to interpretation depending on the person and situation. That said, there needs to be a context for this notion of leadership if it is to be part of what is talked about in group dynamics, and in the spirit of this need for a shared understanding that is also somewhat open ended and flexible, we offer a description:

- **Leadership requires technical competence.** Whatever the skills or knowledge required to operate in a given field, the leader must be skilled and knowledgeable in that field. Just as you expect competency from the civil engineer who designed the bridge you are about to drive over, so others should be able to expect you to possess the skills necessary to lead your activity. A person, however, does not need to be the most technically skilled member of a group in order to be an effective leader; the nature of leadership is diverse enough that the leader can become respected for talents well beyond physical skill or mental prowess.

- **Leadership involves relationships.** Perhaps too often leaders have a disproportionate amount of the responsibility for the group placed on their shoulders. While a significant degree of responsibility is warranted, especially when group members are children and youths, there is no need for leaders to get caught up in the hero syndrome. Remember that there can be no leader without followers. Any meaningful interaction within the group involves leaders and followers contributing to the group and affecting each other in multiple ways and in multiple directions.

- **Leadership is a goal-oriented process.** Groups must have a purpose for maintaining their existence, and leaders must always be aware of their group's central reason for being—the *raison d'etre*. In this regard, leadership is about initiating, motivating, directing, and facilitating actions that will help the group achieve its goals (of course, this means that it is helpful if the group's goals are clear and shared by all the group members!).

One element that so far has been left out of the description of leadership is the question of whether people should be ethical, or a force for good, before they can be considered leaders. When you think of a person who embodies the description of leadership, the person who comes to mind might be someone who is positive, eschews violence, is concerned about members of the group, and acts in the best interests of the community and society. While it would be nice to restrict the label of *leader* to this type of ethical person, doing so would make it more difficult to understand why some people are able to surround themselves with willing followers even when their motivations are purely selfish and lack integrity. Discussion on leadership in a book on group dynamics certainly favors ethical leadership, but in real life there is a continuum of leadership not only in terms of the quality of leadership (how good a leader is) but also in terms of the morality (whether the leader uses the position for good or evil). Thus, it is quite possible (and history has shown this) that a very effective leader can move a group—with or even without the group's consent—toward harmful goals.

Learning Activity

In a small group, discuss whether it's necessary to be ethical in order to be considered a leader. What implications does including or excluding an ethical stance have on your acknowledgement of a leader? Did the leader you admire most have an obvious ethical position?

FOLLOWERSHIP

Followership has been defined simply as a position of submission to leadership, but it is much more complicated than that. It's true, perhaps, that followers usually gain guidance from leaders and feel compelled to follow the direction provided by leaders. However, this kind of followership may not be an ideal way for a group to improve its functioning.

Inherent in the description of leadership is an understanding of followership. In contrast to the image of a passive receiver of instructions and a simple worker within a group, a good follower actively engages with other group members, including leaders. Good followers challenge actions and suggestions that may be harmful to the group's goals or members. An exceptional follower shows elements of leadership through displays of initiative and courage and contributions to the maintenance of group relationships. A person who says that a group member shows leadership qualities is identifying a good follower. In fact, in some flat-structured groups with high-quality followers, it can be difficult to distinguish between good followership and good leadership. This means that leaders should look for opportunities to also become good followers.

LEADERSHIP THEORY

Although leadership is perhaps one of the most studied and least understood phenomena in social life, and although there are scores of leadership theories, sometimes with opposing conclusions, there is something to be gained from becoming at least familiar with the mainstream thoughts in the area. After all, most of what is taught in leadership training courses is based on the conclusions of one or more research findings in the study of leadership. Learning a variety of leadership approaches will allow a group leader to draw on more tools when attempting to facilitate effective group dynamics.

Trait Theory

The earliest theory in leadership attempted to explain how people became leaders. The focus was on historical military, political, and industrial leaders. What theorists wanted to know was what type of men (early theory centered almost entirely on men) rose to positions of leadership in society. The assumption at this stage was that leaders are born, not made. In other words, the thinking was that certain people are born with particular physical or personality traits that surface later and show them to be the leaders they were born to be. The challenge for these researchers was to identify which traits predisposed men to leadership. Physical characteristics proposed for leaders included age, height, and attractiveness. Men who were older, taller, and more pleasing in appearance were said to

Toolbox Tips

If part of your goal for the groups you work with is to develop more leaders, employ the leadership transparency technique. For a selected time, verbalize your thoughts and decisions as a leader. For example, if you work in a leadership team, often you and the other leaders will have to converse to choose a course of action. You might try having this discussion in front of your group members if the subject matter doesn't include sensitive information or judgements about individuals. Whether deciding to call an extra practice for a softball team or deciding it is safe to run a set of rapids, allowing your group members to observe the discussion can give them great insight into the everyday life of a leader—you! You might find that group members not only understand and appreciate the challenges of being a leader but also begin displaying leadership behaviors themselves.

have the right characteristics for leadership. On the psychological side, leaders were identified as being more intelligent, self-confident, extraverted, and assertive. A type of trait theory, the great man theory, posited that history has been forged by individuals who possess an abundance of personal leadership qualities in proper balance. One of the best known proponents of the great man theory was Thomas Carlyle, who is reported to have said "the history of the world is but the biography of great men." However, research was unable to demonstrate that any one trait or combination of traits could consistently predict that a given individual would become a leader in all situations. Consequently, in the late 1940s and early 1950s, theorists looked for other variables to explain the emergence of leaders in groups.

Style Theory

A classic study by Lewin, Lippitt, and White (1939) developed a threefold typology that is still used and taught in many leadership training programs. The theorists, led by Kurt Lewin, arranged for children to be guided by an adult in arts and crafts activities. The adult leaders displayed one of three styles:

- **Authoritarian or autocratic leadership.** Authoritarian leaders are directive, making decisions for the group with no input from group members. Communication is often unidirectional (from the leader to the members) and does not include justification or explanation of the leader's actions and decisions.
- **Democratic or participative leadership.** Democratic leaders actively encourage input from group

members and may share responsibility for the decision making.

- **Laissez-faire or abdicratic leadership.** Abdicratic leaders sometimes are not even seen as leaders because they offer little or no guidance to group members and remove themselves from the process of decision making within the group.

While there is a common misperception that democratic leadership is the most effective, Lewin, Lippitt, and White noted in their study that responses to leaders were not universal among the children. For example, some group members responded well to authoritarian leadership, seemingly needing significant direction, while others reacted negatively to the autocratic leadership. Through your own experiences with groups, you may know people who seem to thrive with little or no direction, tapping into some latent creativity that shines under laissez-faire leadership. Conversely, you may recall others who do not enjoy participating in decision making, preferring instead to follow instructions. Ultimately, effective leadership appears to involve factors beyond either personal traits or leadership style. Recognizing this, theorists set out to study leadership in terms of the relationship between the leader and the group.

Contingency Theory

Fiedler (1967) based his theory of leadership on the assumption that an interaction exists between the leader's preferred style and three contextual variables. This interaction between the leader and the group context is a departure from placing the responsibility for the group's effectiveness solely with the leader.

The leader's preferred style is divided into two categories: relationship oriented and task oriented. The leaders are classified by means of the Least Preferred Coworker (LPC) Scale. The scale consists of a series of pairings such as "pleasant, unpleasant" and "efficient, inefficient" and asks the survey taker to choose which word in each pair describes the least preferred coworker. Positive responses score higher than negative ones, and an overall high score indicates that the leader is relationship oriented, or more concerned with maintaining good relationships within a group. Lower scores indicate a task-oriented leader whose primary focus is the task at hand.

The three contextual variables in Fiedler's theory are the following:

1. Leader–member relations. This variable describes the state of the relationships between the group and the leader and among the members. If there is little conflict and the relationship between the group and the leader is positive, leader–member relations are good. If the reverse is true, leader–member relations are bad.

2. Task structure. Characterized as either structured or unstructured, this variable refers to whether the task is straightforward and well understood (structured) or vague and indeterminate, possessing more than one possible correct result and perhaps requiring a nonlinear approach (unstructured).

3. Position of power. This variable is the degree to which the leader has access to real power over the group members (e.g., ability to promote, hire, fire, or bestow privileges); it is determined to be either strong or weak.

Taken together, these variables depict what Fiedler called *situational favorability*. In contingency theory, neither relationship-oriented (high LPC) nor task-oriented (low LPC) leaders are considered superior. Rather, task-oriented leaders are more effective in very high situational favorability and very low situational favorability. Relationship-oriented leaders, on the other hand, are more effective in situational favorability that is somewhere in the middle (see table 9.1 for an overview of situational favorability and matching leadership style).

Contingency theory holds that leaders should be matched to appropriate levels of situational favorability in order to maximize the effectiveness of the group. Fiedler's model has been well studied in leadership theory, and it has received both support and criticism. The result is that no definite conclusions can be made regarding its consistency across different leader and group situations.

Situational Leadership

Similar to contingency theory, situational leadership theory accounts for the relationship among leader, group, and situation. One significant difference between the two theories is that while contingency theory assumes leaders have a dominant style, situational leadership theory maintains that leaders should

Table 9.1   Situational Favorability and Leadership Styles of Fiedler's Contingency Theory

	Leader–member relations	Task structure	Position of power	Situational favorability	Leadership style
I	Good	Structured	Strong	High	Task oriented
II	Good	Structured	Weak	High	Task oriented
III	Good	Unstructured	Strong	High	Task oriented
IV	Good	Unstructured	Weak	Moderate	Relationship oriented
V	Bad	Structured	Strong	Moderate	
VI	Bad	Structured	Weak	Moderate	Relationship oriented
VII	Bad	Unstructured	Strong	Moderate	
VII	Bad	Unstructured	Weak	Low	Task oriented

be able to adopt different styles of leadership depending on what is required. In this regard, situational leadership explains how leaders can demonstrate behavioral flexibility as the situation changes.

Hersey and Blanchard (1982) introduced four leadership styles (S1-S4) that involve varying degrees of direction and support given to followers in order to address the followers' development levels (D1-D4), or maturity. Figure 9.1 illustrates the relationship between leadership styles and development levels. The four leadership styles are as follows:

- **S1: Telling or Directing.** When followers are unable (low competence) but willing (high commitment), leaders should take a highly directive role, making all the decisions and providing structure for the tasks. Leaders are focusing on getting group members started and are not overly concerned with supportive behavior at this stage.

- **S2: Selling or Coaching.** At this stage, followers possess basic skills but lack the motivation or confidence to complete the task. Leaders should employ high levels of directive behavior and provide a great deal of support (e.g., praise for building self-esteem).

- **S3: Participating or Supporting.** At this stage in the group's development, followers are highly skilled, but motivation is variable. Individuals do not

require much skill development, but the leader should focus on relationships in order to build confidence or motivation.

- **S4: Delegating.** When group members are confident, motivated, and highly skilled, leaders may step back from decision making. Much of the control over the task is left to the group and much less relationship building is needed because of the followers' high self-esteem and confidence in their abilities.

Situational leadership theory is an influential model in management circles and has found acceptance in part because of its simplicity and its recognition that leaders can adapt to situations. Nonetheless, critics dispute the theory's claim that supportive behavior and directive behavior require different emphasis rather than more equal weighting. Once again, there is no real consensus as to the model's ability to predict effective leadership.

Transactional and Transformational Leadership

Transactional leadership theory considers the relationship between leaders and followers to be a form of give and take in which members within a group

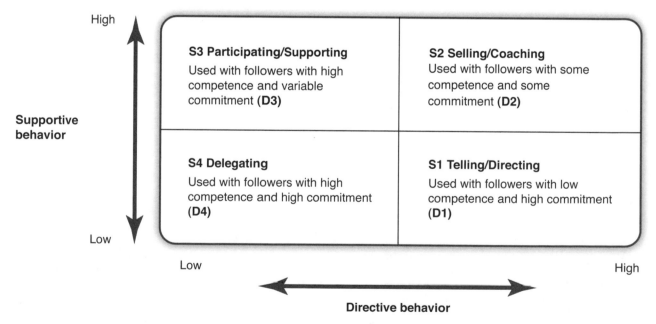

Figure 9.1 Relationship between leadership styles and development in situational leadership.

Adapted from P. Hersey and K. Blanchard, 1976, *Management of organizational behavior: Utilizing human resources,* 4th ed. (Englewood Cliff, NJ: Prentice Hall).

Learning Activity

Invite a few friends who have seen you act as a leader and are honest with you to give you some feedback on your leadership style. Ask them to respond to questions such as the following: What am I most consistently good at in my leadership? How would you describe my dominant leadership characteristics? What themes have you seen in my relationships with those I'm leading? What would you say describes my goals as a leader (what does it look like I'm out to accomplish)? What do you know or have heard about that is most needed in my leadership? What is your favorite story about me as a leader?

From the answers to these questions, you can begin to get a clear picture of your leadership. Make notes and revisit this process as your leadership style matures.

form unique relationships with one another and with the leader. Leader–member exchange (LMX) is one well-known theory that has helped explain group connections as more than a collective relationship between the leader and the whole group. In LMX theory, leaders may get along better with some members than they do with others, creating a difference in how members may report overall satisfaction with their participation.

At the core of the LMX and transactional leadership theory is the idea that members and leaders consider themselves to be part of a transaction, exchanging something for something else of value. For example, followers who identify positively with the leader are rewarded with more privileges and responsibilities and tend to work harder. Members who do not have a good working relationship with the leader are less motivated and more likely to leave the group. The stereotypical job with a boss and a group of employees is an excellent representation of transactional leadership. The employer receives benefits in terms of labor and creative input that add value to the employer's business, while the employees exchange their participation for monetary gain. Those employees favored by the boss receive further benefits such as a year-end bonus and promotion. Those who fail to impress the boss receive little else than a paycheck, if they keep their jobs.

Transformational leadership, on the other hand, seeks to change the world, or at least that part of the world that immediately surrounds the life of the group. Burns (1978, 20) described transformational leadership as a process in which "leaders and followers raise one another to higher levels of morality and motivation." Bass (1997) also grounded transformational

leadership in morality and included the presence of a charismatic leader who elicits powerful emotions from followers that give them a sense of identification with the leader. While Burns believed that transformational leadership moves both leader and followers toward more honorable values, Bass made room for leaders unmotivated by such high principles. Adolf Hitler is the classic example of a man who was able to inspire many for ugly intentions.

Not categorized as transformational leadership theories per se, more recent theoretical developments are flourishing with the addition of ethics and morality in the dialogue on what constitutes good leadership. Taoist leadership, feminist leadership, and servant leadership are a few relatively new areas of study in leadership theory, and all start from the assumption that ethics and leadership should be fused.

APPLYING LEADERSHIP THEORY

Unfortunately, there is no method for sorting through the information and theory on leadership and constructing an appropriate approach to leading a group. All of the theories presented in this chapter have some truth to them and can provide insight into how you might interact effectively with a group. On the other hand, if you read the chapter critically, you might have spotted problems with each theoretical approach. You might have drawn on personal experiences that confirm part of one theory for you and yet remembered other events that didn't seem to match a theorist's explanation of how a situation should be handled. You will need practice and reflection in order to synthesize what works for you in the circumstances you find yourself in. Remember that you will make mistakes—every leader does. The better leaders are those who not only learn from those mistakes but also watch for them. They try new ways to practice and refine their leadership skills and are aware that becoming an excellent leader is a lifelong project. The subtleties of how knowledge of leadership—or of virtually anything—can contain paradoxical truths was described well by onetime U.S. Senator Everett Dirksen, who said, "I am a man of fixed and unbending principles, the first of which is to be flexible at all times."

SUMMARY

Leadership is inevitable. Leaders will always either emerge or be appointed in social situations, and it is beneficial to understand leadership so that you may effectively facilitate group goals and help maintain group relationships. Leadership is understood from a variety of perspectives and has no universally accepted definition. In this chapter we described leadership as a position requiring technical competence, a process involving relationships, and a goal-oriented process. In addition, leadership and followership are linked inextricably, and good followership can overlap and resemble leadership.

This chapter presented a number of theories on leadership, including trait theory, style theory, contingency theory, situational leadership, and transactional and transformational leadership. The chapter ended by reinforcing the vague and imprecise nature of leadership, noting that the practice of leadership and the reflection on leadership theory should be reassessed continuously.

RESOURCES

Bass, B. 1997. Does the transactional-transformational leadership paradigm transcend organizational and national boundaries? *American Psychologist* 52(2): 130-39.

Burns, J. 1978. *Leadership.* New York: Harper & Row.

Carlyle, T. 1888. On heroes, hero-worship and the heroic in history. New York: Frederick A. Stokes & Brother.

Fiedler, F. 1967. *A theory of leadership effectiveness.* New York: McGraw-Hill.

Hersey, P. and K. Blanchard. 1982. *Management of organizational behavior: Utilizing human resources.* 4th ed. Englewood Cliffs, NJ: Prentice Hall.

Lewin, K., R. Lippitt, and R.K. White. 1939. Patterns of aggressive behavior in experimentally created 'social climates.' *Journal of Social Psychology* 10(2): 271-301.

Simpson, S. 2003. *The leader who is hardly known: Selfless teaching from the Chinese tradition.* Oklahoma City: Wood N' Barnes.

CHAPTER

10

Environmental Factors Affecting Groups

As the events of May 10th and 11th, 1996, unfolded, the high-altitude mountaineering world was rocked by the news that eight people (including three professional mountain guides) from two separate expeditions had perished atop the world's highest mountain, Mount Everest (elevation 29,028 feet, or 8,848 meters, above sea level). A severe storm had caught the climbers high on the mountain and several hours away from the relative safety of their tents. The extreme cold, high winds, and blinding snow made the descent nearly impossible. Although the climbers were prepared for the environment, wearing down climbing suits for warmth, using crampons (metal cleats on their boots) for traction on the ice, and carrying bottled oxygen to battle hypoxia and hypothermia (lack of oxygen to the brain and drop in core body temperature, respectively), the extreme nature of the sudden storm caught them off guard.

Did group dynamics play a role in the May 1996 disaster on Mount Everest? As is the case with many horrific events like this one, a combination of poor group dynamics and severe environmental conditions contributed to the deaths of eight climbers.

Both as individuals and as group members, people are exposed to different environmental factors that affect their experiences. Think about how many times in a single day people transition from one environment to another—people leave their homes in the morning, travel to work, get some exercise, and return home again. Each of these experiences is affected by environmental factors such as weather, noise, temperature, perceptions of personal space, and even seating arrangements. The social conditions of the environment also affect an individual's or group's ability to work or play effectively. Understanding how environmental and social conditions influence group functioning is important, as the environmental context is often a large part of a group's experience, particularly when the group is engaged in recreation, leisure, and experiential education activities.

PHYSICAL ENVIRONMENT

People can't escape the physical environment. Part of being human is living on the earth and surviving in whatever atmosphere is present. Individuals go about their daily activities wearing a raincoat or wearing sunscreen, shivering in the cold or complaining that the air conditioner is broken, listening to the wind blowing through the trees or plugging their ears as a police car goes by with its siren wailing, sinking into a leather lounge chair with a martini or feeling uncomfortable because the wallpaper doesn't match the curtains. These are all examples of how people navigate changes in both natural and man-made environments.

Whether natural or built, environmental factors help shape individual and group behaviors as well as expectations about what happens or what can happen in a particular place at a particular time. Think about what happens when university students walk into a large lecture hall. Most people would assume that the students who sit up front are the serious students, while those who choose the back row care less about their studies. Once students have chosen a seat, they will most likely sit in the same place for the remainder of the course and may become acquaintances with those students who sit nearby. Most people would also assume that the person standing behind the podium is the instructor and that the primary purpose of entering the lecture hall is to take notes, listen to the instructor talk, or take an exam. The lights are dimmed to watch a video, the air conditioning comes on when the temperatures outside are warm, and the heat comes on when temperatures outside are cold. Seating is usually heavy duty, institutionalized, and uncomfortable, causing students to fidget to improve blood flow to various extremities.

When people are comfortable in their environment, they devote their energy to the task at hand, to the speaker lecturing, or to playing basketball to the best of their ability. When people are uncomfortable in their environment, they tend to experience stress or feel emotionally, cognitively, physically, or behaviorally agitated. Although doing so is not always possible, manipulating the recreation, leisure, and experiential education environment so that people are comfortable will allow groups to perform to the best of their ability!

Temperature

Most people are comfortable in temperatures ranging from 60 to 80 degrees Fahrenheit (16-27 degrees Celsius). If it gets much cooler or warmer than that, people tend to feel uncomfortable and are unable to work as effectively or efficiently (Bell 1992).

As people who go winter camping might attest, one of the toughest things to do is climb out of a warm sleeping bag and get dressed at –20 degrees Fahrenheit (–29 degrees Celsius). People who camp in the winter spend a lot of their time staying warm or getting warm. They spend much mental energy and physical resources dealing with the cold. Imagine if these people had to accomplish a goal such as snowshoeing to the top of a mountain or finding a lost skier. Both the task and the relationship functions of the group become more difficult as people have to devote more resources to dealing with environmental conditions. The people climbing Mount Everest in May 1996 were certainly concerned about the environment that they were in—temperatures were well below 0 degrees Fahrenheit (–18 degrees Celsius), winds were forceful,

and snow was blowing. Many of the climbers, except for the guides and the more experienced clients, were concerned only about their personal safety and their need to survive. Group dynamics and concern for others were not at the top of their list of things to worry about.

While not everyone winter camps or chooses to spend time in extremely cold environments, most people have experienced the uncomfortable feeling of being in a room that is too hot. Hot temperatures cause equally stressful situations as well as create demands on the body that affect individuals and groups. People start to feel anxious and irritated and attempt to remove themselves from the situation or minimize the time they spend in the hot environment. Tempers tend to flare in hot temperatures, as is evidenced by the increased number of riots, protests, and group acts of violence that occur during the warmer months of the year. Other typical complaints accompanying hot conditions include irritability, fatigue, sadness, and lethargy—all things that can affect a group's effectiveness in its work.

Noise

Noise is another environmental factor that affects group functioning. Most people are uncomfortable with noise, or unwanted sound, that is greater than 80 decibels. For reference, a busy city street registers about 80 decibels, a chain saw is about 100 decibels, and a jackhammer is about 130 decibels. Sounds that are 50 decibels (e.g., a moderate rainfall) or less do not bother most people (Cohen and Weinstein 1981). Groups may be able to function briefly during loud noises by simply ignoring the noise. In the long term, however, individuals and groups soon expend unnecessary energy in coping with the noisy environment and devote less energy to the task at hand. Long-term effects such as headaches and interpersonal conflict may arise from exposure to continuous loud noise. From a practical standpoint, loud noise gets in the way of effective communication, which further curtails group productivity.

For the people climbing Mount Everest in May 1996, the wind certainly played a role in their ability to communicate, particularly as several climbers were trapped high on the mountain. Jon Krakauer, in his personal account of the tragedy, noted that the winds were of hurricane strength and that the wind sounded

The noise of a busy city street is distracting.

like jumbo jets going overhead (1999). The extreme noise from the wind, coupled with the flapping and shaking of the climbers' tents, was enough to make communication impossible, even though the tents were no more than a couple of yards (or a couple of meters) apart. In this extreme case, noise certainly played a role in how effectively a group was able to respond to a situation that required repeated and clear communication.

Weather

General weather conditions may also influence a group's ability to be effective and efficient. Weather is particularly important to recreation, leisure, and experiential education professionals, as many activities occur in the outdoors where weather is a factor. A freak blizzard may stop a group from holding an important meeting or may force group members to spend unexpected time together. Strong winds may create too much noise, blow materials away, or knock down a tent a group had planned to meet in. The sun may also affect people's ability to work in a group setting. As mentioned, people do not work well in hot temperatures, and dehydration from prolonged

exposure to the sun may strain relationships and affect the group's ability to make decisions.

Preoccupation with current or anticipated weather conditions may also affect a group. In many places that receive heavy snow, reports of an impending storm cause people to focus their energy on the weather. Individuals begin to wonder if they will make it home for the evening or if their children will be stuck at school. Many organizations, agencies, and schools close early in preparation for severe weather. As group members leave early to avoid the weather, the ability of the group to complete its work is compromised.

Groups that work or recreate in environments in which weather plays a prominent role often have established ways of coping with the weather. Teleconferences, Internet meetings, and e-mailing enable groups to deal with difficult weather situations. Groups frequently have risk management plans that outline specific procedures for dealing with weather emergencies. Often these groups hold formal training sessions in which they practice what to do in case of severe weather. These groups promote good communication among members, stress cooperation and watching out for other members, and working for the

Altitude and weather can influence group dynamics.

common good of the group. Positive outcomes of going through perceived or real weather emergencies include increased sense of group identity, positive cohesion, and enhanced ability of members to work together.

The Mount Everest climbers certainly were prepared for moderate weather variations. Their clothing and equipment were designed for the environmental conditions in which they were climbing—to a point. The sudden storm and accompanying snow and wind were too much for the climbers and overwhelmed the capability of their equipment to help them with their situation.

Altitude

While most recreation, leisure, and experiential education professionals are not exposed to high altitudes, there are some cases in which changes in altitude may affect a group's ability to function. Rapid changes in altitude (going from a lower elevation to a higher elevation) cause physiological responses, such as increased heart and breathing rates, as the body tries to get more oxygen into the blood. For example, people in a tour group that departs from a city near sea level (zero feet or meters in elevation), flies into Denver, Colorado, and then drives to the top of one of the mountain passes in Rocky Mountain National Park (11,500 feet, or 3,505 meters, in elevation) may experience shortness of breath, headaches, dizziness, and nausea. In extreme cases, people may develop high-altitude pulmonary edema (HAPE) or high-altitude cerebral edema (HACE). In both instances, fluid begins to leak into places it shouldn't (into the lungs in HAPE and into the brain in HACE). As their bodies work harder to adapt to decreased oxygen levels at higher elevations, people focus more on their physiological needs, and their ability to concentrate on group needs and tasks declines. Cognitive processing is also compromised, making decision making, problem solving, and communication difficult.

From an administrative or a programming perspective, professionals should plan to gain elevation slowly when working with groups. Additionally, appropriate risk management and first aid plans should be in place for groups that are visiting high elevations that they're unaccustomed to. For example, many people like to drive to the top of Pikes Peak (elevation 14,110 feet, or 4,300 meters) outside of Colorado Springs, Colorado. Upon reaching the top and getting out of their cars, some people feel the effects of gaining elevation too quickly. There are emergency medical technicians on duty at the summit to assist these people. The most effective way to deal with the negative effects of altitude is to descend to a lower elevation.

Setting

The physical setting in which a group works or recreates may have a profound effect on how the group performs. Imagine walking into a room that has trash on the floor, is dimly lit, smells bad, and has an air-conditioning unit that turns on and off every five minutes. This setting does little to attract people to use it. Now imagine a sunny room that has comfortable furniture, smells clean, and is tastefully decorated. This setting will most likely attract more people.

The atmosphere, or ambiance, of a particular setting affects how the people and groups using that space feel. This in turn influences a group's ability to function effectively. For the most part, people evaluate their physical setting in terms of how hectic or calm they perceive it to be as well as how enjoyable they feel that it is. Most people prefer a setting that is of appropriate size, has comfortable furniture, and is pleasing to the eye. While personal tastes and cultural preferences guide these perceptions, people prefer settings that are well lit and clean.

Another component of the setting that affects group operations is how enjoyable the location is for individual group members. A setting that is overstimulating may distract group members from group work, while a place that is understimulating may create boredom or lull a group to sleep. Stimulating settings may overload an individual's and a group's ability to process information. Many people experience this as tunnel vision, or a state of suspended animation. Their experience is limited to the information they are able to process. Ensuring that a group's setting suits the task at hand and meets the needs of group members will promote group success. While professionals might not be able to work with groups in a setting such as a home living room, they should make preparations to ensure that a pleasant environment exists. Such an environment allows people to feel more comfortable with their surroundings and to focus more on what the group is doing.

Seating Arrangements

Many interactions within groups and among different groups occur in formal settings. A common feature of these settings is a large table surrounded by chairs. The traditional conference room is a good example of this meeting environment. Researchers have found that where people sit in relation to one another affects their interactions and their expectations of the relationships they form with other people around the table (Russo 1967; Sommer 1969). Figure 10.1 shows the four orientations to group process that may arise from seating arrangements, including cooperative, competitive, coactive, and conversive (Sommer 1969).

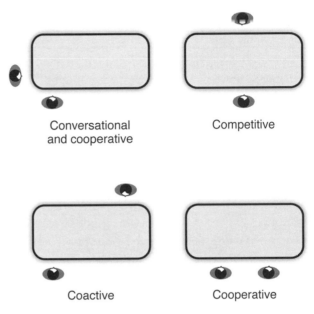

Figure 10.1 Four orientations to group process that might arise from seating arrangements.

Seating people appropriately helps to maximize the effectiveness of a group's experience. A cooperative seating arrangement has individuals sitting at the corner of a table so that they can see one another as well as any documents on the table in front of them. Another variation of a cooperative seating arrangement has individuals sit on the same side of a table. This variation is less effective because it makes it more difficult for individuals to see the other participants and the documents on the table at the same time. When people sit across the table from one another, the seating arrangement sets a competitive tone. This is particularly true when the physical distance is great because people are able to see nonverbal cues less clearly and may misinterpret this information. When people share the same physical space but work on individual tasks, they are in a coactive environment. A seating arrangement in which two people sit on opposite sides but at different ends of the table is best for this. This arrangement allows each person to work with minimal distractions from the other. Both people have their own space in which to conduct themselves as they wish and are free from encroachment by the other person at the table. Finally, a conversational atmosphere may also be established by having people sit at the corners of a table.

Several other patterns of interaction occur depending on where people sit. These patterns have potential ramifications for the recreation, leisure, and experiential education professional facilitating a meeting or work group using a traditional seating arrangement. Generally, the person at the head of the table is attributed power and status (consider the traditional family seating arrangement with the father at one end of the table and the mother at the other). People who are used to being a leader or want to control a situation usually sit at the head of the table in order to be able to influence others, make eye contact more frequently, and take advantage of the societal notion that the person at the head of the table is the leader. Sommer (1969), a researcher who studied the effects of seating arrangements, referred to the power ascribed to the person sitting in this location as the *head-of-the-table effect* and suggested that the distinction of the seating position as well as societal expectations give power to this person.

People who sit toward the middle of the table are more apt to contribute to group discussions, while those who sit toward the ends are less likely to participate. In general, comments are aimed at those sitting toward the center of the seating arrangement. One way to prevent people from engaging in idle chitchat and dominating the discussion is to seat them on the same side of the table with one or more others between them. Doing so uses the characteristics of the seating arrangement to the benefit of the group. Another consideration is to ensure that there are not any empty seats, as these create artificial boundaries that may inhibit interaction among group members.

A seating arrangement used in many recreation, leisure, and experiential education settings is a circle of chairs with no table. This seating arrangement allows participants to see each other, does not distinguish a position of power (such as the seat at the head of the table), sets up a more intimate and trusting atmosphere, and allows speakers to direct comments to the center of the circle for all to hear. While many meetings occur in traditional meeting

rooms, circular seating may be used as an alternative, particularly if the chairs in the room can be moved away from the table.

While the physical environment, including temperature, weather, altitude, setting, and seating arrangement, play a role in a group's ability to function effectively, so does the social environment in which a group operates. As shown in figure 10.2, groups function within the intersection of the physical and the social environments. The challenge for professionals is to ensure that the overlap of these two environments allows the group to operate effectively and efficiently. If either the physical environment or the social environment is ignored, a group will not work to the best of its ability. The next section addresses how the social environment can affect the group.

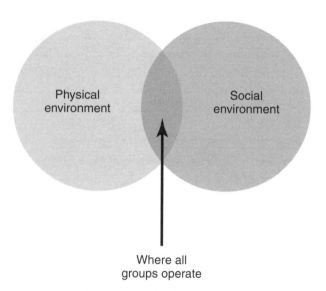

Figure 10.2 Interaction of the physical environment and social environment.

SOCIAL ENVIRONMENT

Like the physical environment, the social environment affects individuals and groups. Most people have experienced the uncomfortable feeling of walking in on a group argument or of overhearing a coach yelling at a team after a big mistake. The social environment, or the feelings people have about their relationships or potential relationships with others, affects a group's ability to function effectively. The study of how individuals interact with others in their group as well as interact with their group as a whole is called *small-group ecology.* Two parts of small-group ecology are of interest to professionals: personal space and group space.

Personal Space

Personal space is the intersection of the physical environment and the social environment on an individual level. The study of how individuals use, structure, and define personal space is called *proxemics* (Hall 1963). Personal space may be thought of as the invisible boundary that people construct around themselves—a better term may be *interpersonal space,* as this space is defined by the distance between the individual and the others nearby. The size of this boundary changes as the physical environment changes. Interpersonal space is also affected by the individual's relationship with the other people or groups of people the individual is interacting with. Think about what happens when you're sitting in a movie theater. How would you feel if most of the seats were empty and someone came in and sat right next to you? Do your feelings change if the theater is almost full? Do your feelings change if you know the person who sits down next to you? Hall (1963) described four interpersonal zones: intimate zone, personal zone, social zone, and public zone. Forsyth (2006) added a fifth zone, the remote zone, to this list. Table 10.1 summarizes the characteristics of interpersonal space zones.

Intimate Zone

The least formal of the interpersonal space zones is the intimate zone. Given its name, it is easy to guess that the boundary of this zone is 18 inches (46 centimeters) or less from another person. Usually this zone is reserved for very close family members, lovers, and very close friends. If a person enters an individual's intimate zone, the individual usually focuses on the other person and nothing else, as having someone in the intimate zone heightens awareness and limits the ability of the senses to attend to other stimuli. The term *in your face* may best describe the interactions in this zone, especially if the people who find themselves in each other's intimate zone are acquaintances or strangers. Sometimes people unwillingly enter each other's intimate zones, but they are socialized into doing so. For example, as a subway car becomes more and more crowded during rush hour, straphangers grow more lenient about letting others enter their intimate zone. Subway riders understand that during rush hour interpersonal space is at a premium. However, during off-peak hours, commuters feel less comfortable with others entering their intimate space (remember the movie theater example).

Personal Zone

The personal zone is defined as 1.5 to 4 feet (.45-1.2 meters) of space around an individual. Recreation and

Table 10.1 Interpersonal Space Zones

Zone	Space	Characteristics
Intimate	0-18 in. (0-46 cm)	This zone is close personal contact reserved for intimate friends, family, or spouse. Attention is focused on the person in this space. This is the least formal zone.
Personal	1.5-4 ft (.45-1.2 m)	This zone is used for conversations with friends. Groups that have been together are comfortable in this zone.
Social	4-10 ft (1.2-3 m)	This is the most frequently used zone. Many everyday interactions occur in this interpersonal space.
Public	More than 10 ft (More than 3 m)	This zone is used most often for interactions such as lectures, speeches, or performances. It is the most formal zone. Recreation and leisure groups may use this zone frequently, as many activities such as organized sports on playing fields use this zone.
Remote	Varying locations	With the advent of communications technology, this zone allows people to interact without being in direct physical contact with one another.

leisure group members who know each other well will use this zone. Conversations occur naturally among individuals in this zone, as people are close enough to talk without having to raise their voices. Communicating from this distance also allows individuals to see nonverbal cues such as facial expressions and gestures. Yet people are far enough away that they do not feel their intimate zone has been invaded by another person. If the group isn't too large, this zone is optimal for group processing activities such as debriefing chats, sharing expectations, and decision making. Larger groups may be broken down into smaller working groups to allow individuals to communicate effectively.

Social Zone

The social zone, or an interpersonal distance of 4 to 10 feet (1.2-3 meters), is used for interacting with strangers and new group members as well as for large group meetings. It grows increasingly difficult to communicate effectively and be a part of a group as you move toward the 10-foot (3-meter) edge of this zone, particularly if environmental conditions create loud noises or obstruct sight lines between group members. People who interact at this distance are more likely to become distracted by the things going on around them, as their visual field includes more than the other person. A good example of group interactions in the social zone is a party in which people are able to speak with each other at a normal volume and carry on conversations with others across the room. Recreation and leisure activities often occur in this zone, as groups often need space to play a game or complete an event. Many times seating at restaurants is organized with this spatial organization in mind.

It allows groups of diners to feel as though they have their own space while maximizing the number of tables in the restaurant.

Public Zone

The public zone is interpersonal space that is 10 feet (3 meters) or more. Communication becomes difficult in this zone, as people may have trouble hearing one another and nonverbal cues such as facial expressions and gestures may be difficult to see. Smaller recreation and leisure groups most likely won't use the public zone in their interactions. There are several examples of recreation and leisure events that necessitate the public zone. Large lectures, movies, theatrical productions, and concerts require a large space for the audience. The theater or symphony tickets for the first few rows of seats near the stage are often more costly than those for the seats farther away, and for good reason. Close-up seats allow the audience members to see the facial expressions of the performers as well as hear the subtleties of their intonations. The nosebleed and bleacher seats usually are priced lower, as they are farther away from the action.

Remote Zone

The final interpersonal space zone, the remote zone, is characterized by physical disconnection among group members. The remote zone has become more prominent in recent years, as the Internet, wireless communication, and computers allow people to interact without fact-to-face contact. Groups working in the remote zone must rely on verbal or written communication. One detriment of interacting in the remote zone is that nonverbal cues cannot be inter-

Learning Activity

Watch the video *Space Invaders: Strategies for Life in a Crowd.* Then answer the following questions in a small group.

1. What techniques do individuals use to deal with personal space issues in crowds?
2. What strategies could you use as a recreation, leisure, and experiential education professional to help people become more comfortable in crowded situations?
3. What strategies do you as an individual use in crowded situations?

preted. Many people become angry after reading an e-mail message that they have misinterpreted, only to find out later from the author that the intended message was very different from the message that was received. In the *New York Times* best seller *Eats, Shoots & Leaves: The Zero Tolerance Approach to Punctuation,* Lynne Truss (2003) comments on how the misuse of grammar and punctuation leads to misunderstandings of the written word. The wording of both verbal and written messages exchanged in the remote zone must be carefully thought out to ensure that the intended message comes through. Depending on the context, the remote zone may range from formal to informal. E-mail exchanges among members of a corporate work group may take a formal tone, while exchanges on a message board for rock climbing may be less formal.

Other Factors Affecting Personal Space

There are several other factors that affect interpersonal space, including gender, culture, and status. Men and women use their interpersonal space differently, partially because of biological differences (men are generally larger) and partially because of behavioral differences. Men tend to take up space by assuming open body positions such as sitting with their legs open or stretched out in front of them (Pearson, Turner, and Todd-Mancillas 1991). They also use broader, sweeping gestures that require more room. Women tend to keep their arms close to their body, sit with their legs crossed, and assume closed body positions (Pearson, Turner, and Todd-Mancillas 1991). Women are more likely to sit closer to another person, regardless of the other person's gender. Men, however, tend to prefer more interpersonal space when sitting near other people, particularly if the other person is a man (Sommer 1969). Women tend to be socialized to accept interpersonal relationships more readily and thus may be more willing to allow others into their interpersonal space (Beebe and Masterson 2000).

People from different areas around the world have varying expectations about interpersonal space. People who are from high-contact cultures are more likely to share their close interpersonal space with others. People from low-contact cultures like to have more interpersonal space (Hall 1976). People from the Middle East, Latin America, and the Mediterranean

region are thought to be from high-contact cultures. Americans, Canadians, Germans, and Scandinavians generally are considered to be from low-contact cultures. These are generalizations and might not hold true in every situation. For example, people might treat others from their culture differently based on religious preference, skin color, or other perceived differences. Professionals who are aware of cultural notions of personal space can smooth the way for more effective group functioning. Leaders and facilitators might choose seating arrangements based on cultural norms or ensure that people have adequate personal space so that they focus on the task at hand and not on how uncomfortable they feel.

Status may also play a role in how people feel about their personal space. Generally, people feel more comfortable sharing their interpersonal space with others of the same status. People are less comfortable with those of a higher status. For example, when professionals attend conferences, they prefer to share a hotel room with people of similar rank from their organization. A seasonal recreation employee would most likely feel uncomfortable sharing a hotel room with the executive director of the county recreation department!

While it is important to understand how individuals interpret their personal space, it is also important to understand how a collection of individuals interprets group space. Leaders and facilitators should be aware of the intersection of personal space needs and group space needs.

Group Space

Territoriality is the sense of owning a particular space (Engleberg and Wynn 2000). Individuals have territories that they claim as their own and attempt to prevent others from accessing. For many students, the seat they claim on the first day of class becomes "theirs" for the rest of the semester. Students even go so far as to mark the location as theirs by labeling it with graffiti or by putting objects down to hold their place until they return.

Just as individuals claim personal territories, groups claim group territories. An easy example that comes to most people's minds is gang territories. Gangs claim particular geographic areas that have some meaning to them. They mark the fringes of their territory with tags and defend the territory against rival gangs.

Why should professionals be aware of group space? By understanding how groups construct territories, what benefits there are to territories, and what potential problems may arise out of territories, professionals may design activities and programs that help groups meet their goals and objectives as effectively and efficiently as possible. This allows for the wise use of time and resources as well as allows group members to enjoy participating in recreation, leisure, and experiential education activities. The establishment and defense of territories also provide clues about the cohesiveness of a group. Groups that are more cohesive tend to have well-defined territories and are quick to protect their area. These groups can put aside internal group conflicts more easily than can groups that are not as cohesive, that do not have territories that are as well established, or that are slower to protect their territory.

Territoriality

Groups tend to define territory by physical space. Just as there are types of interpersonal space, there are types of group territory. These include primary, secondary, and public territories (Altman 1976). A primary territory is the home turf of the group. A group has a long-term interest in its primary territory and works to control the admission into or the right to use the area. For example, many well-established basketball leagues have first dibs on a certain time in the location gymnasium based on their historical patterns of use. A league is scheduled on Wednesday nights from 7 to 9 p.m. because it has always been that way. If another league tries to use the gym at that time, the basketball team will fight to keep its traditional space and time.

Secondary territories are more fluid in nature. Groups that use the space on a regular basis consider it to be their territory but allow others to use it if they are not present. For example, several organizations go rock climbing at a New Jersey state park that is near New York City. Many of these groups visit the same climbing locations regularly and have permits to use the park for rock climbing. However, occasionally there is friction between groups over a specific site, as each group claims the rock climbing site is theirs because they use it so often. In reality, the climbing sites are accessed on a first-come, first-served basis. Some groups attempt to defend their claim to the climbing area by questioning whether other groups have the appropriate permit, even though they have no enforcement authority.

The last type of group territory is called a *public territory*. The group has a claim to this territory only when it is physically occupying that location. A campsite is a great example of a public territory. When a group moves into a campsite at its local provincial park, it claims the site but then loses that claim upon leaving. The group may erect territory markers while present but must leave no trace upon departure.

Just as groups can have a physical attachment to a territory, they can develop a psychological attachment to a territory. Although a group may not physically visit a particular site on a regular basis, its members can feel connected to that place on an emotional, a cognitive, and sometimes a spiritual level. Good examples of groups that have a psychological sense of territory are the many friends groups that support local, regional, and national parks in North America (e.g., Friends of Quetico Park, Yellowstone Park Foundation). These groups are organized to protect specific parks and work with park managers and government officials to ensure that the park has the resources and personnel needed to operate effectively. Often these groups work for the preservation and conservation of the natural resources in the park and the surrounding area. Members of these groups have a psychological sense of territory for their park and work to defend that territory from any perceived harm, misuse, or intrusion.

Benefits of Territories

Groups derive benefits from having a territory to call their own. Territories help create group identity and are often a source of pride. They can enhance feelings of connectedness to the group for individual members. Many people brag about their neighborhood and those who live there. When people have defined a territory and can claim it, they feel more at ease interacting and living in that space. It makes sense that an area a group is familiar with creates feelings of safety and security.

Problems of Territories

Territories may create problems for groups. The game capture the flag may be used as an example to explain how territories can cause these problems. Although there are many variations to capture the flag, the basic rules pit two teams against one another. The main goal is for the team members of each team to journey through the other team's territory, capture the other team's flag, and return to their own territory with the flag without being tagged by an opposing team member. Players who are tagged in the opposing team's territory go to jail and can be freed only if they are touched by one of their own team members.

Conflict between groups over established territories is the essence of capture the flag. This conflict can be transferred to real-world settings. For example, many times undeveloped land that is used informally by local residents is slated for housing developments. The local residents may band together to oppose development of that land. Conflict occurs over land use priorities.

Intragroup Territories

Individuals often claim their own territory within a group's space. People prefer to have space (or territory) of their own within the group context. Employees of companies who work on large projects together may have a set of offices in a building that defines their group territory. However, the workers also have their own cubicle—their own territory—that they modify to suit their own personality and needs by putting up pictures, arranging the furniture, as so forth.

In recreation, leisure, and experiential education, a good example of how individual territories emerge within a group's territory is a campsite. A group claims the campsite as a whole as its territory, and other groups are not welcome to enter or much less stay the night in the same site. Group members then claim individual territories within the larger campsite by putting up a tent in a specific location that becomes their personal territory. In this context, many people rely on their tent as they would their house—it is a place for privacy away from the rest of the group. They can do as they please in that personal space.

It is common for groups to define a collective territory and for individual group members to stake out their own personal space within that territory. What happens when the group territory or personal space is entered by another group or person?

Learning Activity

Go outside and play a game of capture the flag. Be sure each group's territory is well defined, and be sure all players understand the basic rules of the game:

- All players must stay within the boundaries.
- Any player tagged in the opposing group's territory must go to a predetermined area known as the *jail*. A player can be freed from jail only by being touched by a fellow team member who is not in jail.
- To win, a player must return to his own territory with the opposing team's flag (a bandanna or other object) without being tagged.
- No tackling or other rough, physical contact is allowed.

Discuss the following questions upon finishing the game:

1. How did it feel to have a territory?
2. What did your group do to protect its territory?
3. How did you feel about the other group entering your territory?
4. How did you feel about the individuals in the other group?
5. Did you feel a heightened sense of arousal when you entered the other group's territory? Why do you think you felt that way?

Invasion of Interpersonal and Group Space

Individuals and groups do many things when others enter their territory, particularly if those who have entered are trying to take that territory away. Reactions vary depending on whether the territory is the individual's or group's primary, secondary, or public territory. In general, reactions grow in intensity as an intruder gets closer to what a group feels is its primary territory.

If a group's primary territory is entered, members serving as guards may approach the intruders to find out what they want. Often verbal warnings are given, and in extreme cases physical threats or other violence may occur. In capture the flag, opposing team members often call each other names, and in the spirit of the game they tell others to "Get out of town!" or "Leave before we get you!" Gangs often resort to shooting or fighting if others enter their primary territory. When a group's primary territory is entered, most often the group members will focus on repelling the intruder and not on the group process or the task at hand. It may take a while for the group to refocus on its task or relationship function, as heightened vigilance around protecting the primary territory is of paramount concern.

On an individual level, people protect their primary territories as well. They lock their doors, password protect their personal computer files, and create other barriers that make it difficult for others to access their personal space. Some individuals also resort to verbal threats or physical violence. An individual whose primary territory has been invaded often feels violated and compromised in that space.

If a group's secondary territory is entered, reactions will be less forceful than they are when the primary territory is entered. Groups may make comments such as, "We always use this space at this time!" or "Our family has used this campsite every year on this weekend for the past five years!" Good examples of how groups and individuals deal with others who enter their secondary space are the interactions among attendees at the popular summer event in Madison, Wisconsin, the Concerts on the Square, in which the local symphony plays outdoors on the steps of the Wisconsin state capitol building in downtown Madison. Groups and individuals place blankets on the ground to stake out their space for the perfor-

Toolbox Tips

Using the Social Environment to Your Advantage

The following are ways that leaders or facilitators can modify social environmental factors to influence an individual or a group:

- Use a circular seating arrangement with no table to set a friendlier tone. Barriers placed between people create an adversarial tone.
- If individuals or groups claim territory when they enter a room by tipping chairs up to reserve seats or putting objects in the seats besides theirs to discourage others from sitting too close, assign random seating to discourage people from saving seats or space.
- Seat individuals closer to one another to encourage feelings of friendliness.
- Be aware of how men and women sit in relation to one another and encourage alternative seating patterns.
- Encourage groups to decorate or arrange a meeting space to make it their own territory.
- Respect cultural and historical uses of specific places.
- Be sure the temperature, lighting, and ambiance are pleasing to group members.
- Remember the connotations that seating arrangements for meetings might convey. Do you wish to be collaborative or oppositional?

mance—many people put their blankets down hours early to claim their usual space and come back just before the performance starts. It is common to see people moving another's blanket if it intrudes on their secondary space, or the space they are accustomed to occupying for the concert. As these performances are wildly popular, the scramble for space is something to watch!

Finally, there is little reaction if a group's or an individual's public territory is entered. Most people have been socialized to understand that use of public space is fluid and on a first-come, first-served basis. A polite verbal exchange may happen. Rarely do physical threats or violence occur.

CASE STUDY

The tragedy that occurred on Mount Everest on May 10th and 11th, 1996, provides an excellent example of how the physical environment and the social environment combined to create devastating results for mountain climbers. Two personal accounts of the events that led to the death of eight climbers provide a glimpse into how environmental and social factors affect individuals as well as whole groups. These reports are Jon Krakauer's (1999) *Into Thin Air: A Personal Account of the Mt. Everest Disaster* and Anatoli Boukreev and G. Weston DeWalt's (1997) *The Climb: Tragic Ambitions on Everest.* When taken together, these accounts suggest that the social environment, distinguished by the competition between Scott Fischer and Rob Hall, collided with extreme weather conditions to contribute to the events of May 1996.

In the late 1980s and early 1990s, the high-altitude mountaineering world was opening up to the everyday climber who could afford the $70,000 U.S. price tag to ascend the world's highest peaks. Many climbers who chose this route were inexperienced at high altitudes and were relying on the logistical and technical expertise of companies such as Scott Fischer's Mountain Madness and Rob Hall's Adventure Consultants. As the success of these commercial expeditions grew, clients began to assume that buying into a commercial expedition guaranteed a successful climb to the summit. This increased pressure on the commercial companies to get as many climbers as possible to the summit of Mount Everest so they could advertise higher success rates.

Both Krakauer and Boukreev and DeWalt comment on how the commercialization of high-altitude climbing seems to have influenced the social environment of the various expedition groups that were on Mount Everest in 1996. Many climbers seemed more concerned with their own chance of success and less concerned with the dynamics of the group they were with. This was in contrast to Krakauer's and Boukreev's previous experiences, which were more centered on group process and functioning, as this focus contributed to success in climbing a mountain.

How much did the intersection of the physical and social environment contribute to the deaths of eight climbers on Mount Everest in May 1996? Subsequent analyses of this tragedy suggest that there was pressure on the leaders to get as many people to the summit as possible and that the personality type of most of the clients was to move forward with no holds barred. The effects of the high altitude, poor communication among group members because of equipment problems and physical space, and sudden onset of a massive storm certainly added to this situation. Reading *Into Thin Air* and *The Climb* and watching the videos *Everest: The Death Zone* (1998) and *Everest* (1993) make for an interesting case study of group dynamics in extreme environmental conditions.

SUMMARY

Environmental factors such as temperature, noise, weather, altitude, setting, and seating arrangement all play a role in how comfortable people are in a group environment. Extremes in any of these factors affect the ability of both individuals and groups to focus on the task at hand and the relationships among group members. Since people are exposed to environmental conditions all the time, professionals should understand how various environmental conditions might affect a group. This understanding is particularly important for outdoor conditions, where many recreation activities take place.

The social environment can be divided into two dimensions—personal space and group space. Both personal space and group space can be examined through proxemics, or the study of how individuals use, structure, and define space. Individuals have six zones of personal space. These range from the intimate zone to the remote zone. Groups also have zones of space, but these are referred to as *territories*. Most groups have a primary territory, or an area in which they feel most comfortable and at home. Groups defend their primary territories against intrusion by other individuals or groups. A group's secondary territory is space it is accustomed to using but does not have a real claim to. Finally, groups have public territory, which is characterized by fluid possession and use. A group that is in a public space has the right to use it until vacating.

All groups are affected by the intersection of the physical environment and the social environment. Sometimes one of these environments affects a group more than the other does. Professionals should be aware of how groups are influenced by environments and should implement strategies to change adverse conditions when appropriate, particularly if the safety and security of the group are at stake.

RESOURCES

Altman, I. 1976. *The environment and social behavior.* Pacific Grove, CA: Brooks/Cole.

Beebe, S.A., and J.T. Masterson. 2000. *Communicating in small groups: Principles and practices.* 6th ed. New York: Longman.

Bell, P.A. 1992. In defense of the negative affect escape model of heat and aggression. *Psychological Bulletin* 111:342-46.

Boukreev, A., and G.W. DeWalt. 1997. *The climb: Tragic ambitions on Everest.* New York: St. Martin's Press.

Breashears, D., and L. Clark, directors. 1998. *Everest: The death zone.* Broadcast by WGBH TV.

Cohen, S., and N. Weinstein. 1981. Nonauditory effects of noise on behavior and health. *Journal of Social Issues* 37(1): 36-70.

Engleberg, I., and D. Wynn. 2000. *Working in groups: Communication principles and strategies.* 3rd ed. Boston: Houghton Mifflin.

Films for the Humanities and Sciences. 1999. *Space invaders [videorecording]: Strategies for life in a crowd.* Princeton, NJ.

Forsyth, D. 2006. *Group dynamics.* 4th ed. Belmont, CA: Thomson Wadsworth.

Hall, E.T. 1963. A system for the notation of proxemic behavior. *American Anthropologist* 65: 1003-26.

Hall, E.T. 1976. *Beyond culture.* Garden City, NY: Doubleday.

Krakauer, J. 1999. *Into thin air: A personal account of the Mt. Everest disaster.* New York: First Anchor Books.

MacGillivray, G., A. Lorimore, and S. Judson, directors. 1993. *Everest.* Miramax Films.

Pearson, J.C., L.H. Turner, and W. Todd-Mancillas. 1991. *Gender and communication.* 2nd ed. Dubuque, IA: Brown.

Russo, N.F. 1967. Connotations of seating arrangements. *Cornell Journal of Social Relations* 2:37-44.

Sommer, R. 1969. *Personal space.* Upper Saddle River, NJ: Prentice Hall.

Truss, L. 2004. *Eats, shoots & leaves: The zero tolerance approach to punctuation.* London: Profile Books.

Part III

Addressing Issues in the Conscious Group

The final chapters of this book are dedicated to practical, everyday issues that arise when working with groups. Each of the four chapters presents potential pitfalls as well as strategies for avoiding or dealing with these pitfalls. Additionally, each chapter points out the strengths and benefits of working in a group setting while valuing what individual group members bring to the table.

Although people spend a lot of time in groups, especially in recreation and leisure settings, they harbor many common misunderstandings, or myths, about the hows and whys of groups. Chapter 11 turns a critical eye on the myths that leaders and facilitators often hold onto while working with groups. Chapter 12 examines working with large groups such as crowds, which is often a part of the professional's job, and discusses people's behaviors in crowds at special events, sporting events, festivals, and unplanned large gatherings such as mobs and riots. Chapter 13 takes a look at alternative groups, or groups that strive to be outside of the mainstream, and suggests ways of working with these groups in recreation and leisure settings. The final chapter, chapter 14, discusses diversity in groups and celebrates what difference can bring to successful group process and function. The chapter closes with practical ideas professionals may use while working with diverse groups.

11

Troubleshooting

Ryan and Samantha are working together as outdoor leaders guiding a group of first-time canoeists on a 17-day trip in Temagami, Ontario. During the trip, Ryan and Samantha have turned over more and more of the decision making to the group, an action which has gone over fairly well. For most of the trip the weather has been beautiful—clear days with little wind and warm temperatures. However, as the group began paddling down a relatively large lake, thunderheads started to develop and the wind began to blow head-on into the group, making the canoeing slow going. It is clear to Ryan and Samantha that the group should find a spot to pull off the lake and camp—even though the sky above them is clear, they can hear thunder and the

dark clouds are coming quickly down the lake. They have suggested that the group consider finding a spot to camp. However, the resulting discussion quickly turned into a debate, as some group members feel they can paddle farther down the lake and outrun the storm, while others think they should take a more conservative approach and get off the lake immediately. A few minutes have turned into 10 and then 15 as the group continues to discuss what to do. Meanwhile the sound of thunder is growing louder, whitecaps are crashing into the boats, and the sky is turning a smoky black. Seconds later the rain hits—it is a cold, soaking rain, and Ryan and Samantha direct the group to a campsite a short paddle down the shore.

Groups provide an advantage in many situations. However, there are some situations in which a group creates a disadvantage for individual members as well as for the collective itself. Recreation, leisure, and experiential education professionals must keep in mind the strengths and weaknesses that groups bring to a situation. Professionals must also be aware of commonly held myths about groups, as believing these myths can create unsatisfactory conditions for the group. Ryan and Samantha were caught in a situation in which a group weakness affected each person in the group and may have lasting implications for how the group members interact in the future.

In this chapter we'll explore both strengths and weaknesses of groups. We'll also dispel common myths that surround groups and group dynamics. Finally, we'll cover practical techniques for capitalizing on group strengths and avoiding group weaknesses.

STRENGTHS OF GROUPS

Working with a group of others can be very rewarding and productive. There are several reasons why working with a group is better than working alone.

First, having a knowledge bank built from many people's experiences is better than relying solely on one person's knowledge. A group is able to access information from a number of perspectives and sources. Potential decisions may be analyzed from many viewpoints, and possible pitfalls might be identified more readily.

Second, groups are able to examine the logic used in decision making and problem solving. What appears to be sound logic to one person might be improved by a group. The processes used in decision making and problem solving are more likely to be questioned and bolstered when people work together.

Third, by combining the experiences of its group members, a group can reach a broader understanding of a situation. The group can approach the situation from a number of cultural, religious, gender-based, political, educational, and economic viewpoints. Many blue-ribbon panels established to address challenging situations are composed of people from different backgrounds. This diversity allows these groups to take into account a wide range of factors that the individual members live with on a daily basis and thus know intimately.

Fourth, groups tend to be more creative in their approaches to decision making and problem solving. Groups take calculated risks that have better potential for greater payoffs. Perhaps this is because people feel there is strength in numbers, but it more likely relates to the benefits of groups already mentioned. Groups have more intellectual resources and a greater range of individual personal experiences that they can use to inform their decisions.

Fifth, working in groups enhances learning and comprehension of skills and concepts. Individuals who learn with others are more likely to remember the material being studied. This is because individuals take a more active role in the learning process when they are interacting with others. This is particularly true if an individual is responsible for instructing the others in the group about a particular subject

(Beebe and Masterson 2006). Discussing a topic allows people to hear others' interpretations of that subject and enhances each person's understanding in the process.

Sixth, groups are more likely to be satisfied with the decisions they make and the ways they solve problems. Individuals are more committed to group decisions than they are to personal decisions. This is particularly true for groups that have a strong sense of community and cohesion—people are loyal to the group and so they support the group's plan of action. People are also more satisfied with the outcomes of group decisions than they are with the results of personal decisions. Perhaps it is the feeling of sharing a common fate that leads to this satisfaction. Greater satisfaction may also occur because people realize that the outcome is the result of a decision that used the informational resources of several others. In essence, the outcome is the best it could be because of the group resources that went into directing the group that way.

Seventh, individuals who work in groups often come away with a better understanding of their own strengths and weaknesses. Groups provide feedback that can be used to improve performance in future situations. Groups also give meaning to individuals and may provide friendship, collegiality, and camaraderie. This is particularly true for individuals who attach their personal identity to the group. In recreation set-

Working with a group is often better than working alone.

tings, people often do this in team situations when they refer to themselves by their team name, such as "I'm a Wildcat!" or "I'm a Saber!" People often feel a profound sense of connection to groups—sometimes they feel more connected to their group than they do to their family.

Eighth, groups help individuals do things they can't do on their own. Reaching a goal is often an important part of why people engage in recreation, leisure, and experiential education activities. Whether it is to cross a canoe portage, win a basketball tournament, or solve a homework problem, working in a group can help individuals attain goals that would be difficult or impossible for them to reach on their own.

Finally, working in a group is a satisfying experience in and of itself. Most people feel the need to belong to some type of group and are satisfied through these experiences. Groups can meet basic needs such as safety, self-esteem, and connection. Groups help teach skills, knowledge, and dispositions to members as well as provide a safety network of support. Often groups are used as a sounding board for advice. Many groups today serve as the foundation for social capital, or the currency that goes along with knowing others in the community. For example, if Suzie needs to borrow a truck to deliver a sofa to a friend, she might be able to borrow that truck from a fellow group member. Suzie will return the favor by driving the group member's daughter to school.

Working with a group can be entertaining, fun, and stimulating, while working alone may be boring and stressful. Working with a group has many advantages over working alone or working with just a friend or two. However, there are many weaknesses associated with groups, and professionals should be aware of these.

WEAKNESSES OF GROUPS

Many students groan when their professor assigns them a group project as part of the course requirements. Given all the advantages of working in a group, why is this so?

For many students, it is easier to do the assigned work on their own. They don't have to wait on group members who are late, accept compromises they don't like, or carry the weight for others who don't participate fully in the project. Most students can relate well to these reasons for dreading group

assignments. These same problems can apply to any other group as well.

One of the main weaknesses of groups is the tendency for some people to do the work while others sit back and enjoy the ride. Social loafing occurs when individuals maintain that they are contributing members of the group while letting other group members do the majority of the work. Social loafing limits the group's ability to take advantage of the collective expertise of its members. In essence, social loafing counteracts all the positive benefits that diversity and a broad range of opinions bring to the group. In a related phenomenon, sometimes individual group members take it upon themselves to do most of the work on behalf of the group. They often do so without obtaining the rest of the group's permission. They then feel martyred for doing what they feel is a favor for the group. Often these people need to control the situation, or they think that their solution is the best and work to implement it without collaborating with others.

A second weakness of working in a group is that individual members may feel they have to conform to the rest of the group's wishes. This often results in groupthink, which occurs when a group agrees on a course of action without fully considering the implications of that decision. Groupthink occurs when individuals feel that they have to conform to what they perceive is a consensus in the group or a shared understanding. It usually stems from people's desire to avoid conflict, disagreement, and debate. Groups that understand the benefits of constructive debate and use inclusive decision making can avoid this disadvantage of groups.

Individuals who find themselves in crowds, riots, or mobs might behave in ways they never would when outside of that group. People sometimes get swept up in the heat of the moment and might join the crowd that is storming the field after a winning play-off game to tear down the goalposts. The decisions made by individuals in these groups are unduly influenced by those around them. In everyday situations, these individuals would make completely different conclusions about how to act!

Another weakness is that groups must accept individuals for who they are, including both the positive and the negative. Regardless whether people are always late or hold very conservative or liberal viewpoints, the group has to accept them as long as they are a member even if their personal characteristics don't align with those of others in the group. This is often the most challenging weakness to overcome, especially when people are working with others they did not choose to be with (e.g., student work groups, committees). However, if a group recognizes and values the positive aspects of each individual, this disadvantage may be turned into an advantage.

There is an increased chance for conflict in groups. Some group members may choose to be obstructionist or refuse to cooperate with the other group members. People who work alone are not exposed to such conflict and do not have to compromise or cooperate. A group may be consumed by dealing with conflict and unruly group members and may lose its ability to complete the task at hand or move forward in a timely fashion. This is often the story line of sports movies, in which one player believes he can carry the team. He makes decisions without consulting others, calls plays as he sees fit, and hogs the ball. This inevitably leads to conflict among team members. Usually the conflict ends when the remainder of the team shows the individual that the true strength of the group lies in the collective, not the individual. There is a common saying that describes this situation well: "There is no *I* in *team.*"

Groups move more slowly than individuals do. This observation is often cited as a major disadvantage of group work. In the scenario that opened this chapter, Ryan and Samantha experienced this drawback firsthand. It took the group much longer to make a decision than it would have taken an individual leader. This is true for most group processes, particularly if the group needs to work out operating procedures such as decision-making strategies, leadership arrangements, and communication structures. Group discussions take longer, particularly if the group solicits each member's opinion. However, the time invested in working with a group will often reap great benefits!

Table 11.1 summarizes the advantages and disadvantages of working in a group.

Individuals should weigh carefully these advantages and disadvantages as well as consider the strengths and weaknesses a group brings to the situation at hand. There are times when acting alone is better than working with a group, and there are times when working in a group is better than being alone.

Table 11.1 Advantages and Disadvantages of Groups

Advantages	Disadvantages
Group members can combine knowledge.	One or two people may do all the work while others sit back (social loafing).
Groups can critically examine proposed decisions and solutions to problems.	Members feel pressured to conform to the rest of the group (groupthink).
Groups can reach a broader understanding of the situation.	Groups must accept unwanted characteristics of individual members.
Groups have a more creative approach to problem solving and decision making.	Groups increase the chance for conflict.
Groups enhance learning.	Groups move more slowly than individuals do.
Members enjoy greater satisfaction with outcomes.	Individuals may behave in ways they might not when alone.
Members gain greater understanding of individual strengths and weaknesses.	
Working with other people is satisfying.	
Members develop social capital.	
Groups help individuals reach goals that they can't meet by themselves.	

WHEN TO WORK ALONE

Working with a group often provides greater benefits and enhances outcomes. However, there are certain situations when working alone is more effective and efficient than working with a group. These situations usually involve limited resources, a lack of time, changing conditions, access to information or problems with the nature of group process.

Limited Resources

When resources are limited, it is often better for people to work alone rather than with a group. Groups have a tendency to divide their resources among their members. This tendency may result in members receiving less bang for the buck, as the resources allocated to each may be inadequate to accomplish any part of the task. On the other hand, if one individual had use of all the resources, that person would be able to complete the task. For example, a sports club might not be able financially to send an entire team to a tournament. However, the club could support an individual member going to compete on behalf of the team. In this way, an individual can maximize the use of the resources available.

Lack of Time

If time is limited, it is often best to act as an individual. This is particularly true if environmental conditions are changing rapidly. Think back to the beginning of this chapter and the situation in which Ryan and Samantha found themselves. Had Ryan or Samantha acted individually, the group as a whole would not have gotten wet and cold. In situations like these, it is best for the leader or a designated group member to take control of the decision making and problem solving. Because groups generally need more time to process decisions and come up with potential solutions, when time is of the essence, individual action will most likely ensure that suitable outcomes are generated effectively and efficiently.

Changing Conditions

Professionals often work with groups in situations in which conditions change quickly. The scenario at the beginning of this chapter is an excellent illustration of how changing conditions can affect a group. In situations like these, it is sometimes best for people to work alone or for one person to step up and become a directive leader. In many sports, a coach or captain takes on the role of coordinating the team in conditions that may change from second to second. Leaders need experience and awareness of the potential ramifications of stepping in or not stepping in when conditions begin to change rapidly. In some experiential education settings, conditions are changed intentionally to create adversity for a group. For example, on many challenge courses, facilitators alter the conditions to create a greater challenge for the group. Resources may be removed, people may be blindfolded or forbidden to talk, or additional barriers may be put in place. These changes often lead to an individual taking charge and making decisions or providing direction for the group. In general, when conditions are changing rapidly, it is best for one person to take charge or for people to not work in a group at all.

Access to Information

In the communication age, information is readily available and people can find solutions to problems as well as make appropriate decisions without the help of a group. The Internet, media outlets, and public and academic libraries provide information and resources that individuals can use to get answers and make decisions. When information is readily available, working with a group might not be warranted. Why spend time and money doing what's already been done before? However, if a decision or problem requires in-depth information or if the potential ramifications are severe, then capitalizing on the collective power of many people working toward the same end is advisable. In a related sense, if an expert already has the solution or answer, there is no reason to work in a group. Appropriate direction can be obtained without forming a group by working with appropriate consultants. In fact, consulting is a growing business in the recreation, leisure, and experiential education field. There are a myriad of consultants who can be hired to do anything from figuring out the best swimming pool to install to conducting staff training at a summer camp. Consultants have realized that they can capitalize on their ability to provide clear and concise direction when a group of people unexperienced in that area would waste time and money defining a problem, exploring potential solutions, implementing a solution, and evaluating the effectiveness of that solution.

Nature of Group Process

A final consideration in deciding when to work with a group is whether there are potential problems with group process. There are many reasons why group processes may make it better to work alone. First, the group may be embroiled in conflict that it cannot overcome. This conflict may involve potential courses of action, resource allocation, politics between cliques, or overall group direction. While conflict can strengthen a group in many situations, sometimes working alone will produce more effective and efficient results. Sometimes there are individuals in groups who block productivity. These individuals create an impossible social environment as a result of their personality, their want to control the group, or their unwillingness to relinquish power or status to other group members. If these personality and social issues get in the way of group progress, it might be wise to work outside of the group setting.

While working in a group can provide greater rewards, sometimes it is best to work alone or for one person to take on a directive role in the group. Sometimes a learned dislike of participation in groups, or grouphate (Adams and Galanes 2006), is reason enough to work alone. Grouphate derives from past bad experiences with groups and may often explain why students groan when they hear they have to work on a group project. Table 11.2 summarizes the considerations for working with a group versus working alone.

Many people, especially North Americans, prefer to work alone. North American ideals value individualistic achievement over working collaboratively (Engleberg and Wynn 2003). This ideal makes many individuals reluctant to work with others and may be the root cause of problems with group process. A primary way to overcome this focus on individualism is to be sure the group defines goals that all group members feel are important. Professionals must not only be aware of the conditions that make working with a group counterproductive but also be aware of how North American individualism affects people's approaches to working with groups. The decision to work with a group might be a bad one depending on current conditions or individualistic notions of success. Professionals must assess these factors properly in order to be effective and efficient when working as either an individual or a part of a group.

The choice between working alone and working with groups may be a fine distinction that depends on several considerations. Another factor affecting this choice occurs when people entertain certain ideas about group work that in reality are untrue. While believing in these myths may make people hesitate to work with groups, these beliefs are easy to address.

Table 11.2   When to Work With a Group and When to Work Alone

Group	Alone
Adequate resources exist to support several people working together.	Resources are limited—there's only enough for one person to be successful.
There is plenty of time for people to get together, work through the issue, and implement their decision.	Time is of the essence.
Conditions are relatively stable.	Conditions are changing quickly.
Information about a good solution or decision is unavailable.	Information about a good solution or decision is easy to get.
In-depth information and experience are required to move the group forward.	An expert or consultant already has a best course of action.
The individuals in the group work well together.	Group conflict is impossible to overcome and prevents the group from moving forward.

MYTHS IN GROUP DYNAMICS

Myths, or legends that aren't true, may negatively influence how individuals work with groups as well as how professionals facilitate group experiences. Being aware of the reality of these myths will make a leader's job easier as well as allow the leader to educate group members on the true nature of group work. Inevitably, educating the group members will make the group function more efficiently and effectively.

Leadership Myth

One common myth about groups is that the goals of the leader are the most important. Thus followers simply accept those goals as being important for the group. This, however, is a recipe for disaster. For a group to be effective there must be a sense of positive goal interdependence for all group members (Johnson and Johnson 2003). Commitment by all is of utmost importance. Many people think that when others join a group they do so because they agree with the existing goals of that group. In some cases this is true, but in many situations people join groups so they can reach a goal they can't achieve on their own. Just because a leader sets out a potential goal and objectives, it doesn't mean that everyone in the group will agree with those ideas. For example, a recreation director who establishes a planning committee for a holiday festival may have an idea of what she would like the festival to look like. If the director encourages other group members to accept that idea or, better yet, helps the committee develop its own notion of what the festival will look like, the group will most likely succeed because each member agrees on a common purpose.

Conflict Myth

Another myth is that groups that have no conflict are better than groups that do have conflict. No one likes disagreement. However, conflict can be a healthy part of a group's experience. Positive conflict helps groups to consider all aspects of a problem, decision, or course of action. A solid, grounded decision will most likely be reached if it is accompanied by discussion and debate. A group without conflict is subject to groupthink, or the inability to dissect group decisions or solutions to problems. For more on groupthink, see chapter 6.

A second positive aspect of conflict is that ultimately it allows members to feel comfortable with the group process, communication structure, and leadership configuration. Group members who experience conflict over these issues have the ability to discuss how these issues might affect the future of the group. In the end, most people will feel comfortable with a compromise or will at least understand the rationale for a particular course of action.

Homogeneity Myth

Many people believe that groups of people who are similar are better than groups of people who are different. However, there are many advantages to heterogeneous groups. People bring different life experiences, cultural viewpoints, ethnic practices, educational levels, and political beliefs to groups. This diversity adds depth and flavor to the group's toolbox. Groups with a diverse membership find innovative solutions to problems, vet their decisions more thoroughly, and identify potential outcomes that wouldn't have been noticed by homogenous groups. Although diverse groups might experience more debate and potential conflict, such conflict often results in more desirable outcomes for the group as a whole.

Group-Is-Life Myth

A fourth myth is that a group is an individual's sole focus. However, most people belong to several groups, have limits on their time, and have other obligations. In addition, people may be only superficially engaged with the group. Sometimes group leaders and facilitators get frustrated with the timeliness and apparent loyalty of group members. However, leaders should remember that group members are influenced by many factors outside of the group context. Sometimes people need to take care of their individual needs. On many wilderness expeditions, for example, there are days when individuals don't seem totally plugged in to what the group is doing. Inexperienced leaders often get down on themselves and the person because they feel they are losing that person from the group, when in reality the individual is just distracted by personal needs that have nothing to do with the leader or group. Leaders and facilitators should keep in mind the social, psychological, and physical needs of individual members and the way that these needs influence an individual's focus on the group.

People-as-Machines Myth

Another myth regarding groups and group dynamics is that people can move seamlessly from task to task. In some cases this is true, but in others it is not. It is important for groups to mark their milestones, celebrate their successes, and debrief their negative aspects. Many groups march along and narrow their focus on the task function or the crucial social function of the group. Group leaders and facilitators should acknowledge the need that people have to celebrate, reflect, and integrate their experiences into their individual life and group life. Taking time between tasks also allows people to rest, reenergize, and approach a new task with fresh enthusiasm. Groups that plod along with no time for a break often are full of conflict and are less efficient and effective than groups that rest along the way. Often a rest after a task is an appropriate time for group members to evaluate their roles in the group as well as determine whether they wish to remain a member.

One-Size-Fits-All Myth

Many new professionals accept the myth that all groups are alike and that what works for one group will work for all groups. While the fallacy of this myth might seem obvious, our experience with new professionals suggests otherwise. Many inexperienced leaders assume that a strategy for working with groups is a one-size-fits-all answer to group work. They quickly learn, however, that this is not the case. Each group is a beast unto itself and possesses its own characteristics, working procedures, and identity based on the input of its members as well as the direction and skill of its leader.

A related myth surrounds the role of the leader in a group: One leadership style fits all. A given leadership style, however, does not fit all groups or all situations. In some groups it is OK for a leader to take an authoritative, directive approach. However, many others groups may resent a leader who embraces authoritative style. Many new leaders and facilitators let the title of *leader* go to their head and think that their education, training, and title give them an innate ability to be effective at their job. This is a major pitfall that many young leaders jump into feet first! This myth has several aspects of which to be aware. Most of them are grounded in what type of leadership style is employed by the recreation, leisure, and experiential education professional and how that style translates into group processes.

One way in which inappropriate leadership style manifests in groups is through top-down decision making. In this top-down process, the leader makes the majority of decisions for the group. In some instances this style is warranted, but for most groups, especially those in recreation, leisure, and experiential education settings, a more collaborative decision-making approach is better. Another problem area is communication. If all communication is instigated or mediated by the leader, group members may become disenfranchised with the process. Often new leaders feel that they need to control the flow of information and keep on top of all aspects of the group, when doing so is unnecessary. On the other hand, a leader-centered approach to communication might be appropriate for groups that are new or that are in obvious disarray.

Many students are enamored with Tuckman's (1965) and Tuckman and Jensen's (1977) stages of group development. When asked what they remember about group dynamics, they'll answer, "Forming, storming, norming, and performing." A common myth surrounding group development is that groups naturally progress through these stages like clockwork. People who are new to working with groups often get confused when a group never reaches the performing stage or continually revisits the storming phase. Although current models of group development suggest there are many different ways in which groups develop, new leaders and facilitators seem to want a linear development model to fit all groups. This is not the case, as group development depends on many factors.

One way the myth of leadership affects groups is through the distribution of power. Again, when the recreation, leisure, and experiential education professional does not disperse power to the rest of the group, resentment, disconnection, and lack of commitment may arise among group members. By distributing leadership power (in one way or another) to all group members, the leader can ensure members feel more connected to the group, are more committed to the group goals, and are more engaged in all group processes. This is called *transformative leadership*.

Many people, both leaders and followers, fall prey to the romance of leadership (Forsyth 2006). Often people do not realize just how little influence a leader actually has over a group, and they disregard external factors that can affect a group. This is apparent in professional sports, where football quarterbacks, baseball pitchers, and hockey goalies shoulder much of the glory or blame for the team's success or failure. They often become the scapegoat for a team's loss but reap much of the credit when the team wins. What goes unnoticed (for the most part) is that the remainder of the team contributes to success or failure in the game. It is embarrassing and disheartening for a quarterback, pitcher, or goalie to be pulled from a game before its completion. These players are removed for not moving the ball down the field, for allowing too many runners to reach base, or for allowing too many goals to score. However, often these events are not the fault of the quarterback, pitcher, or goalie. Blockers might be missing their targets, outfielders may be dropping easy pop flies, or defensemen might be failing to clear opposing players from in front of the net. On the other hand, quarterbacks, pitchers, and goalies are the ones seen on the news when the entire team performs well and wins. People who fall prey to the romance of leadership overlook the contributions of others in the group. It is all members who create the success or the failure of the group—not just the leader.

People believe in many myths surrounding groups and group dynamics that can limit the effectiveness of both the group and the individual leader. However, there are several practical techniques that professionals may implement to overcome the negative effects of these myths.

PRACTICAL TECHNIQUES FOR ADDRESSING GROUP NEEDS

While every group is unique and it is impossible to supply one specific way to address the needs of every group, there are some general techniques professionals can employ to meet group needs. This last section of the chapter is devoted to these techniques. Successfully meeting group needs will help the group reach its goals effectively and efficiently.

Techniques for Group Development

Groups need different things at different points in their development. Groups that are newly formed often need greater direction from a leader. During the early stage of group development, referred to as the *forming* stage in Tuckman's (1985) and (Tuckman and Jensen's (1977) model, groups often need help with both the task and the relationship functions of the group process. However, because in this stage group members are still getting to know one another, it is the relationship function that needs the most attention from a leader or facilitator. One technique leaders can use to help meet group needs is to hold a discussion about what people's expectations are for the group and for the various group processes that need to be established. Spending part of the first group meeting working on team building and setting the tone for how the group wishes to conduct itself is a great start on the right path.

Priming the Pump

A leader may wish to prime the pump by sending out information on successful group functioning before the group meets for the first time. While doing this might not be feasible in many situations where groups form randomly, it can help dispel the common myths mentioned earlier in this chapter. A good resource for leaders is "Experiential Learning in Teams" (Kayes, Kayes, and Kolb 2005), an article describing a collaborative team approach to group learning. This

Learning Activity

Think of a group you currently belong to. Write down some of the strengths and weaknesses of that group. Answer the following questions:

1. Are the strengths or weaknesses caused by any of the myths presented in this chapter?

2. How can group members dispel these myths in your group?

3. Are these myths commonly held in other groups you are involved in? Why?

Share your answers with others. Brainstorm ideas on how you can help each other combat myths about groups.

approach includes setting a positive tone, creating shared goals and expectations, and maintaining a respectful environment. These ideals may be transferred to any group in any setting.

Leaders who have access to registration forms or other facts about group members may use that information to gain perspective on the backgrounds of the individual members. A person's background gives the leader possible clues as to why the person is joining the group. While a leader shouldn't rely solely on assumptions made from registration forms, having this information is better than starting from scratch during the first group meeting!

Creating Connections

Leaders and facilitators must be prepared to help individual members determine their roles in the group. Ensuring that people have a meaningful role to help them feel connected to the group helps the group as a whole and meets an individual need. These roles should have some function that helps the group reach its goals—they should not be just a facade for a meaningless position.

As mentioned earlier, both the task and the relationship functions are important group needs. Leaders should ensure that the group as a whole establishes clear group goals that individual members can commit to. These goals help members connect to the group and help define the group as a whole. Many times people join a group that has predetermined goals. For example, sometimes students in university outdoor recreation programs join a wilderness trip group that is part of a course required for graduation. The course requires the students to complete a wilderness expedition in which they practice technical skills and leadership while experiencing small-group dynamics in an outdoor setting.

Creating Process

In creating process, a leader focuses the group on how achieving the predetermined goals will benefit the individual members and the group as a whole. While completing a wilderness expedition might be a once-in-a-lifetime experience for some group members, they can still take away from it leadership skills, the ability to recognize changing weather patterns, an understanding of small-group dynamics, and an

overall appreciation of outdoor recreation pursuits. Thus leaders can tailor predetermined needs to fit individual needs. There is something to take away from every experience, and a savvy leader will help people figure out early on what they can take away.

Leaders can also meet group needs by helping the group determine its operating procedures, such as communication patterns, decision-making processes, and methods of resolving conflict. As each group is different, the leader must decide carefully just how much direction a group needs. Most groups will feel more comfortable with operating procedures they have established. Operating procedures should be coordinated with the technique that fits the needs of the situation. For example, there are many ways to make decisions. However, the decision-making technique that should be chosen depends on the complexity of the decision. As seen in figure 11.1, groups usually make moderately complex decisions and infrequently make simple or very complex decisions. The appropriate time, resources, and guidance must be provided depending on the complexity of the decision, the experience of the group members, and the experience of the leader. Properly matching the decision-making technique with the situation will help the group meet its needs and avoid potential negative conflict and lack of meaningful progress toward goals.

Celebration

A final suggestion is for leaders and facilitators to arrange for debriefing and celebration before a group disbands. Closure for a group experience is important, both for the group as a whole and for individual members. The group might have a party or enjoy one last game together as a team. Some groups might require lengthy debriefing and need help in coming to terms with disbanding. If you think about it, people who have shared positive interdependence, have reached a goal with others, and have put a lot of work into the group have heightened connections with other members. It may take a while for those feelings of connectedness to fade away. The main purpose of school reunions, winter parties for summer campers and their staff members, and other such events is to help people remain connected to the group, as well as help them ease into other facets of life.

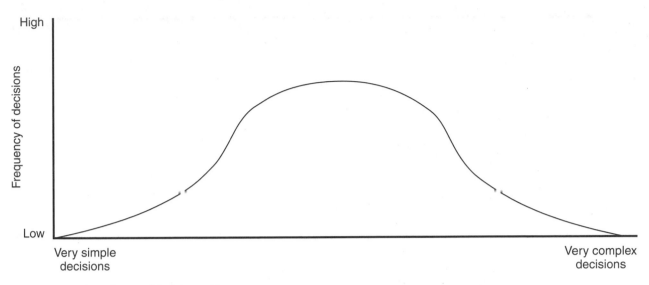

High

Frequency of decisions

Low

Very simple
decisions

Very complex
decisions

Figure 11.1 A continuum of decision making.

Reprinted, by permission, B. Martin et al., 2006, *Outdoor leadership theory and practice* (Champaign, IL: Human Kinetics), 75.

Techniques for Group Processes

There are several techniques that leaders and facilitators can use to help groups meet their needs such as power, conflict, making decisions and solving problems effectively and efficiently, and interpersonal issues. Remember that each group has its own unique characteristics and needs, and these recommendations must be tailored to the group.

Allocating Power

First, power should be carefully allocated to group members. The ways in which people are influenced by others must be appropriate to the situation (Johnson and Johnson 2003). Leaders should help group members understand who has power and why and should ensure that all members have the ability to influence others and the group as a whole when necessary. Leaders can help people understand power differentials by setting a collaborative tone. If the group understands that some people need to exert influence (or have power) in some situations to help the group reach its goal, and that it is a group effort, chances are the people being influenced won't feel as if they don't have any say in the process. Leaders can be sure that group members know that power distribution is part of working with a small group and that power is very fluid in groups—it changes constantly based on the task and relationship functions of the group (Johnson and Johnson 2003).

Positive Conflict

Positive conflict can be a very helpful tool for groups and can help groups meet their needs effectively and efficiently. Constructively debating the merits of decisions and solutions to problems can help the group avoid groupthink, consider the positive and negative outcomes, and examine the logistics and resources needed to implement plans of action. Groups that work through positive conflict, or conflict that is based on good intentions for the group, are usually stronger and more cohesive than groups that don't experience any conflict or must deal with negative conflict. Leaders can serve as the devil's advocate and introduce strategies to help groups to use positive conflict to their advantage. These strategies might include open debates or brainstorming pros and cons. The leader should be sure that the collaborative nature of the positive conflict process remains at the forefront of the discussion, as positive conflict can quickly deteriorate into negative conflict without careful attention. Overall, positive conflict that is managed carefully can help a group meet its needs.

Reading the Situation and the Third Eye

Decision making and problem solving are integral in helping the group meet its needs. The essence of most groups involves decision making and problem solving. Leaders should be well versed in a variety of

Toolbox Tips

Here are some ideas to help you begin to develop a third eye:

- Review scenarios from real-life events. Think about what you would do in a similar situation.
- Volunteer at a local recreation department. Work with an experienced leader so you can see how she handles different situations.
- Take on a more active leadership role in a group you belong to. Practice reading situations as they unfold. Try implementing different courses of action and see what happens.
- Read as much as possible about human behavior in groups and group dynamics!

decision-making and problem-solving techniques. Perhaps one of the hardest skills for new professionals to develop is the ability to read the situation and choose the appropriate tool to implement in that situation. An even harder skill to develop is referred to as the *third eye*. Leaders who have a third eye are able to anticipate and react to group needs before the situation gets out of control. Most often the third eye develops through experiential learning, trial and error, and the school of hard knocks. The third eye helps leaders meet individual and group needs around decision making and problem solving; it also helps leaders implement the appropriate leadership style. Johnson and Johnson (2003) suggest that consensus is the most effective decision-making method, as it encourages participation of all group members, creates community within the group, and equalizes power imbalances. However, the main downfall of decision making by consensus is that it is time consuming.

Interpersonal Issues

The last area in which leaders and facilitators can implement specific techniques to attend to group needs addresses the interpersonal issues among group members. Generally, if leaders can frame these issues in a positive light, the needs of both the individual members and the group can be met. Johnson and Johnson (2003) suggest five approaches to resolving interpersonal issues: problem solving, compromise, smoothing, withdrawal, and forcing. Problem solving involves negotiating a reasonably acceptable course of action for both parties. Compromise means that both people give in a little so that they can reach agreement.

Smoothing includes apologizing, figuring out who thinks their side of the issue is most important and letting them have their way, or humoring the problem. People who withdraw ignore the issue in hopes it will go away. Finally, forcing a resolution to the issue means that one side wins while the other loses. Leaders should monitor interpersonal issues that occur in groups.

Much like process of resolving conflict, the resolution of interpersonal issues can benefit the group and help the group meet its needs. However, professionals need to be prepared to step in and facilitate a solution to these issues if necessary. How this process unfolds depends on the nature of the issue as well as the parties involved. The key aspect of resolving interpersonal issues is keeping a positive, collaborative framework in mind. Although many people are reluctant to do so, sometimes it is wise for them to conclude that they cannot reach a solution and that the recreation, leisure, and experiential education professional should make the decision or impose a solution. In a worst-case scenario, this might include asking a group member to leave the group. However, resolving interpersonal issues will help move the group toward its goals and satisfy its needs.

Working with groups can be very tricky. Leaders and facilitators will be best equipped to deal with groups if they keep in mind the strengths and weaknesses groups bring to different situations. Sometimes a recreation, leisure, and experiential education professional will be better off working alone. Leaders can also capitalize on the strengths of groups by discounting the many myths that surround groups and group dynamics by using some of the practical techniques outlined in this chapter.

SUMMARY

People experience groups almost every day of their lives. The world is a very social place, and individuals are expected to work with others to reach a common goal in a variety of settings. However, there are many strengths and weaknesses to working with groups. Working with a group is a rewarding experience. The collective knowledge, experience, and background of a diverse group enable people to reach goals that are unattainable for individuals. Groups often find more creative solutions to problems, and they are more apt to take risks that pay off with greater rewards. Finally, working with a group can be fun and stimulating. Humans are social creatures and enjoy (for the most part) being with others.

While there are many positive aspects to groups, there are weaknesses as well. Some group members might not contribute as much as others do, and belonging to a group may arouse feelings of having to conform to group norms. When we become a member of a group, we bring along both our positive and our negative attributes. We all have baggage that affects how a group functions. Groups also are a spawning ground for negative conflict that can prevent the group from ever reaching its full potential. Groups also move more slowly than individuals move. Decisions take longer to make, and problems take longer to solve. However, usually the rewards of this extra time spent are well worth it!

There are times when it is better to work alone or to act as an individual within a group context. The reasons to work alone revolve around access to information, available resources, experts in the group, and the time frame required to act. Generally, the more resources and time that are available, the better it is to work with a group. If a clear solution to a problem has already been determined by an expert, it is better to work alone.

This chapter presented several myths surrounding groups and group dynamics. Many people who come to groups have preconceived notions of what a group and group dynamics are all about. Leaders and facilitators can implement the techniques suggested in the last part of this chapter to dispel these myths and cut off any negative aspects of group dynamics and interpersonal relationships before they interfere with individual and group needs. With practice, professionals will develop the ability to read groups and will develop a third eye, or the ability to see trouble before it happens. Through training, practical experience, and trial by error, professionals can develop a host of techniques to improve their work with groups.

RESOURCES

Adams, K., and G. Galanes. 2006. *Communicating in groups: Applications and skills.* 6th ed. Boston: McGraw-Hill.

Beebe, S.A., and J.T. Masterson. 2006. *Communicating in small groups: Principles and practices.* 8th ed. Boston: Pearson Education.

Engleberg, I., and D. Wynn. 2003. *Working in groups: Communication principles and strategies.* 3rd ed. Boston: Houghton Mifflin.

Forsyth, D. 2006. *Group dynamics.* 4th ed. Belmont, CA: Thomson Wadsworth.

Johnson, D.W., and F.P. Johnson. 2003. *Joining together: Group theory and group skills.* 8th ed. Boston: Pearson Education.

Kayes, A., D. Kayes, and D. Kolb. 2005. Experiential learning in teams. *Simulation and Gaming* 36(3): 330-54.

Tuckman, B.W. 1965. Developmental sequences in small groups. *Psychological Bulletin* 63:384-99.

Tuckman, B.W., and M. Jensen. 1977. Stages of small group development revisited. *Group and Organizational Studies* 2:419-27.

CHAPTER

12

Crowd Dynamics

It was the third and final evening of Woodstock 1999, the music festival commemorating the 30th anniversary of the original Woodstock, and things had gone fairly well. Approximately 225,000 people had attended the event from July 23 to July 25. The Red Hot Chili Peppers were on stage for the final performance of the festival, and many concertgoers were given candles to light as part of the festival closing. It was rumored that a special guest band was to close out the show, which created anticipation for a unique closing to the festival. When the house lights came on after a video tribute to Jimmy Hendrix's performance of "The Star-Spangled Banner" during the 1969 Woodstock festival, marking the end of the concert, the crowd was disappointed. At some point, people used their candles to start bonfires, a car was tipped over and set on fire, and other acts of vandalism occurred (Vider 2004).

Of the approximately 225,000 people who originally attended the festival, only about 155,000 remained because many concertgoers had left early to avoid traffic jams. It was estimated that of those remaining, about 500 people actually participated in the riot that occurred at the end of the festival. What caused those people to suddenly act in such a way? Why didn't the remaining 154,500 people participate?

Crowds are often cast in a negative light. Many people picture riots, sport fan violence, looting, and other antisocial behaviors when they think of crowds, especially mobs. However, crowds often create positive feelings and can enhance an experience. For example, most people feel connectedness, pride, and excitement when in the presence of a large number of people cheering for their favorite sports team. Imagine what it would be like to watch a professional basketball game with only a few other people in the arena!

Recreation, leisure, and experiential education professionals work with crowds of various sizes. Many community and municipal recreation departments have special events associated with holidays such as the Fourth of July or Canada Day, which large numbers of people attend. Recreation and leisure professionals often organize large-scale sporting events that involve crowds, including tournaments, the Olympic Games, and marathons. Parades, carnivals, and fairs are other examples where crowds might form in a recreation, leisure, and experiential education context. Therefore, professionals need to understand how people behave in crowds, as well as how a crowd as an entity might act in specific situations.

This chapter defines crowds and distinguishes among crowds, collectives, and mobs. Additionally, this chapter examines the behavior of individuals in crowds and the psychological reasons why people join crowds. It also identifies and examines crowds that are specific to recreation, leisure, and experiential education. Finally, this chapter offers strategies for working with crowds, collectives, and mobs.

COLLECTIVES

A large assembly of people who have similar reasons for being at a particular place but are otherwise unaffiliated is called a *collective*. A collective is an umbrella term that describes several types of groups made up of people who are in the same place, exhibit similar characteristics, and often have the same focus or goals. There are nine types of collectives: crowds, mobs, riots, panics, mass hysteria and rumors, audiences, queues, social movements, and trends (Forsyth 2006). A collective may consist of people who are physically in contact with each other, such as those attending a tennis tournament. A collective may also consist of people who are scattered across a country or around the world. People who belong to fan clubs, listen to the latest music, or wear trendy clothes fit into this definition as well. The factor that determines membership in a collective is that the individual has a shared goal or behavior with others.

Although collectives share many of the same characteristics of groups outlined elsewhere in this book, they are generally more loosely organized than groups. There is often no clear leader or structure through which directions are given, decisions are made, or communication occurs. As a result, collectives are less cohesive and tend to work in different ways from other groups.

Crowds

A crowd is a gathering of people who are in the same place (usually in public) and share a common reason for being in that place. There is a fine line in labeling a group of people as a *crowd*. It takes a specific event, occurrence, or action on the part of a person or people to turn a group of people into a crowd. There needs to be a focal point or some reason to draw people together; otherwise, those people are not really a crowd. For example, people who are at the beach on a hot summer day are not considered a crowd. However, if a suntan-lotion company arrives at the beach and starts giving away free bottles of lotion, a crowd may form.

Crowds often comprise smaller units of people; many individuals in public places are there with other people. However, that doesn't mean that people who happen to be in the right place at the right time will not become members of a crowd. Crowds may not have an identified leader, but there is usually some center of attention or focal point. Many crowds form either a circle or a semicircle, with the bull's-eye being the focal point. Individuals and small groups closer to the center of the circle usually are more intimately involved with the crowd than are those who are on the outer edges.

Membership in most crowds is dynamic—a person or small group might become a member of a crowd for only a few passing seconds, whereas others may be members for much longer. The nature of the occurrence may influence how long a person or small group is a member of a crowd. If the center of attention piques the curiosity of the bystanders, then they are more likely to be a member of the crowd for a much longer time. If a person or small group happens to be at the interior of the circle, they may remain longer; it might become physically difficult to leave because people gathering behind them block an easy exit.

Learning Activity

In a group of six students, go to an outdoor location that many people pass by. One person from the group should stand in an obvious location and look up at a building. Observe how many passersby look up or stop and look up. Repeat the process with two people, then with three, and so on until you have looked up with all group members (except one, who should record how many people look up and how many people stop and look up). Create a graph that depicts the data your group has collected. Then answer the following questions:

1. How many people did it take before passersby looked up?

2. How many people did it take before passersby stopped and looked up (i.e., formed a crowd)?

3. What could your group have done to create a crowd more quickly?

This activity recreates an experiment conducted by Milgram, Bickman, and Berkowitz (1969).

Mobs

A crowd can quickly turn into a mob. A mob is different from a crowd in that its members experience the same emotion at the same time. This emotion is usually highly charged, and people in mobs are often characterized as irrational. Whereas the term *crowd* is often seen as neutral, the term *mob* often has negative connotations. The word *mob* comes from the Latin term *mobile vulgus,* which means "excitable crowd" (Drury 2002). Mobs have been historically associated with lawlessness, uncivilized behavior, and disorderliness. When many people think of mobs, terms such as *hooliganism, lynch mob, unruly mob,* and *mob rule* come to mind. As such, mobs have been associated with prejudice, racial bias, violence, and hatred.

Mobs are not always violent, unlawful, or disorderly, however. In many cities, large street celebrations break out after professional sports teams win major titles. People who dance and drink together at Oktoberfest in Munich, Germany, share the positive experience of having fun. The heightened emotions that arise from groups of parade-goers in Rio de Janeiro during Carnival create a festive atmosphere that doesn't include violence or other negative behaviors.

Riots

Riots are related to mobs but tend to include more participants. They are unruly, unlawful, and often violent. Rioters may exhibit seemingly aimless behaviors, are spontaneously violent, may assault people or property, and are purposefully destructive (Russell 2004). Sometimes riots break out because of a perceived lack of law enforcement. Rioters are tempted by the chance to loot and steal with little or no chance of getting caught. In recreation, leisure, and experiential education settings, particularly those related to sport, riots have become increasingly common. The riot at Woodstock 1999, soccer hooliganism in Europe, and the 1994 riots in Vancouver are examples of this type of crowd in recreation, leisure, and experiential education. The psychology of mobs and riots will be discussed later in this chapter.

Panics

Panics are mobs that are scared or anxious. These feelings increase as members of the group think their chances of succeeding are growing smaller and smaller. Most panics are caused by people trying to get away from a specific situation or environment. Some are caused by people who are trying to secure a limited commodity, such as food or water, after a natural disaster.

In the classic movie *It's a Wonderful Life* (Capra 1947), the main character, George Bailey, comes face to face with a mob that is on the verge of becoming a panic. A crowd forms when people who have money deposited with George's lending company hear word of a run on the bank. This mob is on the verge of becoming a panic because its members are looking for access to limited resources: their deposits in the bank. George explains that the loan company doesn't keep large amounts of money on hand, and through some smooth talking he steers the mob away from violence.

Rumors and Mass Hysteria

Rumors feed the emotions of crowds and mobs. They are often the straw that breaks the camel's back, so to speak, and they lead to aggressive behaviors and violent actions. The rumor circulating about the final act at Woodstock 1999 certainly contributed to the rioting there. In collectives, rumors circulate and are often the only means of communication for the group because there are no formal structures to exchange information. Mobs and riots often believe rumors to be true even though there is no means to verify their accuracy (Drury 2002).

Rumors also contribute to mass hysteria, which is the occurrence of beliefs or actions that happen on the spur of the moment. These beliefs or actions are usually counter to socially accepted norms. The infamous Salem witch trials of 1692 were the result of people believing that a group of young women were witches. Several people were put to death as a result of the rumors about them. The citizens of Salem had to be careful because of the mass hysteria created by these rumors. Anyone could be labeled a witch because people were told that evil was lurking around every corner. This led to skewed perceptions about others, and many of these perceptions led to the assumption that the person was a witch.

Although mass hysteria often is viewed in a negative light, many professionals hope to create mass hysteria about their programs and services. In this sense, professionals can create a positive message and energy about what they are doing and encourage people to act in ways in which they might not normally act. Many marketing and promotion strategies hope that people will become so motivated to participate that they will go to extraordinary lengths to attend an event or a program. Used in a positive way, mass hysteria can be an effective tool for providers of recreation, leisure, and experiential education services.

Audiences

When people gather with the purpose of watching a performance, film, or some other activity, they form an audience. The behaviors of these crowds often are moderated by socially accepted norms. Audiences may clap for the performers upon completion of the show, enter and exit the venue via aisles, and secure a ticket for the performance. Audiences are common in recreation, leisure, and experiential education.

Queues

Queues, or lines of people waiting for something, are another type of collective. Most people are used to

waiting in line, and usually queues are perceived as a minor annoyance. Queues are often used to control access to a specific place or event. These lines may take many forms, from the traditional straight line to the more modern beeper style of line used by many popular restaurant chains, in which patrons are given a beeper that lights up, vibrates, or does both when it is their turn for a table.

Most people in North America accept the idea that they have to wait their turn. Many queues develop their own rules and operating procedures. For example, people who camp out for tickets to a major music concert or for play-off tickets for their hometown sports team become friendly with others in the line near them. They will often save a person's space if that person needs to leave to use the restroom or to eat. Sanctions for those who try to insert themselves into the line without waiting their turn also develop over time. These might include dirty looks, verbal confrontation, or physical action such as pushing. Most people in North America are socialized to understand that they should enter a line at the end and allow those who arrived first to have first access to the event or area.

Toolbox Tips

Using Queues to Your Advantage

Queues inevitably form at recreational, leisure, and experiential education events. Although most people accept that they sometimes have to wait in line, professionals can use this opportunity for a number of purposes. Here are some examples:

- Staff may hand out brochures about upcoming events.
- Instructors can welcome participants and answer any questions they might have about the program.
- Staff may ask participants to fill out surveys while waiting in line.
- Signs placed at strategic locations might indicate admission costs, specify rules or regulations for entry into the event, or ask participants to have identification ready when they approach the service desk.
- Mascots or other characters might greet kids waiting in line in order to keep them engaged and occupied while waiting.

Queues do not have to be negative or boring experiences. They can be fun, be informative, and serve an important administrative function as well.

Social Movements

A social movement is a collective that usually has a longer time frame than other types of collectives have. Social movements are organized with some specific purpose in mind. These movements might try to create different conditions, oppose existing conditions, or oppose a change to conditions that are of direct concern to the group. The civil rights movement in the United States is an excellent example of a social movement. People tried to create change in the U.S. social system by creating conditions that were equal for people of all racial backgrounds. Other social movements include temperance (discouraging the consumption of alcohol) and women's rights.

Trends

A trend occurs when people's actions and beliefs toward something change over time. Common social trends include what clothes are in vogue, what video games are hot, and what cocktail is the latest rage. Trends may be characterized as fads or crazes, which are usually short-term interests in a particular part of society. Trends occur often in recreation, leisure, and experiential education. For many corporations in the early 1990s, challenge courses were used to increase communication skills and decision-making skills. Rock climbers in the 1980s wore brightly colored spandex tights. Today, Global Positioning System units are the rage among hikers and other backcountry travelers.

Collectives describe many of the groups in which people find themselves. The purpose, character, and emotional nature of the group will determine which type of collective it will be. It will also determine how people will act and what influences how they act in that context. The next section describes individual behavior in collectives, and it identifies factors that influence these behaviors.

BEHAVIOR IN CROWDS

Most people find themselves in some type of crowd on a daily basis. Sometimes people unwittingly become members of a crowd when they happen to be in the place where a crowd forms. Other times people choose to be a member of a crowd. For a number of reasons, it is important to understand people's behaviors when they are in a crowd.

First, professionals work with crowds in many capacities. Preparing for how people might behave in crowds can lead to a more positive experience for both the participant and the professional. Understanding collective behaviors is important in planning special events, shows, tournaments, and other programs that large groups of people might attend.

Second, when large groups of people get together, individuals may be influenced by the experience of being in a collective. For example, many people who participate in large bicycle events are caught up in the rush of riding with thousands of others. Heightened emotions and feelings of invulnerability may cause people to behave differently than they would if they were alone or with a smaller group.

Third, as safety concerns have become increasingly important, vast sums of money are spent to provide security, crowd control, and a positive experience for those attending events. An understanding of individual and crowd behaviors can lead to financial savings and create a sense of safety and fun for participants.

Researchers have found it difficult to explain collective behaviors, particularly when these behaviors are negative, such as in riots and mobs. First, it is impossible to know when crowds will engage in negative behaviors. As such, these events are usually studied after the fact (Vider 2004). When such situations do occur, it is often difficult to identify people willing to speak about their experiences because most people do not like to talk about negative behaviors, especially when they may be illegal. Second, anecdotal accounts of these behaviors are usually reported by people who are not trained in crowd psychology. These people often falsely label a *crowd* a *mob* or call a *mob* a *riot*. Third, there is a reliance on computer models and theoretical rationale to explain crowd behaviors, but these do not seem to explain fully what happens. Finally, it is difficult to reproduce the true flavor of a crowd in a laboratory setting. Ethically, it would be irresponsible to create a situation in which a riot occurred since it would heighten the chance for physical harm or property damage.

Most people in North America know how to conduct themselves in a crowd. People have been socialized to exist in an increasingly crowded world. They wait in line until it is their turn, sit in the seat

Crowds are part of many recreation and leisure events.

assigned to them as indicated on their ticket, and respect the personal space of those around them. Earlier in this chapter the definitions for various collectives were presented. When given these definitions, most people could list a set of expected behaviors for each situation and discover that there are common behaviors that occur in all types of collectives. However, some behaviors are exclusive to each type of collective. These have been studied from a variety of perspectives, most of which have focused on the negative behaviors that emerge when collectives turn violent. It is vital to understand the relationship between the individual and the collective as well as the relationship between the collective and the individual (Vider 2004). Determining why crowds form, how crowds turn into mobs, and what psychological factors influence individual behavior in crowds will provide professionals with a better understanding of the dynamic nature of crowds.

Why Crowds Form

Crowds form and disband every minute of every day. People stop on the street to watch firefighters put out a building fire, families attend church on Sunday, theatergoers flock to the opening of a Broadway show, and basketball fans clamor for play-off tickets. Why do crowds form? The simplest explanation relates to the definition of a crowd itself: People happen to be in the same place, and they share a reason for being there. People passing by street performers on a busy summer weekend can illustrate how a crowd forms—there is a shared reason for being in that place (watching the street performer), and people choose to watch or to move along. As the crowd grows larger, the crowd itself causes people to become interested (i.e., potentially share the reason for being there). These people might not see the street performer at the center of attention, but they stop to see what is going on because their curiosity is aroused (i.e., they go to the same place as others). Once they find out that there is a street performer, they might stay and become a member of the crowd, or they move along. Another reason why people might be drawn to a collective is the need for excitement or change.

When a Crowd Becomes a Mob

One of the most studied areas of crowd behavior is crowd violence, mostly associated with mobs and riots. Sport riots have been a particular focus of many researchers in recreation, leisure, and experiential education because they often receive media attention and create an international stir.

What causes a crowd to become a mob or to riot? In 1895, Gustave Le Bon, who popularized the study of crowds with his book *The Crowd: A Study of the Popular Mind,* suggested that people in crowds lose their individual ability to function. They take on the mind of the collective, which emerges as the crowd or mob takes shape. As individuals take on the identity of the crowd, they turn irrational and reckless. Mere exposure to others who tend toward impulsive behavior is enough to persuade people to act the same way. A physician, Le Bon explained these behaviors in terms of a disease that spread from person to person and applied terms such as *feverishness* and *delirium* to the study of crowds (Drury 2002). Le Bon based these assumptions on his perspectives of the French Revolution, which he did not personally experience. The idea of a crowd as irrational was based primarily on fears that the socially elite would be overwhelmed by crazed hordes of revolutionaries (Vider 2004).

This theory serves as the basis for many modern explanations of crowd behavior. Individuals create groups, which in turn influence the individuals' future behaviors. Thus, it is necessary to understand the relationship of the individual to the group and the group to the individual.

Psychology of the Individual in Crowds

Several theories describe how individuals both influence and are influenced by groups and how this influence causes crowds to become mobs or riots. These include self-categorization theory, emergent norm theory, convergence theories, and deindividuation theory.

Self-Categorization Theory

Self-categorization theory suggests that people in groups tend to stress similarities in the group over individual differences (Vider 2004). Although this sounds somewhat like Le Bon's theory, self-categorization theory differs in that people shift their focus from individual identity (which reflects personal values, attitudes, and beliefs) to the identity of the collective (which reflects its values, attitudes, and beliefs). Through this process, the crowd comes to some understanding of appropriate behavior for that collective. These behaviors may range from standing to applaud at the end of a concert to turning over cars and setting them ablaze. How does this happen?

People socially identify with others around them and take on the voice of the collective *we*. This process is influenced both by the individual and by the collective. For example, snowball fights break out during the winter on many university campuses across North America. These snowball fights usually pit one dorm against another, with residents of each respective dorm socially identifying with others who live in the same building. But what causes the snowball fights to break out in the first place? In terms of self-categorization theory, identifying as a resident of a specific dorm is both the cause of the snowball fight and an outcome of the snowball fight. Individuals in a crowd before

the snowball fight starts may be prompted to throw snow at other individuals who identify themselves as living in another dorm. As the snowball fight breaks out and more people join, they are drawn to the collective that is defined by the dorm in which they live, thus feeding the cycle of cause and effect.

Whereas Le Bon's theory suggests that rules don't exist for mobs and riots, self-categorization theory states that members of the mob or riot feel as though new rules apply to their collective based on the attitudes and beliefs of that collective. These new rules develop into norms, which are more loosely defined than norms that small groups develop. Many people in mobs or riots assume these norms are acceptable through two main ways. First, the individual projects personal attitudes and behaviors onto others in the crowd and interprets any similar attitude or behavior as substantiation of this perspective, although this may or may not be the case. Second, bystanders who are not involved with the mob or riot often support violent or destructive actions through cheering, egging on, and pointing out new targets. Members of the mob or riot often interpret lack of condemnation as tacit support for what they are doing. This manifests itself among rioters as well, who are reluctant to point out to others that their behaviors would normally be considered inappropriate. These instances are examples of the false consensus effect.

Emergent Norm Theory

A second theory that describes how crowds turn into mobs and riots is emergent norm theory (Turner and Killian 1972). Emergent norm theory is based on the idea that mobs or riots are caused by the development of temporary norms based on members' shared understanding of the experience around them. Emergent norm theory also suggests that people come to some illusory agreement about what behaviors and actions are acceptable. People in mobs and riots justify their behaviors as acceptable because they help the group reach its goal. These behaviors may not be in line with behaviors of others in the group or with behaviors that are acceptable in normal society. However, people believe that their behaviors are OK because a goal (norm) has been established. Many of these behaviors follow from instigators in the crowd, especially as the crowd grows in size and there is more perceived support for emergent behaviors.

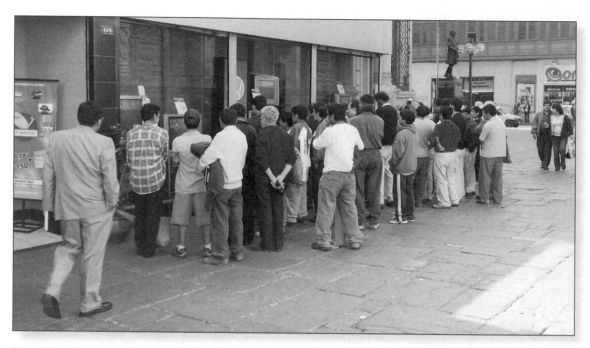

A crowd watches a soccer match in a shop window.

Convergence Theories

Convergence theories are based on the idea that a person is drawn to crowds, mobs, and riots because they are compatible with qualities that the person deems important. People join crowds, mobs, and riots because they view that experience as an opportunity to meet a need or exhibit a quality.

Many people join mobs and riots because the situation has historical connotations of violence or countercultural action. Some people have theorized that the riots at Woodstock 1999 resulted from the historical feelings of countercultural action present at the original Woodstock. Other situations such as riots at universities occur because they are associated with specific events such as homecoming games, Halloween festivities, or end-of-semester parties. People who join mobs and riots out of memory or tradition feel as though they can establish a connection to others who rioted before them, as well as create a meaningful experience for themselves as individuals (Vider 2004).

Deindividuation Theory

A final theory of crowd psychology is deindividuation theory (Zimbardo 1969). People who join mobs and riots are thought to do so because they can escape the norms and expectations of socially accepted behaviors. Deindividuation theory suggests several factors that lead to this phenomenon: anonymity, responsibility, arousal, new situation, group membership, group size, and self-awareness. The first, anonymity, often leads people to participate in destructive or violent behaviors with a mob or riot. People who think they won't be recognized or caught are more likely to join mobs. Many times people who participate in riots wear nondescript clothing or masks to hide their identity. They are comforted by the fact that others won't know who they are and can't report their actions to police or family members. The fact that many people feel uninhibited while wearing Halloween costumes is a testament to how anonymity can affect a person's choice to participate in certain behaviors.

Many people participate in riots because they do not feel responsible for the violent or aggressive behaviors. They see the responsibility for the violence or destruction as being shared with others. In some cases, people deny having any responsibility for their actions, regardless of how destructive or counter these actions are to their everyday behaviors. People are more at ease giving up responsibility because they feel that the norms of the situation allow them to behave in ways that they might normally not—it's justification for participating in the mob or riot.

Deindividuation theory also recognizes the fact that heightened or altered states of arousal influence a person's choice to join a mob or riot. Alcohol, drugs, feelings of euphoria, and feelings of invulnerability contribute to deindividuation. In essence, these states of arousal help to mask feelings, attitudes, and beliefs that might preclude someone from destructive or violent behaviors. Other examples of heightened arousal in recreation, leisure, and experiential education include loyalty to sports teams; a rush from completing a race, event, or competition; or feelings induced by listening to music concerts.

Unique situations also contribute to feelings of deindividuation. People with no experience in a certain context must rely on others for cues on how to behave. If the experienced individuals tend toward behaviors associated with mobs and riots, these actions are deemed acceptable, and inexperienced people will assume these actions are the norm. In new situations, people might not know each other, so conditions of anonymity are more likely to exist.

Group membership also influences individual behavior. Individuals by themselves cannot be deindividualized; it is affiliation with others that allows people to blend in with the group and become anonymous. People are most likely to exhibit mob and riot behaviors with others because they can hide in the pack, which is impossible in smaller groups or as an individual.

Participation in riots and mobs is also influenced by the size of the group. The larger the mob or riot, the more likely people are to participate. A large group allows people to maintain anonymity to a greater extent than smaller groups do.

A final component of deindividuation theory is self-awareness. People who lose self-awareness through lack of concern about what others think, feelings of group unity, performance of unrestrained tasks, and loss of sense of time are more likely to participate in mobs and riots.

There are many explanations for why people behave the way they do in crowds. Sometimes crowds turn ugly and mobs form or riots break out. Although not everyone in a crowd will be impelled to join in violent or destructive behaviors, they are part of a socially constructed experience that affects them and that they in turn affect. Even if someone is not participating in destructive actions, the mere presence of that person signifies support to others. As the size of a mob or riot grows, conditions become more conducive for anonymity, false consensus effects, and feelings of deindividuation. As the mob or riot takes on a life of its own, participants are more likely to assume that the behaviors exhibited around them are normal and use that as tacit support for their own behaviors. Awareness of the psychological factors that influence individuals in crowds, mobs, and riots can assist recreation, leisure, and experiential educators in planning for and dealing with situations that may arise in their programs or activities.

SPORT RIOT MODELS

Several models help define why crowds turn into mobs or riots at sporting events. Although they are intended to apply to sport riots, they can also describe crowds in other recreation, leisure, and experiential education settings.

FORCE Typology

The FORCE typology developed by Mann (1989) suggests that crowds form at sporting events out of frustration, outlawry, remonstrance, confrontation, or expression. People become frustrated for two reasons: injustice and deprivation. These feelings of frustration, particularly when many people feel the same way at the same time, may lead to mobs or riots. People interpret an injustice as unfair, perhaps because they perceive that some person or group has been unfairly sanctioned. For example, certain people might be asked to leave an event because they are being too disruptive. If others around them think this is unfair, they may form a crowd that could turn into a mob or riot. In the second case, people who are deprived may also form a mob or riot. Common occurrences of this would be lack of tickets to an event.

Outlawry is characterized by people or groups of people who use a recreation, leisure, and experiential education setting as a venue for violence in order to gain media attention. Often these groups are encountered outside athletic events.

Remonstrances are rooted in ideological differences among groups. Usually groups supporting a specific political or social agenda will attend certain events to gain exposure. If two or more groups with opposing stances are present, mobs and riots may form.

Confrontation riots occur when groups that have a history of conflict meet at recreation, leisure, and experiential education events. These conflicts usually have religious, racial, class, or economic bases.

Expressive riots tend to occur after an event or a game and are spurred by a team's win or loss. The heightened emotional state of fans and bystanders causes a mob or riot to form. The 1994 riots in Van-

couver after the Stanley Cup play-off loss of the Vancouver Canucks is an example of an expressive riot.

Issue-Oriented Versus Issueless Riots

Another model that is used to classify sport riots was developed by Smith (1983). This model categorizes sport riots into two types: issue-oriented riots and issueless riots. Figure 12.1 shows the subcategories of riots that make up these two types. Issue-oriented riots can be traced to two causes: structural sources

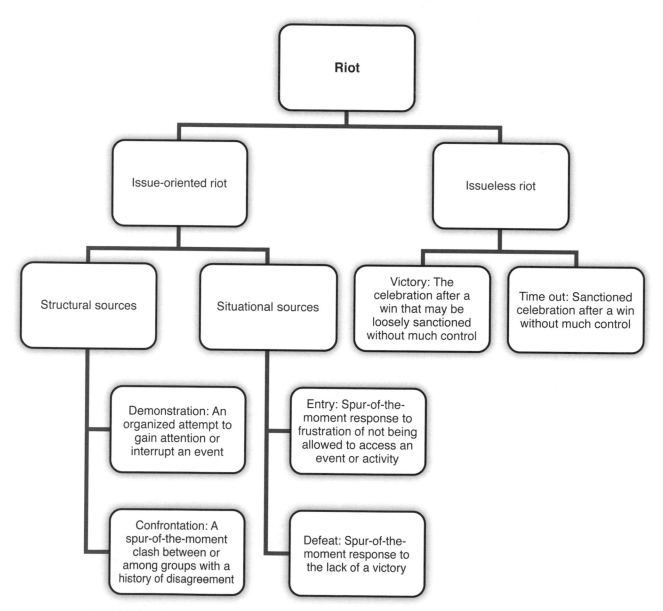

Figure 12.1 Smith's (1983) classification of sports riots.

Adapted from M.D. Smith, 1983, *Violence and sport* (Toronto, Canada: Butterworth).

and situational sources. Riots rising from structural sources usually result from people or groups trying to gain access to a sporting event or from two groups that have longstanding problems with one another. For example, many sport fans from rival teams will get into fights and cause small riots. Situational sources of riots include crowd response to a loss or defeat and a response to not being allowed access to a game.

Issueless riots are caused by celebrations after a team wins. Fans get out of control and overturn cars, smash windows, and set garbage bins on fire. A time-out is a riot that erupts from a sanctioned event during which control is temporarily lost, whereas a victory riot results from an unsanctioned event during which control is lost.

These two classifications of riots that occur in sport settings may be useful to professionals when trying to understand why a crowd might turn into a mob or riot. Looking at the underlying issues that a crowd perceives to be true will give insight as to what strategies might be implemented to dispel anger and misunderstanding before violent or destructive behavior begins. The next section gives examples of approaches to working with crowds in recreation, leisure, and experiential education settings.

STRATEGIES FOR WORKING WITH COLLECTIVES

Professionals might use many strategies when working with collectives. These include entrance restrictions, alcohol bans, physical restrictions, humor, role models, and the use of civilized nature.

Entrance restrictions have been used for crowd control since the 13th century, when attendees of knight tournaments were banned from entering the grounds with weapons that might be used to instigate fights and riots (Russell 2004). Ticket sales in general are a form of crowd control, particularly when the tickets are high priced. Some events are held in locations that are not served by public transportation in an effort to keep out troublemakers. However, many of these strategies are based on stereotypes and thus are biased, prejudiced, and sometimes illegal.

Alcohol bans are another form of crowd control. In Ontario, many provincial parks ban alcohol from campgrounds for two weeks around major summer holidays such as Canada Day. This restriction helps keep intoxicated people from creating disturbances, bothering others, or instigating others to take action to keep them quiet. At many sporting events, tailgate parties are a common part of the experience. To many pregame revelers, the tailgate party is what going to the game is all about. However, some stadium officials have banned the consumption of alcohol outside sporting arenas as a means of preventing trouble inside the event. Many stadiums also have alcohol-free seating areas, which are intended for families and for people who do not want to be in the presence of fans under the influence of alcohol. Event staff members should be trained in methods of effectively talking to people under the influence of alcohol or drugs so they can prevent fights and riots from breaking out.

Professionals can use physical restrictions to help control crowds as well. Most people are familiar with fences, hedgerows, and gates that either allow or restrict access to specific parts of an event. Sometimes event attendees are purposefully segregated from one another as a means of minimizing contact. At many university football games, tickets are sold in blocks to fans from the visiting university. Physical restrictions in terms of security personnel may also serve as crowd control. However, the mere presence of security personnel might provide a point on which mobs can focus their aggression and cause a riot.

The use of humor by event personnel in dealing with unruly crowd members may also dissuade crowds from becoming too aggressive. Security personnel should be trained to deal with aggressive attendees in a personable and professional manner. Many disturbances that get out of control are because of perceived conflict between event personnel and attendees who feel slighted or that the event personnel are exercising too much authority. However, event personnel should also be trained to deal with people who might need to be removed physically from a situation in order to prevent fights, violence, or destruction. In some cases, event personnel might experience better luck with crowd control by letting some instances go unaddressed. The littlest thing can serve as the straw that breaks the camel's back and leads to a crowd, mob, or riot.

Role models might also help control crowd behaviors. These people may take on the role of good-natured cheerleaders or serve as liaisons between security personnel and crowd members. Role models can also alert event personnel to the undercurrents and rumors that inevitably precede mobs and riots. Professionals might consider hiring people specifically for this role or planting employees in the crowd to serve as role models.

A final crowd-control technique that professionals might use is civilized nature (Wright 2006). This process uses carefully designed site layouts to prevent crowds from accessing areas they shouldn't or from forming mobs or riots. For example, many of the backstage areas of Walt Disney World do not have signs restricting access but instead use natural features such as long curves, changes in light, or untamed nature to suggest that access isn't allowed (Wright 2006). Other ways civilized nature might be used is through the choice of colors, light, and sound. Some colors, lights, and sounds may prompt people to behave in ways that could lead to aggression. Creating conditions that appear calm and orderly will help in maintaining crowd control. Although some crowds will inevitably turn into mobs or riots, these strategies provide a place for professionals to start while making plans to control crowds at events. Some of these strategies may also be helpful for people who inadvertently find themselves in the midst of a crowd that is growing angry!

SUMMARY

For many recreation, leisure, and experiential education professionals, working with collectives is a daily part of the job. Sometimes these professionals might not even know that these types of collectives (e.g., queues) exist in their programs. Understanding the characteristics of different collectives will help professionals understand how people in those situations might behave. Self-categorization theory, deindividuation theory, emergent norm theory, convergence theories, and Le Bon's notion of crowd psychology provide insight into the inner workings of crowd members' minds.

This chapter identified several key factors, such as the false consensus effect, rumors, and perceptions of a *we* mentality, that influence individual behaviors in crowds, mobs, and riots. Two models of classifying sport riots were presented, as were specific strategies for controlling crowds in recreation, leisure, and experiential education.

RESOURCES

Capra, F., director. 1947. *It's a wonderful life.* Liberty Films.

Drury, J. 2002. 'When the mobs are looking for witches to burn, nobody's safe:' Talking about the reactionary crowd. *Discourse and Society* 13(1): 41-73.

Forsyth, D. 2006. *Group dynamics.* 4th ed. Belmont, CA: Thomson Wadsworth.

Le Bon, G. 1895. *The crowd: A study of the popular mind.* Repr., London: Transaction Publishers, 1995.

Mann, L. 1989. Sports crowds and the collective behavior perspective. In *Sports, games and play.* 2nd ed., ed. J.H. Goldstein. Hillsdale, NJ: Erlbaum, 229-327.

Milgram, S., L. Bickman, and L. Berkowitz. 1969. Note on the drawing power of crowds of different size. *Journal of Personality and Social Psychology* 13:79-82.

Russell, G.W. 2004. Sport riots: A social-psychological review. *Aggression and Violent Behavior* 9:353-78.

Smith, M.D. 1983. *Violence and sport.* Toronto, ON: Butterworths.

Turner, R.H., and L. Killian. 1972. *Collective behavior.* Englewood Cliffs, NJ: Prentice Hall.

Vider, S. 2004. Rethinking crowd violence: Self-categorization theory and the Woodstock 1999 riot. *Journal for the Theory of Social Behaviour* 34(2): 141-66.

Wright, C. 2006. Natural and social order at Walt Disney World: The functions and contradictions of civilising nature. *The Sociological Review* 54:303-17.

Zimbardo, P.G. 1969. The human choice: Individualization, reason, and order versus deindividualization, impulse and chaos. *Nebraska Symposium on Motivation* 17:237-307.

CHAPTER

13

Alternative Groups

Darek wasn't sure if his success as a recreation coordinator for a seniors' center was because he was good or just lucky. He had started the volunteer position a few months ago when the center lost its funding for a paid recreation director. Darek didn't know what kinds of recreation opportunities were available for older adults or even how people a little older than he was thought they should spend their free time. He chuckled to himself thinking that he was probably going to learn more about recreation from them than they were going to learn from him. He couldn't quite believe that the center agreed to take him on—he figured the center must be desperate to fill the position.

Darek decided that if he didn't know all the answers (or in his case, almost any of them), he would simply help the participants to become the experts. He had read somewhere that if people stay mentally active they tend to stay sharper for longer in life. So, with a vague plan, Darek went to the center for his first day to meet one group of septuagenarians. He was informed that this group was a little difficult, and although the group members participated in the activities organized by the previous recreation director, they never seemed quite happy about it. When he had introduced himself to the group, Darek asked, "So, what do you folks like to do?" The response was rather pointed: "That's your job, Sonny!"

After a disastrous first day, Darek reflected on what went wrong and reformulated his plan. The center's director had told him that in the past, this group had always let the recreation director plan the events. She also let him know that many members had shown interest in sudoku, a type of number puzzle that wasn't overly active and tended to be a solo pastime. However, Darek was interested in changing the way the group members interacted with each other. The physical activity could come later, when they were more motivated. The challenge for Darek was taking them from a passive, uninterested group to a collection of involved and motivated seniors engaged with planning their own activities.

The next time he met the group, Darek proposed a group sudoku tournament. Virtually everyone looked surprised, and two newer members of the group said they'd never even heard of sudoku. Darek had anticipated and even hoped for this because it allowed him to put his plan into effect. He explained that he had an idea for a team approach that would have groups of three or even four members trying to solve the puzzle together instead of individually. Then he asked for a volunteer to show the whole group how sudoku was played. Second, he suggested that because they knew each other better than he did, they should divide themselves into fair teams. The group members got busy and in no time were ready to start. The tournament was a big success and everyone left with a smile, including Darek.

Over the next few weeks, Darek helped the group move away from being dependent on him to being able to generate its own activities. The director of the center mentioned that she'd never seen the group so happy and involved. But more importantly, the group members recognized the benefits of taking responsibility for their own planning and learning—they became reinvested in living their own lives again, and their relationships with each other improved. Eventually, the group reached the point of simply informing Darek what would be happening the next week and asking him if he would mind picking up a few things that were on the other side of town. Darek didn't mind at all—at least the seniors still needed him for something!

Alternative groups exist in virtually every aspect of social life that encourages the formation of groups. Alternative music, art, dance, medicine, education, lifestyle, family, media, dispute resolution, legal sentencing, and even mathematics all have groups that have formed around the principles and ideas driving them.

For the most part, this book has dealt with groups that fit within mainstream recreation (e.g., summer camps, organizational committees). But a surprising number of people have attempted to organize themselves into groups that seek a different way to conduct their activities, to relate to each other, and to simply *be*. From street gangs to communes, the desire to form associations that run counter to the larger societies they exist in is worthy of attention. There are lessons to be learned from groups that do not conform to social norms.

To get a feel for being part of a group that is intentionally different, first we will consider what is mainstream and then we will visit alternative approaches to organizing groups that have some relevance for the recreation field. Although there are many examples even in this narrowed field, we will focus on two types: consensus-based and participant-centered groups.

ALTERNATIVE GROUPS DEFINED

What does it mean to be alternative? The concept of alternativeness is steeped in contrast. In order for anything to be considered alternative, it must be different and stand apart from something else. In this chapter, the word *alternative* is used to convey that which is considered in contrast to the mainstream, conventional, or accepted practice. In the context of groups, it's important to decide what is mainstream

and what is not in order to reduce confusion between the uniqueness—the individual character—of all groups and those that are truly different. All groups are unique, and so it could be said that each one is also alternative to some degree, but there is a fuzzy dividing line that makes some groups more alternative than others.

Something that is considered to be mainstream generally represents the current thought and practices of the majority, or at least of a large and accepted minority. In some situations, it is clear whether a group is part of the mainstream or is alternative. For example, a basketball, soccer, or hockey team usually is considered mainstream, whereas an Ultimate Frisbee league usually is considered alternative. Going to the beach is a fairly mainstream summer activity, but taking advantage of clothing-optional beaches is still a pursuit for a relatively small number of people.

On the other hand, it's not always evident whether something is alternative. A developing trend, for instance, may be gaining in popularity and transitioning from alternative to mainstream. Environmental concerns such as climate change were largely the domain of tree huggers and scientists before the year 2000, but they have received much more media attention since then and have gained prominence as a matter of social importance. Still, it is difficult to say whether concern over environmental issues has translated into mainstream practices. Although many positive initiatives are occurring, it can also be said that consumption and the production of harmful wastes are at unsustainable levels.

The notion of alternativeness is complicated further by its relation to the social and cultural context used to describe it. What is alternative in one part of the world might be mainstream in another. For example, from a Western perspective, faiths other than Chris-

Learning Activity

Reflect on groups you've been part of in your lifetime. Describe common elements in how those groups are organized (e.g., whether they all have leaders, how they make decisions, what kinds of goals unify the members). Did the way in which the group was organized make a difference in how the group members related to each other? Now describe groups that you know about that seem to be organized differently than most are organized. What makes these groups seem different? Do you think the differences help the groups accomplish their goals?

tianity are not part of the mainstream—the widely celebrated holidays in North America emphasize this fact. However, Hinduism is mainstream rather than alternative in India, and historically, paganism was mainstream in Ireland before the arrival of St. Patrick and the Holy Roman Empire.

In a recreation context, snowboarding was considered alternative, even radical and undesirable, not that long ago. Many ski resorts initially did not even allow snowboarders on the slopes. Today virtually all ski resorts not only accept snowboarding but also spend time and money catering to this style of downhill fun. Snowboarding is big business and despite its alternative roots, it can be argued that snowboarding has now become part of the mainstream. That said, in order to speak about anything alternative, there must be a starting point from which to provide the contrast, and we make the admission that alternativeness is seen from the perspective of this text and its authors' rootedness in North American culture of the late 20th and early 21st centuries.

In addition to the activities and leisure pursuits that people choose to get involved in, the way in which groups organize themselves can be traditional or alternative. The standard game of Ultimate has no referee, a purposeful choice that was made to foster cooperation and integrity among players, even in the context of fierce competition. This has been modified in more recent times, especially for high-level play, but many players still adhere to the principles, and refereeing is not the norm among recreational leagues.

Even in mainstream activities, groups can organize themselves in alternative ways. From alternative school models that emphasize student empowerment in directing their own education to companies breaking the mold of the traditional workplace environment by allowing pets to accompany employees, there is a great deal of room to organize groups in ways that differ from the mainstream but meet the needs of members. At the beginning of the chapter, we mentioned summer camps as mainstream, but that doesn't mean all camps are mainstream or that mainstream camps are limited to mainstream organizational structures. Breaking the mold can come in the form of relatively minor adjustments, such as the director of a small camp asking each staff member to run one camp meeting over the summer. Such a small difference in organization could have ripple effects in terms of how staff members see their own potential for administrative leadership in the future. The possibilities are endless; what you are encouraged to do with this chapter is to take in the general principles of the alternative groups outlined here and reflect on how they may apply to your situation. This chapter focuses on two alternative approaches to the organization and function of groups that could be applied in a variety of settings.

CONSENSUS-BASED GROUPS

In its simplest form, consensus is arriving at a decision that all group members can support. It tends to avoid or even reject voting as a way of making decisions, and it is predicated on the idea that cooperation and a commitment to the group will make for a better outcome. Many groups operating within a consensus

In most recreational games of Ultimate, players referee themselves.

Gurumustuk Singh—www.sikhphotos.com

framework do so in keeping with this understanding, but in a loose and unstructured fashion. They do not impose many rules or employ systematic protocols in coming to their decisions. For many groups, consensus means that everyone in the group needs to agree on the outcome. These groups generally are using informal consensus. Formal consensus, on the other hand, can involve complex procedures for discussion and decision making, rivaling the elaborate processes of parliamentary procedure. (Governed by *Robert's Rules of Order* and majority voting, parliamentary procedure is the norm for conducting most meetings and other formal business not only in the corporate world but also in other organizations, including community groups that have a seriousness of purpose.) Groups that have chosen formal consensus for conducting their meetings generally are unsatisfied with what they see as the competitive and hierarchical principles that govern parliamentary procedure and believe that a different set of values should govern their interaction.

Principles of Consensus

Proponents of consensus-based groups maintain that members of these groups are more involved in making

a decision and that they are more likely to help implement it when it is reached. A commitment to the group and equality among members are hallmarks of consensus. With this in mind, let's outline these underlying principles.

Commitment to the Group

Consensus begins with a commitment to the group and its purpose, goals, and objectives. A fundamental principle driving successful consensus groups is that members must give up self-interested participation. That isn't to say that people must melt into a group identity, but members must ask themselves if they are presenting positions that are best for the group as a whole. Of course, personal interests and group well-being should be aligned to some degree—or else there is little reason to be part of the group—but consensus decision making rejects the attempt by group members to bend the interests of the group to fit their own.

Consensus is not about compromise. A misconception about consensus decision making is that it results in watered-down solutions that attempt to make everyone happy. If everyone's personal needs must be satisfied before the group members all agree, then it is true that a poor decision may be reached. However, true consensus asks participants to shed their selfish interests. In other words, if your original position is shown to be less aligned with what is best for the group, you should be happy that a better decision is in the making. Ultimately, whatever solution arises out of the discussion should be oriented to the purpose, goals, and objectives of the group, and if members are truly committed to the group, there is no need for a compromise. In consensus, a decision is not about protecting your own ideas or your own ego. Instead, it is about using everyone's experience and brain power to come up with the best solution to the problem.

Included in a commitment to the group is a commitment to open,

Members of consensus-based groups are committed to making decisions that are best for the group.

© Human Kinetics

respectful dialogue. Most consensus-based groups have either an informal or a more structured understanding of how people should participate and speak to one another. The details of this are covered in the Process of Consensus section on this page, but the basic principle of respectful dialogue helps to ensure that a safe environment exists for anyone wishing to participate in a discussion.

Egalitarian Participation

Egalitarianism, the belief that all group members are equal and so deserve equal rights and opportunities for input, is a dominant theme in consensus. Consensus decision making does not allow for hierarchical structures within a group. There is no permanent boss or chairperson, and ideas are judged on their merit, not on who voices them. Because each member of the group is considered of equal importance, and each person is committed to the group, no one person should be given any more value—or power—than another. In addition, valuing all members also means valuing their input, so active participation in discussions is sought. In true consensus, it is rare that a person does not say anything, especially when discussing important matters.

No actions are taken until all members agree with a decision or at least support it enough not to obstruct it. In consensus, anyone with a valid concern has the power to block a decision from being adopted. This principle supports the idea of egalitarianism, giving each person the same level of power in the group. It also promotes a shared responsibility for decisions. Group members are more likely to work toward the implementation of a decision if they feel connected to its creation. Conversely, if a particular solution does not work out well, no one should be able to reprimand the rest of the group by saying, "I told you so." Perhaps most significantly, this principle suggests that a better solution is more likely to surface if everyone is equally responsible for its development.

Process of Consensus

There is no universally accepted method of conducting group business by consensus. Groups must decide how they wish to implement this form of decision making and alter the process as needed to make it work in their particular circumstances. Despite not being standardized, there are accepted practices followed by most groups. As mentioned, informal consensus involves a casual approach with a general understanding that everyone should agree before proceeding. The exact method of how the group reaches that agreement is loose and the process is open.

Formal consensus is a more conscious approach and consists of specific steps in the course of making a decision. No universal code exists by which all formal consensus groups must abide, but there are some generally followed practices. The steps outlined next provide a fairly common foundation for putting consensus decision making into effect.

Introduction

As with any other formal organization, items for discussion should be introduced to the membership within a reasonable time before a meeting. Distributing the item (in writing if possible) with accompanying information demonstrates respect for group members and allows people time to reflect on the issue in advance.

Clarification

In this stage, the item is introduced (or reintroduced with a brief explanation of its history if it has been discussed previously) and a call for clarification is made. This is an invitation for people to ask questions that will enhance understanding of the issue. The questions should focus strictly on increased comprehension of the issue at hand and should not become sidetracked by concerns related to an outcome. Once the questions of clarification have been satisfied, a discussion on the item ensues.

Discussion

The discussion phase is when concerns about the item and questions of compatibility with group goals are raised. The discussion may range from the philosophical to the specifics of logistics and implementation. It may even be wise to organize the discussion in a way that moves from the general to the concrete, especially if the item is complex, but doing so is not necessary. Questions and concerns should be added to a list as they arise. It is during discussion that each person is encouraged to speak. Additional information may be added, questions answered, and concerns addressed.

Being open to the substance of the discussion is of particular significance in this part of the process; it is an opportunity to look at the issue from different points of view. Those who initially attended the meeting leaning toward the proposal should reflect on the inherent problems it may bring. Conversely, anyone entering with a negative sentiment would benefit the group by attempting to recognize the benefits of the proposal. Once there is a general sense that the group may be moving in a certain direction with regard to the item, a call for consensus can be made by the facilitator.

Call for Consensus

The call for consensus may happen in a variety of ways. Some models involve each member voicing agreement or disagreement or holding up a color-coded card indicating the same. Butler and Rothstein (1991) explain a process in which the facilitator asks if there are any further concerns. Consensus is then reached if, after an appropriate amount of time, there is silence from all group members. If there are outstanding concerns, focused discussion on those concerns is warranted. The process then repeats itself until all concerns have been addressed and consensus is reached.

Throughout the decision-making process, a proposal may be modified as a result of discussion and information that comes to light. For complex issues, it is often seen as a positive sign that an original proposal is modified, because modification represents progress toward a solution that reflects the collaborative efforts of the group members. In other words, carefully considered modifications most likely indicate a superior decision. Once a decision is made, everyone commits to working toward its successful implementation. Figure 13.1 shows how decisions are achieved in formal consensus and provides options when consensus is difficult to reach.

If Consensus Can't Be Reached

Group members have several options if consensus is not forthcoming. First, if time is a concern, the item can be referred to a committee. The committee can be given the responsibility to deliberate on the topic at a later time and then report at the next meeting any further insights it might have generated. If the discussion is intense, referring to committee may also lower the level of anxiety.

Second, any member may decide to stand aside. Such a decision is taken if a concern has been discussed completely yet has no resolution. A member may not agree with a proposal but also not disagree enough to block its adoption. In formal meetings, the disagreement is noted along with the larger decision. This action gives the concern the ability to be raised again at a later date.

A serious disagreement by any member may result in that member blocking the proposal. As mentioned earlier, every participant has the authority to veto a proposed action. A block, especially when it is delivered by one person, is a serious prospect, and group members are encouraged to think about their reasons for doing so. Reasoning must be considered valid in order to block a proposal, with the definition of valid reasoning up to the group in setting out its process and procedures. The rationale for demonstrating the validity of a concern is that it prevents members from blocking proposals for selfish reasons. With this requirement, one person or small group cannot stubbornly hold a concern without a reasonable explanation. In other words, it is not sufficient for people to simply say they are blocking a proposal simply because they don't agree with it.

Roles and Responsibilities

Because there is no permanent leadership position within true consensus groups, the roles that help meetings run smoothly are assigned on a temporary, rotating basis. The key role of facilitator involves making sure that the agenda is covered, procedures are followed, and members abide by the agreed-upon rules of discussion. Additionally, facilitators are usually charged with watching the tone of the group in order to gauge when to call for consensus. Normally, a facilitator will avoid direct participation in a discussion. If facilitators wish to speak to a proposal, they are required to pass on the role, at least temporarily.

Timekeeper is another important role in consensus meetings. This person keeps the discussion on track by watching the time during discussions. Because meetings almost always cover more than one topic,

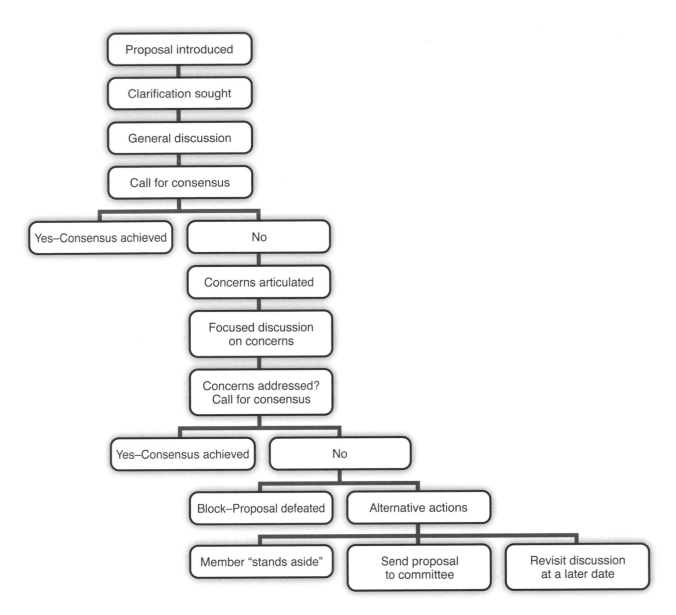

Figure 13.1 A decision-making flow chart for formal consensus.

adequate time must be allocated to each one. It is the timekeeper's responsibility to monitor this aspect of the meeting and to announce when time is running short. In conjunction with the facilitator, the timekeeper may also ensure that certain people do not dominate a meeting by speaking for an excessive amount of time.

Much like a secretary in mainstream meetings, the note taker is responsible for generating a written record of the meeting and its decisions. In most consensus groups, emphasis is placed on recording the discussion and any dissenting positions registered

during the meeting. Unresolved concerns and reasons for a member's decision to stand aside, for example, are entered along with the discussion record and the adoption of any proposal.

Benefits and Pitfalls of Consensus

Several benefits are claimed by practitioners of consensus decision making, and a way of doing things would not be complete without its critics. Here are some of the common declarations made on either side.

Benefits

When followed with integrity and an atmosphere of openness, the process of consensus contains a variety of advantages. Though not an exhaustive list, some of the common advantages are the following:

- It almost always leads to decisions that are well thought out. Active participation by all members in a group increases the number of minds working toward a solution and reduces the passivity that may exist in more mainstream groups.

- It is one of the most inclusive forms of decision making.

- It reduces intragroup competition and strategizing. The philosophical orientation of consensus is toward collaboration and cooperation, so if group members act on this principle, the tendency toward competition is reduced at the outset. The requirements for reaching consensus—the ideal of unanimity—are concrete applications of this philosophical position, and, if followed, meetings cannot be dominated by anyone nor can decisions be sabotaged.

- It creates increased commitment because members all agree with the decision on some level.

Pitfalls

Critics claim that the ideals put forward by consensus models do not necessarily translate into effective outcomes. The following are some of the recurring issues:

- The process is time consuming. Being so methodical and inclusive in making decisions can become inefficient and bog down discussion. There are times when a decision simply needs to be made.

- A possibly unrealistic level of commitment is required. If not all members are committed to the process, there is no point in proceeding because the underlying principles will be compromised anyway. For instance, if certain members within the larger group have no desire to work for the good of the collective and are focused on personal interests, any decision will be compromised and is unlikely to receive full support in its implementation.

- If the group lacks common purpose, commitment will decrease and discussion can become burdensome. This can be true of any group, but especially so for consensus-based groups.

- Achieving consensus in large groups is impractical.

These points are not facts, but are contentions made by proponents and critics of consensus. For example, proponents claim that group decisions on any complex issue are always time consuming, no matter what method is used. Although the decision itself can be made rather efficiently by a leader, many would argue that unless the people who are to implement that decision feel represented, the decision may be ineffective in the long run. If you are interested in consensus as an organizational approach for a group you work with, there are resources that go into greater depth regarding not only the principles and philosophy but also concrete steps for putting consensus decision making into practice (see Butter and Rothstein 1991; Snyder 2001; and Susskind, McKearnan, and Thomas-Larmer 1999 in the Resources, page 169).

Examples of Consensus Groups

Consensus has been implemented in a variety of groups that have sought an alternative approach to the issues that face them. Two examples are provided in this section. The first involves an environmental action campaign that relied on a constant inflow and outflow of people at the base of operations. This setup meant, of course, that the group membership was continuously changing, often on a daily basis. The second example introduces consensus as a mainstay of a stable community life that has been practiced in this tradition for generations.

Franklin River Blockade

In 1981 and 1982, the Tasmanian Wilderness Society organized a continuous human blockade of the Franklin River, preventing materials from being barged to a proposed dam site. People traveled from all across the country to a site in southwest Tasmania to receive a mandatory three days of nonviolent action training before moving on to a riverside camp where they could string themselves across the river in small rafts. When the protestors were arrested, they were replaced with more from the pool of volunteers. The organizers captured the imagination of the country and were able to keep up a blockade over months of the campaign. Ultimately, the activism was successful. A national election was under way at the time and the leader of one party promised to stop the construction of the dam. That party won the election and fulfilled the promise. The Franklin River success has been a model for other groups in planning their own activism.

Every morning at the training site, a meeting was held with everyone who was in residence. Information was provided on the progress of the protest and news on the issue was reported from around the country. Any decisions, including matters of strategy, were made by consensus of those in attendance. Even press releases were discussed during these meetings. Considering the transient nature of the training camp, this was an incredible accomplishment. Thousands of people were trained and subsequently arrested. All of these people not only offered their bodies for a blockade begun by the Tasmanian Wilderness Society but also had an equal say in how the campaign should be run. In the end, the attachment of the participants in the Franklin River protest helped create a momentum that placed an environmental issue at center stage during a national election.

Religious Society of Friends

Also known as *Quakers,* the Religious Society of Friends is a religious organization that was begun by George Fox in England in the 17th century. Friends believe that all people have equal access to spiritual messages and that there is no need for a hierarchical structure within a spiritual community. Quakerism also states explicitly that women and men are equal, and the belief that women could provide ministry was controversial for its day. Quaker meetings are run following a consensus structure.

One of the key tenets that is illustrated consistently in consensus-based groups is a lack of leadership—no one person or collection of persons occupies permanent positions that provide direction for a larger body of people. The positions of chair and secretary, for example, are rotated among members of the Society of Friends so that no one person or small group controls the agenda or the way minutes are recorded. All members are expected to contribute to the decisions affecting the community.

PARTICIPANT-CENTERED GROUPS

In participant-centered groups, the group activity focuses on the participant, meaning that the activities should meet the participants' needs and goals rather than the leader's conception of what should happen. Most formal groups are centered more on the leader, even among groups that think of themselves as participant centered (Estes 2004). In leader-centered groups, both the process and the outcome are driven by the leader and other external forces. The typical classroom in most schools is an example of a leader-centered group. The teacher sets the lesson and delivers information based on a curriculum that is set by experts who have a great deal of knowledge and training but little or no knowledge of the community the school exists in or of the particular class and its teacher. By contrast, in participant-centered groups, each person is the most important part of the equation—not the externally developed program or curriculum.

A participant-centered approach should begin by asking what the person wants and needs from the experience. The answers are used as a starting point for designing and implementing the experience. However, the leader does not simply take that information and create the plan; rather, he tries to act as a resource and a mentor, providing feedback and questions to encourage participants' development. In doing this, teachers and leaders move from directing an activity to facilitating an activity, which is at the heart of participant-centered experiences.

Alternative educators and researchers have been responsible for much of the development of student-centered learning, a participant-centered approach that is specific to education. Student-centered learning consists of the following characteristics:

- Students are intrinsically motivated to learn.

- Students are involved in their own learning; they are not passive receivers of knowledge.

- Students take responsibility for what and how they learn.

- Students assess themselves and the work they produce.

- Students work in collaboration with teachers and other students while learning instead of working at the direction of the teacher.

Students learn best when they are involved and the material is meaningful to them.

- Teachers act as facilitators, asking questions designed to stimulate problem solving.

- Teachers acknowledge different learning styles among students in order to facilitate individual learning.

John Dewey, an education philosopher, argued that students do not learn well as passive receivers of information. In order for real learning to occur, the information has to be relevant to the students and their lives, with the students integrating what they learn into experiences beyond the classroom. Jean Piaget, a developmental psychologist, maintained that knowledge does not merely arrive from the world outside of learners; instead, learners take in information and test it against what they already know. In a sense, people are active in the construction of their knowledge because they are free to accept, modify, or reject what they encounter. Lev Vygotsky, a Russian developmental theorist who is perhaps less well known to Western audiences, wrote about the intersection among knowledge, the child, and culture. In developing a theory referred to as *cultural mediation,* Vygotsky looked at how children constructed meaning out of events and objects that are part of their culture.

Taken together, the ideas of these three theorists influenced progressive educators as they reformulated how children learn and therefore how education should be practiced. If you take the perspective that people learn best when knowledge is relevant beyond the immediate lesson and that learners are active participants in the generation of knowledge that has meaning for them, you may begin to question the way in which lessons have been delivered.

The tenets of participant-centered learning hold true for recreation groups. Many proponents of experiential education say that good recreation and good education may not be separate if the participants are actively engaged in the experience, appropriately challenged, and reflecting on the experience as potentially transformative. Many recreational pursuits and settings involve learning, particularly in organized recreation. Skills and technical competence, knowledge of rules and operational procedures, and navigation of social norms are some shared elements that involve learning in recreation and leisure settings. In addition, if participants are to stay interested and involved, facilitating recreational experiences requires that participants fully engage in an activity that has relevance for them.

A participant-centered approach is particularly relevant for those who are striving to foster a conscious group. If group members become empowered and more involved in planning the outcomes for themselves, they are also required to take on more responsibility for realizing those outcomes. They are obligated to become more aware of their roles and what is needed to reach the goals that they set for themselves and the group. Experiential education with participant-centered principles for learning and solving problems can lead to a more conscious group dynamic. Recall the opening scenario with Darek and the success he achieved with his group. Another reading of Darek's situation will reveal that the group became more participant-centered and, as a result, self-aware. It was at that point that the group was able to see the solutions to problems. In becoming more conscious, the group also became more effective. A participant-centered approach is one way in which facilitators can help groups move in this direction.

WORKING WITH ALTERNATIVE RECREATION GROUPS

Any recreation group will need to reflect on how its administrative and decision-making structure will be affected by the group's purpose and the goals driving its existence. If you belong to a group that is partially or wholly alternative in its approach, here are some hints that will allow you to function more effectively, especially if your experience with that group is limited:

• **Be patient with others and with yourself.** If you have never been exposed to an alternative group and how it functions, there is a good chance that you may become frustrated with processes and norms that are different than what you have known. Many people have felt anxious at a perceived lack of progress in trying to make decisions by true consensus, for example. Ask yourself if there is a need to feel frustrated with what is happening.

• **Try to understand the underlying rationale for the alternative approach.** Understanding the underlying philosophy of the group and what it hopes to achieve will undoubtedly help in deciding whether the approach is warranted by the guiding theory or doctrine of the group.

• **Get to know the procedures and alternative norms.** Feeling lost in a group culture that is so different from previous experiences can be disconcerting. Once you learn the expectations of interaction, the situation will begin to feel normal. Don't be afraid to ask questions. Put forward in a tone that indicates your desire to understand the process, your questions will not only orient you to the group but also require group members to validate their own practices.

Whether you join a group that is intentionally alternative, become a member of a group that has little or no experience in alternative approaches but would like to explore the idea, or are asked to implement an alternative decision-making structure for an agency you work for, the concepts and advice in this chapter will provide you with a good start.

SUMMARY

Alternative groups may be less visible because society's focus is on the mainstream. However, difference is now more celebrated and alternative groups can be found everywhere in social life. This chapter explored what it means to be considered alternative: intentionally in contrast to the dominant thoughts and practices of the larger society. Two examples of alternative groups were presented (consensus-based groups and participant-centered groups) and explanations of how these types of groups operate and organize themselves were provided in some detail. Finally, some practical advice for functioning as a member of an alternatively organized group was offered.

RESOURCES

Butler, L., and A. Rothstein. 1991. *Conflict and consensus: A handbook on formal consensus decision making.* Tacoma Park, MD: Food Not Bombs Publishing.

Daniels, H., ed. 1996. *An introduction to Vygotsky.* London: Routledge.

Dewey, J. 1938. *Experience and education.* New York: Macmillan.

Estes, C. 2004. Promoting student-centered learning in experiential education. *Journal of Experiential Education* 27(2): 141-61.

Piaget, J. 1955. *The child's construction of reality.* London: Routledge & Kegan Paul.

Robert, H.M. 2000. *Robert's rules of order newly revised,* 10th ed. Cambridge, MA: Perseus Books Group.

Snyder, M. 2001. *Building consensus: Conflict and unity.* Richmond, IN: Earlham Press.

Susskind, L., S. McKearnan, and J. Thomas-Larmer, eds. 1999. *The consensus building handbook: A comprehensive guide to reaching agreement.* Thousand Oaks, CA: Sage Publications.

CHAPTER

14

Diversity

It is the first day of a three-week adventure sailing trip up the Inside Passage of British Columbia to Alaska. People on the trip are expected to help out with sailing, cooking, and other chores. Clients have been loading their baggage and getting to know one another on deck. A van pulls up and a man and woman get out, unload and get into their wheelchairs, and bring their luggage to the boat. One of the clients who are already on board approaches Kat, a crew member, and says, "I didn't know people with disabilities were going to be on this trip! I sure hope they can help out as much as I can, because I didn't come on this trip to take care of a couple of cripples!" Kat isn't sure how to respond—she hasn't had much experience working with people with disabilities. In fact, the people she's worked with on previous sailing trips have been pretty much the same. Kat thinks to herself, "What do I do now? I have to spend three weeks with this group of clients, and I've never had to work with such a diverse group of people!"

Diversity is the spice of life! Imagine what the world would be like if all people were the same—everyone would eat the same food, think the same thoughts, wear the same clothes, and play the same games. Without diversity, the world would be a stale, uninteresting place, particularly in terms of recreation, leisure, and experiential education. Individuals can benefit from engaging in recreation, leisure, and experiential education activities with diverse groups of people. Leaders and facilitators don't need to know everything about all the diverse types of people they might work with. However, group leaders and facilitators who know a little about how diverse groups work and how to capitalize on the positive aspects of diverse groups will find that this knowledge makes their jobs easier. Additionally, this information will allow leaders and facilitators to design and deliver programs that are friendly and inviting to a wide range of people.

Chapter 2 opened with a meeting of a typical recreation, leisure, and experiential education committee. This committee was responsible for planning, running, and evaluating the Waterfront Extravaganza that was six months away. The people who were on the committee were there for a number of reasons, but not much other information was given on how these people varied. What if these people were different in terms of race, ethnicity, sexual orientation, religious beliefs, disability status, gender, and age? Would vastly different backgrounds and personal characteristics affect how the committee functioned? Would diversity affect the way in which the leader worked with the committee? This chapter examines diversity and looks at some of the benefits of working with groups that are made up of people with different characteristics.

THE SHRINKING WORLD

The population of North America is very diverse. The United States prides itself on being a melting pot where people from around the world make their dreams come true. North American history is filled with tales of how people with diverse backgrounds have affected the economy, industry, and fabric of society. If you visit any part of North America, you can see how people of diverse backgrounds have integrated into the everyday life of society. Recreation, leisure, and experiential education professionals are in an ideal position to capitalize on what diversity brings to the modern world.

With the increased use of the Internet, video conferencing, computer technology, and wireless communications systems, the world is becoming a much smaller place. Transportation and international business have also helped form connections among nations and people—connections that were almost nonexistent less than 25 years ago. It is common for corporations to have branches in several countries around the world. This globalization of the marketplace requires a diverse array of people who speak a number of languages and are familiar with how consumers use products and services in different regions of the world. Through globalization people are exposed to different forms of recreation, leisure, and experiential education, which they then integrate into their own practice.

Understanding dissimilarities and focusing on similarities help diverse group members to work together.

Most of society will begin interacting more and more frequently with people who are increasingly diverse in a myriad of ways. A glance at the magazines and newspapers sitting on a newsstand in any city in North America provides an idea of the existing diversity of languages, ethnic and cultural backgrounds, political affiliations, religious beliefs, and other lifestyle choices. As individuals become members of the global society, facilitators and leaders must become equipped with the skills and knowledge to work with diverse groups of people, particularly when the people in the group might not be as practiced, skilled, or knowledgeable in working with diversity.

TYPES OF DIVERSITY

Diversity is the similarity and dissimilarity occurring among group members. A group that shares characteristics or whose members are very similar is a homogeneous group. A group that has characteristics that vary is a heterogeneous group. Often, diversity is framed in terms of how dissimilar people are. However, people in recreation, leisure, and experiential education groups usually are more similar than they are different, and if there are differences, these differences are usually

negligible! Diversity is something to be recognized, but it should not become the overwhelming focus of a group's existence. By understanding dissimilarities and focusing on similarities among individual group members, groups will be much better suited to do whatever it is they are intended to do.

There are as many sources of diversity as there are ways in which people are different. However, it is possible to make some generalizations and narrow down these differences into a few discrete categories. For the purposes of this text, there are five types of diversity: personal characteristics; cultural characteristics; race and ethnic characteristics; generational characteristics; and characteristics based on abilities, skills, and knowledge. Each of these categories of diversity includes different facets of diversity as well. While the list included here is not exhaustive, it does give foundational information that you can use while working with diverse groups of people.

Personal Characteristics

People have many different personal characteristics that make them unique individuals. The intersection of these characteristics is what gives people their own essence. Personal characteristics include gender; motivation; sexual orientation; values, attitudes, and beliefs; education; personality; focus on task or relationship function; leadership style; and political beliefs. While there are many other characteristics, this list is a good starting point for determining how an individual's personal characteristics contribute to diversity.

As a leader or facilitator, you should remember that personal characteristics aren't easy to change. People are born with many of these characteristics (i.e., gender, race), and they develop the others throughout their lifetime (i.e., personality type, leadership style, task or relationship orientation, political beliefs). People develop personal characteristics based on where they live, who they live with, and what resources are available to them (e.g., education; money for food, shelter, and clothing; information).

There are many evaluation instruments leaders can use to understand the diverse characteristics people bring with them to the group context. These instruments usually come in paper and pencil format, and most people have filled out some type of personal characteristics evaluation instrument sometime in their life (usually in school). One well-known example of an evaluation instrument, the Myers-Briggs Type Indicator (Briggs Myers 1987), sorts people into 16 different personality types depending on the combination of traits they exhibit. These types are broken down further into eight types that are at either ends of four continuums.

Most people are familiar with the introvert–extrovert continuum. Introverts are quiet, prefer to work on their own, and feel less comfortable in social situations. Extroverts are more outgoing, like to work with others, and feel more comfortable in social contexts. The thinking–feeling continuum relates to how people go about decision making. Feelers make decisions based on how they perceive others perceive a situation or how a certain course of action will affect others. Thinkers are more logical in their approach to decision making, taking into account facts and evidence about the decision at hand. The sensing–intuiting continuum relates to how people go about collecting information regarding a particular situation. People who are on the sensing end of the continuum like concrete information, while those who are more intuitive prefer theoretical information and are characterized as imaginative. Finally, the perceiving–judging continuum refers to how people manage things. Judgers like to make a plan and follow that plan with little or no deviation. Perceivers are more spontaneous and have difficulty making decisions.

The Myers-Briggs Type Indicator is one example of an instrument that professionals may use to better understand the personal characteristics of their group members. These instruments are available in a wide range—some are free while others must be purchased. Other types of evaluation instruments include leadership style inventories, self-concept scales, life-effectiveness instruments, and leisure preference scales.

Some people will be more flexible in accepting the personal characteristics of others, while some individuals will have difficulty accepting others. Understanding how to match different personality styles in group settings will be an advantage for leaders and facilitators. This information may also be used to ensure that group members have the skills and knowledge to work with others who might have different personality traits. Ultimately, when working with diverse groups, professionals should shift their approach to meeting the needs and expectations of the group as a whole and not the personal needs of the individual group members or themselves.

Cultural Characteristics

When most people think of diversity, cultural differences are one of the first things to spring to mind. A definition of culture depends on the framework in which it is examined. From a group communications perspective, culture may be defined as "the system of beliefs, values, and symbols and rules that underlie communication patterns within a discernable grouping of people" (Adams and Galanes 2006, 197). Culture may also be defined as "the common characteristics and collective perceptions that distinguish one group of people from another" (Englberg and Wynn 2003, 65). Finally, "culture is a learned system of knowledge, behavior, attitudes, beliefs, values and norms that is shared by a group of people" (Beebe and Masterson 2006, 101-102). Regardless of the framework through which culture is defined, people who belong to the same culture share specific traits of some kind. It is through the people's own definition that the essence of their culture takes shape.

Most people do not focus on their culture because they are immersed in the society created by that culture.

However, once people are removed from that society, they tend to notice differences and start to think about their own culture. For professionals, it is important to realize that group participants may feel outside of their culture when placed in various recreation, leisure, and experiential education contexts. Some activities and programs will feel comfortable to people from a variety of cultures, while others will make people feel uneasy with themselves or other group members. This uneasiness stems from perceived differences among group members and may come from a variety of cultural dimensions. There are six dimensions of culture, including the power distance, individualism–collectivism, masculinity–femininity, uncertainty avoidance, short-term–long-term, and high-context–low-context dimensions (Engleberg and Wynn 2003). Figure 14.1 depicts these dimensions of culture.

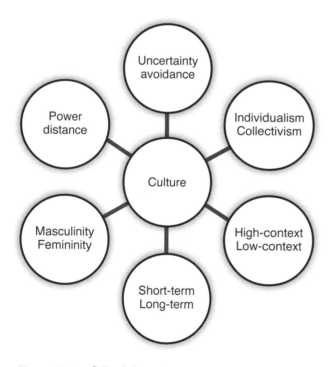

Figure 14.1 Cultural dimensions.

Every person in the world exhibits some of these dimensions of culture. Much like the recipe for stone soup, in which the outcome depends on what ingredient each individual adds to the pot, every person will be slightly different based on his home location, available information sources, religious beliefs, socioeconomic status, and education level.

Power Distance

Power distance is the degree to which people in a particular culture portray power and status differences among individuals. People from low–power distance cultures believe that everyone should have equal say in decision-making processes and equal protection under the law and that leaders and followers should have equal power in group situations. People from high–power distance cultures believe in a hierarchical structure in which some people are afforded more power and status because of their place in society. People in high–power distance cultures believe that leaders should make decisions, that followers should not have a say in group decision making, and that followers should conform to what those who have power say and do.

Individualism or Collectivism

The individualism–collectivism dimension of culture relates to how much emphasis is placed on people doing things they like to do and not considering the wishes of the larger group or society. Individualistic cultures value people who are independent, outspoken, and autonomous. Collective cultures value those who put the group before the self, conform to societal and cultural norms, and avoid dissent. In general, the cultures of the United States and Western Europe are individualistic, whereas Asian, Latin American, and Native American cultures are collective.

Masculinity or Femininity

The masculinity–femininity dimension of culture is in some ways similar to the individualism–collectivism dimension. There are three areas that differentiate masculine cultures from feminine cultures. Masculine cultures value assertiveness, focus on the task function, and champion individual-oriented behaviors. Feminine cultures value sharing, focus on the relationship function, and prefer cooperative behaviors (Adams and Galanes 2006). These statements are only generalizations, as these values and behaviors vary for each individual and across cultural groups. As mentioned in chapter 8, there are other differences in how women and men approach working with groups.

Uncertainty Avoidance

Some cultures are more relaxed about time, logistics, plans, and the pace of life. Cultures with low uncertainty avoidance are more comfortable with fluid plans and relaxed perceptions of time. Cultures with high uncertainty avoidance value routines, rigid plans, and absolute perceptions of time.

Short Term or Long Term

The short-term–long-term characteristic relates to the time frame in which people expect to receive outcomes from their behaviors. Short-term cultures expect immediate feedback and reward from their actions. Cultures such as the United States exhibit this characteristic. Long-term cultures do not expect immediate feedback or cessation of their needs. People from long-term cultures, such as members of Asian cultures, are more likely to exhibit this characteristic.

High Context or Low Context

This dimension of culture relates to how important nonverbal cues are in communication and interaction. A low-context culture places more emphasis on verbal communication and the actual meaning of words. A high-context culture emphasizes nonverbal communication cues such as gestures, context, and facial expressions. People from high-context cultures might not be comfortable with the lengthy verbal descriptions individuals from low-context cultures give to explain a situation or thought. Individuals from low-context cultures may not be as adept at interpreting body language or other nonverbal forms of communication. Figure 14.2 depicts where various cultures fall on the context scale.

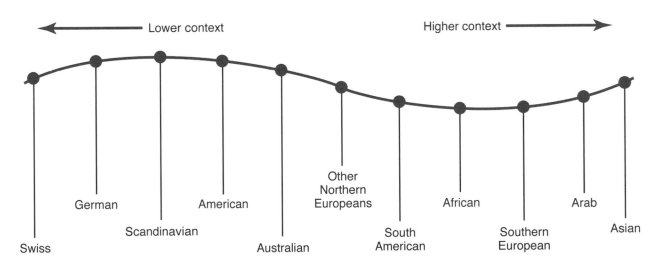

Low-context cultures: Information must be provided explicitly, usually in words. Members of such cultures

- Are less aware of nonverbal cues, environment, and situation
- Lack well-developed networks
- Need detailed background information
- Tend to segment and compartmentalize information
- Control information on a "need to know" basis
- Prefer explicit and careful directions from someone who "knows"
- View knowledge as a commodity

High-context cultures: Much information drawn from surroundings. Very little must be explicitly transferred. Members of such cultures

- Respond to nonverbal cues
- Share information freely
- Rely on physical context for information
- Take environment, situation, gestures, and mood into account
- Maintain extensive information networks

Figure 14.2 Cultural context scale.

From Beebe, S.A. and J.T. Masterson. Communicating in small groups: Principles and practices, 8e. Published by Pearson Education, Boston, MA. copyright © 2006 by Pearson Education. Reprinted by permission of the publisher.

Table 14.1 summarizes the six dimensions of culture, gives examples of associated behaviors, and provides recommended adaptations for working with groups that include people from different cultural backgrounds. Later in this chapter, we will discuss specific strategies that professionals might use when working with groups of people from diverse cultural backgrounds.

Race and Ethnic Characteristics

If you travel anywhere in North America, you will see people from a wide variety of racial and ethnic backgrounds. Problems caused by perceived differences among racial and ethnic groups seem to receive much attention in the news, in governmental affairs, and in politics in general. One reason why these perceived differences are spotlighted so frequently is that racial and ethnic differences are often the first thing that comes to people's minds when thinking about diversity. While there are differences, there are more similarities among racial and ethnic groups than most people think! This is particularly true in North America, which has a long, proud tradition of being a place where people or groups of people could come to better their situation.

Most professionals work with people from a wide range of ethnic and racial backgrounds, and so you should be open to working with people from different backgrounds. Don't be afraid to be yourself and experience others being themselves too! While it is possible to make cautious generalizations about people from certain ethnic or racial backgrounds, these are generalizations and not absolute truths. Each person is unique in her own way and lives life in the context of her race and ethnicity in her own way. In North America, the major ethnic and racial groups include African Americans, Asian Americans, Hispanic Americans, Native Americans, and European Americans. Table 14.2 summarizes some characteristics of each of these groups. Knowing how people's race and ethnicity affect interactions with others will help professionals understand the context in which they are working when they are interacting with people of diverse backgrounds.

Many African Americans, Asian Americans, Hispanic Americans, and Native Americans communicate in their own racial and ethnic contexts as well as in the contexts of European Americans,

which tend to dominate interactions in North America. However, often European Americans are not exposed to the communication contexts of other racial and ethnic groups, which may lead to misunderstanding and uncomfortable feelings. Professionals working with groups should recognize that people in the minority (and this could be you!) might feel uncomfortable and unable to participate in the group process if they do not understand the racial and ethnic context of the other group members. By understanding why people from different racial and ethnic backgrounds interact with others the way they do, professionals can allay some of the fears and misunderstandings that might exist among group members. This will allow the group to focus on what it intends to do.

Generational Characteristics

Recreation, leisure, and experiential education programs serve people of many ages, including children and senior citizens. While age is certainly a factor in how programs are developed and delivered, the generation from which people come will also affect how they approach and interact in a group context. Societal factors and events that occur during a person's life influence how people perceive working with others in a group. For example, people who were born early in the 20th century experienced two World Wars and the Great Depression. Those born in the early 1970s were influenced by several governmental scandals, the rise of computers and technology, and television.

There are four dominant generations in North America: the builders, the boomers, the Xers, and the N-geners (Hicks and Hicks 1999). Each of these generations exhibits general characteristics. A basic understanding of these generational characteristics will help professionals design better programs, facilitate groups more effectively, and decrease potential conflicts among group members. For most people, the easiest way to think about generational differences is to look at the family. How do grandparents differ from parents and grandchildren? How do parents differ from their kids? Most children live their lives much differently than their parents did. This is often the result of parents deciding to raise their kids differently from the way they were raised and the result of societal influences on children. Increased reliance on technology certainly has influenced how later

Table 14.1 Cultural Dimensions of Group Participation

Cultural dimension	Definition and examples	Participant behavior	Recommended adaptations
Power distance	Extent of equity or status among group members *High power*: Inequality between high- and low-status members; Mexico, India, Singapore *Low power*: Equity and interdependence among group members; New Zealand, Denmark, Israel	High–power distance members try to take charge and make decisions; low–power distance members seek consultation and consensus.	Establish clear norms for member behavior. To what extent will members participate in decision making? How will specific tasks be assigned? How and by whom will members be evaluated? Who will serve as leaders?
Uncertainty avoidance	Extent of comfort in uncertain situations *High uncertainty avoidance*: Prefer rules, plans, and routines; Japan, Belgium, Greece *Low uncertainty avoidance*: Comfortable with ambiguity and unpredictability; Jamaica, Hong Kong	High-uncertainty avoidance members require structured tasks and spend more time on details; low-uncertainty members want less structure and can work independently with little supervision.	Provide clear instructions to the high-uncertainty avoidance members and give low–uncertainty avoidance members opportunities to function unaided.
Individualism or collectivism	Prefer to act independently or interdependently *Individualism*: Value individual achievement and freedom; United States, Australia, Canada *Collectivism*: Emphasize group identity; Asian and Latin American countries	Individualistic members work alone and seek credit for their own work; collective members work in groups and try to help each other. Collective members may prefer face-to-face discussion instead of virtual discussion.	Encourage collectivism but make sure that individualistic members understand that they are part of a larger group that needs their input and participation to achieve a shared goal.

(continued)

Table 14.1 *(continued)*

Masculinity or femininity	Concern for self and success versus a focus on caring and sharing *Masculine:* Assertive, decisive, dominant; Japan, Venezuela, Italy *Feminine:* Nurturing, cooperative; Sweden, Norway, Denmark	Masculine-oriented members focus on the task and personal success; feminine-oriented members focus on member relations and respect for others.	Balance masculine and feminine values in order to achieve task and social goals. Do not forgo action in order to achieve total cooperation and consensus.
Long term or short term	Expectations for and timing of rewards *Long term:* Value patience, planning, and postponement of rewards; Asian countries *Short term:* Value immediate returns and rewards; English-speaking countries	Long-term members engage in long-term planning for future success; short-term members can become impatient and need immediate feedback and reinforcement.	Involve long-term members in planning and skill building and let short-term members pursue immediate and measureable objectives.
High context or low context	Directness of communication in specific circumstances *High context:* Favor implied and context-sensitive messages; Japan, China, Greece, Mexico *Low context:* Favor explicit, factual, and objective messages; England, United States, Germany	High-context members consider background, nonverbal cues, and interpersonal history when communicating; low-context members want facts and clear, direct, explicit communication.	Give high-context members time to review information and react; demonstrate the value of going beyond just the facts to low-context members.

Adapted, by permission, from I. Engleberg and D. Wynn, 2003, *Working in groups: Communication principles and strategies*, 3rd ed. (Boston: Houghton Mifflin), 65-66.

Table 14.2 Racial and Ethnic Characteristics in North America

Group	High or low context	Collective or individualistic	Communication patterns
African Americans	High context	Collective	Interactive, emotional communication; open sharing of feelings; narrative style
Asian Americans	High context	Collective	Indirect and ambiguous verbal communication; direct and clear nonverbal communication and actions
Hispanic Americans	High context	Collective	Communication through networks; person in leadership position communicates for group
Native Americans	High context	Collective	Indirect and ambiguous verbal communication; direct and clear nonverbal communication and actions; narrative style
European Americans	Low context	Individualistic	Prefer factual information; prefer eye contact when speaking; need specific background information

From K. Adams and G. Galanes, 2006, Communicating in groups: Applications and skills, 6th ed. (Boston: McGraw Hill) 207-208. Adapted with permission from The McGraw-Hill Companies.

generations perceive the world and interact in group settings.

The oldest generation, referred to as the *builders,* includes people who were born from 1901 to 1945. These people were influenced by World War I and World War II and the Great Depression. Years of living frugally caused this generation to be vigilant about spending money. Builders are also team oriented—they will contribute toward a common goal, often at their own expense. People from this generation may be seen as overcautious and old fashioned.

Members of the next generation, the boomers, have received much attention in the media, as they are reaching retirement and may have a great effect on health care, tourism, and recreation and leisure services. Boomers were born between 1946 and 1964 and were influenced heavily by the Vietnam War and the civil rights movement. Boomers are characterized as being self-important, as their builder parents tried to provide them with things to make their lives easier. While boomers are willing to confront challenges and put in the effort required to complete a task, they also expect immediate fulfillment of their needs. As a generation, boomers have one of the highest divorce rates. This affects their children, the Xers.

The Xers, or people born from 1965 to 1976, were affected heavily by how their parents, the boomers, raised them. Boomer parents often devoted a lot of time to work, often compromising family for work obligations. Thus Xers are more individualistic than

previous generations were, a characteristic that translates into the "me first" attitude of this generation. Xers are not as committed to work, as they see work only as a way to reach other goals. Xers usually are technologically savvy and are more open to diversity than their parents and grandparents are. However, the N-geners are even more adept at technology and even more open to diversity.

The N-geners, or members of the Internet generation, are the youths of today. Most of the people who read this textbook will be N-geners. While the effects this generation will have on society are yet to be realized, the use and integration of technology into everyday life is a key characteristic. N-geners are skilled at group work but also need quick feedback and easy access to answers, as they are influenced by the speed of acquiring information on the Internet. N-geners will most likely hold a greater variety of jobs and live in a greater variety of places than their parents or grandparents did. Because technology and the speed of travel have made the world more accessible, N-geners are truly members of a global community that values diversity. Table 14.3 summarizes the characteristics, strengths, and weaknesses of the major generations in North America.

The ebb and flow of generational influence changes over time and location and depends on context. In some situations, the beliefs and values of the builders will benefit group process and output, while in other cases the positive characteristics of the Xers and N-geners will be most influential. Professionals must

Table 14.3 Dominant Generations of North America

Generation	Characteristics	Strengths	Weaknesses
Builders (1901-1945)	Major influences are Great Depression and World War II; cautious about spending money; work hard at a single task until finished; put own interests aside for common good	Careful with resources (e.g., money); plan ahead; reliable, dependable; disciplined	Too cautious with resources; lack spontaneity and flexibility
Boomers (1946-1964)	Major influences are TV, Vietnam War, the Pill, assassinations, civil rights movement, size of generation; major consumers, value the good life, self-absorbed, believe they're special; work is an end in itself, expect to be fulfilled at work; value education	Confident; willing to put in whatever time a task takes; willing to challenge old ways of doing things; willing to take on big causes	Think they're right all the time; expect others to hold similar beliefs and values; may break rules of ethics if they think it's best for them
Xers (1965-1976)	Major influences are rising divorce rate, Watergate, Pentagon Papers, MTV; distrust institutions, particularly government; comfortable with diversity; work is a means to an end; value family (broadly defined); comfortable with technology; endure education	Independent thinkers; sensitive to people; value relationships; tolerant; accept competing points of view; comfortable with change; highly computer literate	Appear pessimistic and negative; unwilling to put personal life and concerns aside to complete task; may seem alienated and unmotivated
N-geners (1977-1997)	Major influences are AIDS, technology and the Internet, death of Princess Diana; still young and forming; value diversity, highly tolerant; major consumers; non-linear thinkers; value family	Open minded and tolerant; welcome different viewpoints; completely savvy with technology and media; optimistic; innovative; comfortable with collaborative work and networking	Seem to lack initiative; seem unmotivated; unlikely to conform to bureaucracy, hierarchy, and organizational rules

From Engleberg, Insa N., Dianna R. Wynn. Working in Groups: Communication Principles and Strategies, 3e. Published by Allyn and Bacon, Boston, MA. Copyright © 2003 by Pearson Education. Reprinted by permission of the publisher.

remember to value the input and perspective of people from different generations. While the lens through which some people view the world might be a little older, life experience is a good teacher!

Abilities, Skills, and Knowledge

The last type of diversity—ability, skills, and knowledge—is one that doesn't get noticed much when people initially think about diversity. Today, most people who work in a group context are experts in their chosen field of study. It is rare to find someone who is a jack-of-all-trades and has a broad base of abilities, skills, and knowledge. Even the recreation,

leisure, and experiential education profession has become specialized. For example, at one time outdoor recreation professionals were skilled in numerous outdoor activities and could safely and successfully plan and conduct programs in these various areas. In the contemporary world, outdoor recreation professionals are more likely to focus on one or two particular skill areas (i.e., rock climbing, white-water rafting). It is rare to see a job posting that doesn't require specific expertise in a skill area.

Professionals working with people possessing a diverse array of abilities, skills, and knowledge have an easy job *if* they can identify the individuals' strengths and develop effective connections between people.

For example, a therapeutic recreation service provider may establish a working group of employees who have the abilities, skills, and knowledge to provide holistic treatment for clients. The working group may be made up of a social worker, an occupational therapist, a therapeutic recreation specialist, a medical doctor, and a physical therapist. Each of these people has specific abilities, skills, and knowledge that strengthen the capability of the working group to provide patient services.

Professionals may apply the same principles when working with volunteer groups, committees, or student groups. A diverse group will have various abilities, skills, and knowledge that people in the group bring to the table. By making connections and using the complementary abilities, skills, and knowledge of the group, professionals can help group members understand each other better, reach their goals, and complete the task the group is working on.

While there are many potential benefits to working with groups of people from diverse backgrounds, there are many shortcomings as well. The next section examines some of these benefits and shortcomings and offers suggestions for working successfully with diverse groups of people in recreation, leisure, and experiential education contexts.

BENEFITS OF DIVERSE GROUPS

Diversity can add immensely to a group's success, particularly in recreation, leisure, and experiential education settings. However, the positive effects of diversity are tempered by the type of diversity present in the group. Diversity may affect a group in terms of successfully completing tasks, making decisions, and solving problems and in terms of how group members relate to each other.

Often a group is formed to accomplish something. In recreation, leisure, and experiential education settings this something may range from planning an event to playing a game to completing a team-building initiative to finishing a canoe trip. How does diversity affect the group's success in accomplishing its task? The answer depends in part on the task itself and in part on the ways in which the group members differ from one another.

Generally, groups performing decision-making tasks make higher quality decisions if they are more diverse. The wider variety of perspectives provides different types of information that can be used to make the decision. In diverse groups, some people may not be as familiar as others are with the context, information, and nature of the decision to be made. These people may ask seemingly naive questions that help clarify the context of the decision for all group members. Group members who are familiar with the context of the decision may explain the situation to those who don't understand it as well. By describing the context to others, everyone in the group will have a clearer understanding of it. Those who are familiar with the context may remember something forgotten or clarify their understanding of the decision to be made by explaining it to another person. For those who aren't as familiar with the context, the explanation given by others provides foundational information to set the stage for the decision-making process. In decision making, diversity allows the group to think outside of the box by questioning common

Toolbox Tips

Here are some ideas you can use when working with diverse groups to encourage everyone to participate:

- Keep the lines of communication open.
- Use group decision-making techniques. Be sure everyone's voice is heard!
- Keep all group members involved. Find out what skills people have and get them to use those skills to contribute to the group work.
- Make sure everyone is aware of group goals. Revisit them every so often to ensure that they are still relevant for the group.

beliefs, values, and traditions that may influence the decision. Too often groups fall into the trap of ignoring new information in favor of old information that has worked in the past. Groups with members from diverse backgrounds are better equipped to avoid this trap.

Although research is limited, it appears that groups with diverse members are able to complete tasks more effectively. In recreation, leisure, and experiential education settings, sports teams in particular benefit from including members who have a wide range of skills. Tasks are completed better by diverse groups that meet more frequently than by groups that meet less frequently. Having people with a wide range of skills in a group gives members a chance to capitalize on symbiotic relationships, or relationships that are complementary. For example, in an outdoor recreation setting, pairing a good map reader with a strong canoe paddler exploits the strengths of both people and helps them to get to their intended destination in a timely manner.

People who belong to diverse groups are able to use other members as measuring sticks with which to compare their individual performance. If some group members are succeeding at completing tasks or giving input, others will strive to do the same, particularly if the group is cohesive and members feel a sense of obligation to the group. This process of group members evaluating their performance against other members is called *social comparison*. Professionals can help groups to complete tasks by encouraging them to use the abilities, skills, and knowledge of all members. Professionals can also encourage a homogeneous group, or a group whose members are more similar than they are dissimilar, to recruit new members who have the needed abilities, skills, and knowledge to help the group complete its task. Often the person or people recruited will add diversity to the group.

Diversity has other benefits for groups. Groups that include members with diverse characteristics are more likely to deal with unexpected dilemmas effectively and efficiently. Diverse groups are better suited for brainstorming, coming up with new ideas, and developing methods of implementing decisions and programs. A diverse group may also emerge as a stronger, more cohesive group, as its members must work through their differing viewpoints in order to reach a common understanding. Groups with a diverse membership also tend to take more risks.

Following a riskier course of action often results in better outcomes for the group.

While diversity can benefit a group, it may also create shortcomings. The next section delves into the disadvantages of diverse groups.

SHORTCOMINGS OF DIVERSE GROUPS

One of the major issues affecting diverse groups occurs when group members are unable to work through their perceived differences and get caught in an unending cycle of debate, argument, and uneasy feelings toward one another. Group members may constantly position themselves to represent their own interests or make sure their voice is heard. This may be particularly true for people who are a minority in the group and feel they are being overlooked.

One factor affecting how group members perceive one another are the generalizations people make about others who exhibit specific characteristics or are thought to be members of a distinct group. These generalizations are called *stereotypes*. Most people use stereotypes as a quick means of processing information. Stereotypes are used to reduce the amount of brain power required to deal with meeting new people, reacting to others in a different environment, or comparing one group to another group. While stereotypes can be a useful cognitive processing tool, they can also create misunderstandings among members of a diverse group and thus affect the group's ability to attend to its task.

Prejudice may also affect diverse groups. Prejudice is having a negative attitude toward another person only because that person belongs to a specific race, religion, sexual orientation, gender, nationality, or cultural background. Prejudice among group members may hinder the group's ability to complete tasks, make decisions, and work through interpersonal conflicts.

Stereotypes and prejudice lead group members to focus on their differences rather than their similarities. If group members are unable to overcome their preconceived notions of others and get to know other members on an individual level, the group will never become very cohesive or productive. Recreation, leisure, and experiential education groups often need to reach their full working potential in a short length of time. For example, members of a basketball team who don't play as a team because of stereotypes or prejudice win few games. Committees are hard pressed to plan and conduct special events without the entire group working together as a cohesive unit.

Another shortcoming to working with diverse groups is culture clash (Johnson and Johnson 2003). Culture clash occurs when group members from different cultures disagree on the importance of beliefs, values, and issues. What is important in one culture might be less important in another. Culture clash may be particularly disruptive if minority group members feel that their beliefs and values are underrepresented in the group or are automatically discounted by the majority of the group. Many established groups that have a clear majority of members from a specific culture find it extremely difficult to change traditions and history to include the values and beliefs of new members. Confronting this situation is one of the primary challenges for professionals working with diverse groups of people.

Another shortcoming of diverse groups is that their tendency to make riskier decisions may get them into trouble. A diverse group may talk itself into believing that its decision is appropriate based on the input from members, the understanding of environmental conditions and available resources, and the perceived ability of the group to implement the decision. Homogeneous groups, or those comprising people who are more similar than dissimilar, are more limited in their thinking, as they do not have the broader perspective and experience of heterogeneous groups. It is a fine distinction between being aggressive and taking too great a risk. Diverse groups need to consider carefully the true extent of the risk associated with their decisions.

WORKING WITH DIVERSE GROUPS

Capitalizing on the benefits and avoiding the shortcomings of diversity in groups require attention from professionals. There are strategies professionals may use to maximize the potential of diverse groups while staying away from the downfalls. These include developing a positive group identity; encouraging members to spend time getting to know one another; promoting an atmosphere of inclusion; developing an inclusive

system of communicating; encouraging group members to learn about other cultures, religions, ethnic groups, and so on; focusing on similarities instead of differences; and discussing how differences can be a positive aspect of the group.

Professionals can help diverse groups develop a positive group identity. This identity should include elements that represent all members of the group. This process often requires time to complete. The goal is not to force individuals to become homogeneous but to reach a common understanding of what the group is about and who the group represents as a whole. The group is together for some intended purpose, and the group's final identity should focus on that purpose rather than the characteristics of the people who make up the group. Most people know of groups that have successfully developed a positive group identity. These groups stand out: Their members are happy, their job gets done, and people refer to the group by its collective identity instead of the individual traits of its members.

A second strategy that professionals might implement while working with diverse groups is to encourage individual members to get to know one another. In the movie *Remember the Titans* (Howard 2000), football coach Herman Boone (portrayed by Denzel Washington) required his African American and European American players to learn something personal about every other team player. Coach Boone's strategy was unique, as racial tensions were high after two high schools were integrated into a single school in 1971. Ultimately the team members came to see each other as brothers and go on to a winning season. By developing an understanding of others in a diverse group, members gain some understanding of each person's background, culture, and ethnic influences. This understanding will encourage group members to develop respect for others' beliefs, attitudes, and values.

Promoting an atmosphere of inclusion is a third strategy for working with diverse groups. All group activities should be as inclusive as possible. While ensuring inclusiveness might require additional meeting time or the help of technology, doing so avoids hurting people's feelings and reassures people that their beliefs, values, and issues have not gone unheard. The process of developing an atmosphere of inclusion should not be patronizing. Being patronizing can hamper the effort to promote inclusion by causing

Learning Activity

Watch the movie *Remember the Titans*. Answer the following questions in a small group of 5 to 6 people:

1. What factors initially got in the way of the Titans working together as a team?
2. How did this diverse group go about dealing with its differences?
3. What strategies did the coaches implement to get the team members to work together?
4. What strategies were successful?
5. What strategies were unsuccessful?
6. If you were Coach Boone, what would you have done? Why?

negative feelings among group members, particularly those in the minority. A primary way to develop inclusion is to be sure that the group has agreed on goals that are cooperative. To reach these goals, all members of the group will have to work together.

Although it is related to promoting inclusion, developing an inclusive system of communication is important to recognize as its own strategy. Groups should use communication networks that include all members, especially when important decisions are made and solutions to problems are implemented. Including every group member in a communication network is not enough; the network should also reflect the values, attitudes, and beliefs of the group members. The communication styles of different group members should be accommodated as well. Some people might prefer to read a written communication while others prefer to hear a verbal message. Language choice should also be monitored, especially when communicating with group members who are not speaking their primary language. These members might translate some words or syntax into a different, offensive meaning. Likewise, body language and certain hand gestures mean different things in different cultures. While groups do not need to reconstruct communication networks and styles each time a new person joins, when welcoming a new member it is a good time to revisit communication procedures to ensure that they are truly inclusive.

Professionals can encourage group members to learn about other cultures, religions, and ethnic groups. Each group meeting might start or end with the sharing of food, customs, and other information about the ethnic backgrounds of different group members. With the ease of access to information via the Internet, local libraries, and television, group members can also explore other cultures and ethnicities on their own time. Recreation, leisure, and experiential education service providers can offer programs that highlight the customs of different cultural and ethnic groups as a means of promoting understanding. During the summer in New York City, tourists may attend major street festivals and parades sponsored by a wide variety of cultural and ethnic groups. Facilitators and leaders can suggest group members attend events such as these to gain a better understanding of others.

A sixth strategy that professionals might use is to focus on similarities rather than differences among group members. This strategy involves looking at the individual aspects of each person and not using stereotypes or prejudices to form impressions of others. If group members rely on outward signs or depend on what they think they know about others' cultures or ethnicities without focusing on similarities, a group will not be able to capitalize on its diversity. Looking at each individual as a person and not as a member of a particular race or culture may uncover many similarities in values, interests, and beliefs. Group members may also reach a common understanding of why people are interested in the group. As mentioned, one commonality that professionals can focus on is the group's purpose. By focusing on what the group is supposed to do, group members can focus on how their similarities and individual aspects can enhance the group as a whole.

A final strategy professionals may implement is to discuss how differences can be a positive force for the group. This chapter presented several reasons why diverse groups may be stronger than groups with less diversity. When group members are aware of how diversity benefits group performance, they will be more apt to accept diversity. Group members can be educated on the benefits of diversity in many ways. First, group members can be given readings on how diversity affects groups in a positive way. Second, group members can brainstorm ideas on how having diverse members in the group is a positive quality. Third, the recreation, leisure, and experiential education professional can remind the group at strategic moments how diversity has helped, and not hindered, the group. Finally, the professional can promote the idea that diversity adds to an individual's life experience. Exposure to new cultures and ethnicities creates an exciting opportunity to learn about others in the world!

SUMMARY

Many people feel nervous when diversity is mentioned and are apprehensive about joining groups that include a diverse array of people. Many people interact daily with others who are more similar than they are dissimilar. As the world continues to shrink, people increasingly need to interact with others from different races, religions, cultures, sexual orientations, ethnicities, and genders. Professionals must understand what diversity is and how people are different. While becoming an expert in diversity is not necessary, a basic understanding of how people with different backgrounds interact will go a long way in ensuring a group's success.

This chapter has provided several generalizations about people from different cultures and ethnicities. Remember that these are only generalizations and that each person has a different personal history and lived experience. Generalizations are useful as a starting point in learning more about specific people and their backgrounds. Professionals are uniquely positioned to encourage others to look beyond their differences and focus on their similarities. Recreation, leisure, and experiential education programs allow people to focus on having fun, playing a game, traveling through the wilderness, planning events, or sharing a picnic table together instead of focusing on the perceived differences existing among the group.

Recreation, leisure, and experiential education professionals can implement any of several strategies to promote the strength of diversity in their groups. By focusing on inclusive communication and decision making as well as on similarities and individual characteristics of group members, a group may realize the positive potential of its diversity.

RESOURCES

Adams, K., and G. Galanes. 2006. *Communicating in groups: Applications and skills.* 6th ed. Boston: McGraw Hill.

Beebe, S.A., and J.T. Masterson. 2006. *Communicating in small groups: Principles and practices.* 8th ed. Boston: Pearson Education.

Briggs Myers, I. 1987. *Introduction to type: A description of the theory and application of the Myers-Briggs type indicator.* Palo Alto, CA: Consulting Psychologists Press.

Engleberg, I., and D. Wynn. 2003. *Working in groups: Communication principles and strategies.* 3rd ed. Boston: Houghton Mifflin.

Hicks, R., and K. Hicks. 1999. *Boomers, xers, and other strangers: Understanding the generational differences that divide us.* Wheaton, IL: Tyndale House Publishers.

Howard, G.A. 2000. *Remember the titans.* Walt Disney Productions.

Johnson, D.W., and F.P. Johnson. 2003. *Joining together: Group theory and group skills.* 8th ed. Boston: Pearson Education.

Index

NOTE: An italicized *t* or *f* following page numbers indicate that there is a table or figure to be found on that page, respectively.

About the Authors

Timothy S. O'Connell, PhD, is an associate professor in the department of recreation and leisure studies at Brock University in St. Catharines, Ontario, Canada, where he teaches outdoor recreation and group dynamics courses.

With over 20 years of experience as a wilderness guide, O'Connell has developed firsthand experience of the workings and outcomes of group dynamics. As an instructor at the high school and college level, he has taught group dynamics for 15 years. O'Connell is currently conducting research on the social psychology of groups as well as developing a new outdoor recreation curriculum to include group dynamics courses.

O'Connell is coeditor for the *Journal of Experiential Education* and a member of the Association for Experiential Education, the National Recreation and Parks Association, and the Council of Outdoor Educators of Ontario.

O'Connell and his wife, Dr. Mary Breunig, reside in Ridgeville, Ontario. An avid outdoor recreationist, he has led over 100 wilderness trips, including integrated trips of people with and without disabilities, with Dr. Breunig, coauthor of *Outdoor Leadership Theory and Practice* (Human Kinetics).

In his free time, he enjoys rock climbing, sea kaying, and home brewing.

Brent Cuthbertson, PhD, is an associate professor and director in the School of Outdoor Recreation, Parks, and Tourism at Lakehead University in Thunder Bay, Ontario, Canada, where he teaches courses in outdoor leadership and experiential education.

Cuthbertson has over 25 years of experience as a wilderness adventure educator and guide. In both 2002 and 2004 he received the Lakehead University Merit Award for Excellence in Teaching. He is also the associate editor for the *Journal of Experiential Education*.

Cuthbertson enjoys wilderness canoeing and sea kayaking, woodworking, and walking with his dogs. He resides in Thunder Bay, Ontario.